UPON
THIS ROCK

For my beloved wife and family, my teachers and the Orthodox Mission of St Boniface, Ryde, Isle of Wight.

UPON THIS ROCK

Doctrine, Dogma, and Orthodox Church Authority

David Dale

ISBN 1-928653-08-1

Cover Photo: Mausoleum of Galia Placidia.
Ravenna, Italy

Regina Orthodox Press
P.O. Box 5288
Salisbury, MA 01952
1-800-636-2470
FAX: 978-462-5079
www.reginaorthodoxpress.com

CONTENTS

CONTENTS

ABOUT THE AUTHOR

After training at the Royal Military Academy, Sandhurst and serving in a cavalry regiment David Dale first read for the English Bar and then read theology for ordination in the ministry of the Church of England. He later took an honors degree in history at the Open University and went on to do research at Oxford in the biblical and patristic understanding of revelation. He was a parish priest and school chaplain for 35 years until he left the Church of England in 1998 and was received into the Orthodox Church in 2000. His last parish was the largest on the Isle of Wight where he earned a reputation as a pastor and preacher and a trainer of laity in the lay vocation. He is a prolific journalist and an experienced lecturer. He has conducted several parish training weeks for laity and he has twice been a lecturer at a John Keble Conference specializing in dogmatic theology. He has also delivered a series of lectures on dogmatic theology onto camera for use in traditionalist Episcopalian seminaries.

He has been married for 40 years to Jillian and they have three children, Andrew, Kate and Emma and two grandsons, Daniel and Jack.

PREFACE

It is hoped that this study will enable the reader to understand the criteria by which the Church decides if doctrinal propositions are true or in error and to understand that the question needs to be studied. There is a glossary of the principal technical words at the back in case the reader is unfamiliar with any of them. There are also appendices seeking to give an insight into the way the debate has gone and continues to go or to provide basic dogmatic statements and other information. The same or similar issues occur again and again in a subject like this. The result is that there is sometimes some repetition of treatment and argument. This is inevitable. It is not possible to present a fair and rounded account of the arguments without some repetition.

If anything I have written is inconsistent with the Apostolic Faith, the teaching of the Orthodox Church or is deemed authoritatively to be a doctrinal error I unreservedly and humbly withdraw it. Where I have said that such and such a doctrine or practice is Orthodox I have done so because wiser and more experienced writers have said so.

David Dale
June, 2001

INTRODUCTION

If we define the function of something as what will not happen if it is absent—so that the function of a light bulb, for example, is to give light—then we can say that the function of the Church of Christ is to bring men and women to salvation. There are many ways in which we can describe the nature of the Church but if we lose sight of its function as the agent of salvation then we wander into serious errors.

The Church exercises its function by preaching and living the Gospel of the Lord Jesus Christ and by incorporating people into the way of salvation. The Church is able to do this because it holds to certain truths that are summed up in the Creed of the Apostolic Church and in the various dogmatic definitions of the Councils of the Church. The Creed and the dogmatic definitions are expressed as concepts, a particular way that we shall explore in chapter one.

The Faith of the Church is, however, not a set of concepts. It is a reality lived out and it has been lived out from the time of the Incarnation. It has always been known, even if not always clearly defined. We can be sure that it has always been known because the Apostolic life has always been lived; there have always been those who lived an authentic Christian life—and it is only possible to do that if one holds to the Apostolic Faith. It is the truth of this last assertion, i.e. that the authentic Christian life can only be lived if the Apostolic Faith is believed, which is at once disputed and also leads to concern with doctrinal error.

We find that many people do not see the connection between what is believed and the way one lives one's life, nor is it easily possible to demonstrate this truth. We shall explore this further below. It is possible, however, to demonstrate through reason that certain propositions, if true, make the saving work of Christ of no effect. If, for example, it is believed that the Lord Jesus is either not truly a man or not truly God then, for reasons we shall examine, salvation through the work of the Lord Jesus is not possible. We shall examine this also.

The second point—concern with doctrinal error—and more particularly the process by which doctrinal disputes are resolved is the main topic of this essay. Nobody disagrees with such vigour as do Christians over matters of doctrine. A dispute over a point of doctrine brings out the very worst in people. They abuse their opponents. They accuse them of bad faith and dishonesty. At terrible times in the past Christians have tortured and killed their doctrinal opponents forgetting that we must conquer by love. The fights are remorseless and no quarter is given. There is even a name for such disagreement—*odium theologicum*--the hatred generated by theological and doctrinal difference.

These disagreements and the vigor with which they are prosecuted are a source of confusion and scandal. Many people cannot understand why such fierce battles should take place. They cannot understand how doctrine can be that important. Even if people understand the importance of doctrine they cannot understand the ferocity of the debate. Most people believe that one should be able to discuss doctrinal differences without getting angry. That is reasonable enough. Less reasonably it is assumed that it is a mark of being a Christian that one is tolerant of differences in doctrine. It is not understood that the vigour with which the debates are conducted is caused by the gravity of the issues. People do not see how much hangs upon the result of the debate. The fact is that truth and error in doctrine are not matters of personal preference or taste or what one can most readily fit into one's understanding of life. Doctrine concerns the salvation of souls. Error in doctrine threatens to frustrate the whole purpose of the sacrifice of Christ. The issues, therefore, could not be more serious.

We are asked to be tolerant of doctrinal differences. The secular virtue of tolerance is put to us as the ideal that should mark our relationships with other Christians. The belief that tolerance should play a central part in ecumenical relationships makes real progress towards the unity of the churches almost possible. Certainly we do not advocate persecution. Too many orthodox Christians have been persecuted too much for anyone to want to see persecution spread or to be a party to it. Nor can physical violence towards one's doctrinal opponents ever be contemplated or defended. We need to understand, however, that the alternative to violence, harassment and persecution is not tolerance of error or indifference to error. There is nothing more cruel than the tolerance of error or seeking to persuade others that error in doctrine is a matter of no importance. There is a third way. We need not persecute those with whom we disagree nor need we tolerate error in doctrine, which leads people away from their salvation. The alternative to persecution or damaging tolerance is the application of recognised processes and the use of accepted criteria for resolving doctrinal differences. There are well-established principles for deciding the truth in doctrinal disputes. The failure to apply them leads to disorder and confusion in the Church and puts the salvation of souls at hazard. This failure is usually leads to disaster.

What prevents the use of these processes and the application of these criteria? Why do we not see the criteria by which doctrinal orthodoxy is measured used in discussions on doctrinal innovation? It would seem a sane and godly thing to do. Decisions on doctrine are sometimes made on grounds which differ markedly from the grounds upon which the dogmatic definitions of the early centuries of the life of the Church were made. We shall see in the discussion which follows that from time to time the accepted criteria are abandoned and decisions made with what is best described as a sort of frivolity. We see innovations defended by arguments that ignore every accepted basis upon which a doctrine can properly be taken to be part of the Apostolic Faith. The decisions are then enacted without anything more than a hollow gesture to the venerable principle that a doctrine must be accepted and received by the whole Church before it can properly be understood to be orthodox. This defective process has tragic effects upon the Christian community that conducts its affairs in this way.

Two blind spots in the minds of some contemporary Christians prevent the application of recognised processes and criteria for resolving doctrinal conflicts. Because of these blind spots they do not to speak the language of doctrinal orthodoxy and the question of the orthodoxy of a doctrine is not among those to which they give weight in their deliberations.

The first blind spot, to which we have referred, is the failure to recognise that doctrine is of central importance to the life of the Church and that there is a direct link between error in doctrine and error in following the Christian way. The second blind spot is that many of those whose task it is to teach theology and to give guidance in the resolution of doctrinal differences are unaware of, or choose to ignore, the processes and criteria for deciding whether a doctrine is true or not. We shall refer to some examples of this. They seem not to know that there are sound and tested ways of discerning the orthodoxy or error of a doctrine. This is not surprising since the concern of much contemporary theological teaching is not the exposition and passing on of the Apostolic Faith within the terms of the contemporary culture. It is rather the changing of the Apostolic Faith to conform to the mores, morals and beliefs of the contemporary world.

It has been seriously proposed, for example, that there is much of value in the Christian message even if we leave out belief in the Resurrection.[1] It is a short step from that extraordinary proposition to leaving out belief in the Resurrection altogether. The Resurrection is, after all, a very unlikely sort of story to modern ears. It does not fit in easily with contemporary ways of looking at the world. The truth is, however, that there is no Christian message without the Resurrection. Remove the Resurrection and there is nothing left. The Church has nothing to say to anyone unless it can preach and live the Resurrection. It is the task of the Church to conform the world to our Lord Jesus Christ, not so to dilute the Apostolic Faith that the world finds it easy to swallow.

The processes and criteria for discerning the orthodoxy of a doctrine seem not to be generally known and so are not generally applied. They are not known and so not applied because the truth of doctrine is not thought to be important. The desired quality of a doctrine is believed to be that it is reasonable not that it leads to salvation. The important characteristic of a doctrine is thought to be that it is believable and acceptable to non-believers not that it is true. That path leads to disaster.

One of the secondary purposes of this study is to show that doctrine is centrally important to the life of the Church. We must regard the subject with absolute

---

[1] The present Anglican Bishop of Rochester in his diocesan newsletter and in an interview in 1998. The bishop stressed that he believed in the Resurrection. The strange part of his remarks was that there was plenty of good stuff left in the Christian message without the Resurrection.

seriousness. Despite the danger of serious conflict it is, in fact, more damaging to ignore the significance of doctrine and to adopt the view that doctrinal differences do not matter than it is to tackle the differences in established ways. The tragic decline in the beneficial influence of the Church and Gospel in much of Western society, arguably a result of the abandonment of the Apostolic Faith, shows us the result of ignoring the significance of true doctrine. It brings home to us the need to ensure that the doctrines we hold and teach are orthodox. It is wiser to take time to understand the ways in which doctrinal disputes are properly resolved than to paper over cracks which will bring the house down in due course. The criteria and processes which have historically been applied to come to decisions about the truth or otherwise of doctrine are known or can be relearned if they have been forgotten. We must understand them clearly and start to apply them.

The view that discussions leading to a union of churches—ecumenism—can be conducted as a doctrinal negotiation in which one side gives up something in return for a matching surrender by the other side is also misguided. The body that results from such a union has abandoned what was believed to be true and bases itself on the lowest common doctrinal denominator. The criterion here for the holding of doctrine is not its truth but its acceptability. This is one of the principal causes of playing down the significance of doctrine and the increasing readiness of churches to abandon essential doctrines. It is incorrect to suppose that there is a real and living unity of churches to be brought about by doctrinal negotiation. The process by which it is attempted will inevitably be damaging to the integrity of the Apostolic Faith. It will, further, diminish the significance of doctrine. Administrative arrangements are becoming more important to churches than the truth of doctrine.

The discussions which led to the union of the Church of England and the Baltic Lutheran Churches, although conducted by honest men and women, illustrate the disastrous nature of this sort of ecumenism. Churches with almost nothing in common, with different dogmatic bases, different order and a radically different history came together by fudging on fundamental matters of faith and order. Many schemes of unity lack any principle except that union of some sort is to be achieved at all costs. Such unity, based upon something other than the truth of the Apostolic Doctrine, leads to collapse—and that collapse can be observed although survival is, in fact, the main dynamic of many union schemes.[2] Lutherans in the U.S. resisted union with the Episcopal Church because they believed it was too heterodox. They knew what they believed.

Doctrines, and the order and conduct which flow from them, are either necessary for salvation or should not be held at all. Doctrines are not negotiable luxuries.[3]

---

[2] Cf. the observations of Archimandrite Constantine, below.

[3] Cf. J.H.Newman's Letter to Bishop Ullathorne as quoted in Butler, *The Vatican Council 1869–1870* (London, 1962), p. 182. In the light of the later discussion of papal infallibility an extended quotation might be helpful: "When we are all at rest, and have no

If they are necessary to salvation they cannot be surrendered. To give up a doctrine that one believes is necessary to salvation is a sin, a monstrous sin. To hold as essential a doctrine which is not necessary to salvation is folly, grave folly. Tolerance in doctrinal matters is a disastrous virtue. It inevitably leads to tolerance of error. The tolerance of error is not an expression of love any more than the tolerance of a life threatening condition is an expression of love. It is, at some level, the very denial of love. The trouble with tolerance in doctrine or in ethics is that it has no boundaries. We cannot know when to stop being tolerant or when tolerance denies love—as it does more often than many would like to admit.

The belief that ecumenism can properly be conducted in the way we have described can only proceed

---

doubts, and—at least practically, not to say doctrinally—hold the Holy Father to be infallible, suddenly there is thunder in the clear sky, and we are told to prepare for something we know not what, to try our faith we know not how. No impending danger is to be averted, but a great difficulty is to be created. Is this the proper work for an ecumenical council? As to myself personally, please God, I do not expect any trial at all; but I cannot help suffering with the various souls which are suffering, and I look with anxiety at the prospect of having to defend decisions which may not be difficult for my private judgement, but may be most difficult to maintain logically in the face of historical facts. What have we done to be treated as the faithful never were treated before? When has definition of doctrine *de Fide* been a luxury of devotion, and not a stern painful necessity?" We shall explore below the odd proposition that the definition of a doctrine believed to be necessary to salvation may be inopportune. The last two sentences are quoted below in the section on infallibility.

from the belief that the purpose of God is for people and nations to live at peace and that the function of the Church is to bring that about. The achievement of such an end, utterly desirable in itself, is not the purpose of preaching and living the Gospel. It is a side effect, a result, which follows from the achievement of the primary purpose.[4] Small groups of monks and nuns at prayer contribute more to world peace and the preservation of the environment than a hundred conferences, resolutions and pamphlets. In that life of prayer orthodox doctrine is central.

Doctrines are maps that lead us to salvation, truths that bring us to God. Changing the doctrines changes the maps, and that means that we may not come to salvation. The old ways are known and tested. Innovations in doctrine and order are not.

If we reject doctrinal negotiation as a means of resolving differences we must turn to an examination of the nature and exercise of authority in the Church. This is the only other way of resolving doctrinal differences. That is the principal concern of this study. Article 20 of the Articles of Religion of the Church of England says that "the Church hath authority in controversies of faith". It was Dr Carey's misquotation of this article which led the Church of England Synod to vote for the ordination of women to the priesthood. Whether his misquotation was deliberate or inexcusably negligent, the result was to persuade the Synod that it had an

---

[4] Cf. the opening pages of Archbishop Michael Ramsey's *The Gospel and the Catholic Church* (London, 1939).

authority that it did not, in fact, possess. His error was to quote Article 20 as "The Church *of England* hath authority in controversies of faith."[5] In doing so he confirmed, perhaps inadvertently, the fact that the ordination of women was a matter of faith.

Efforts have been made since to suggest that it is not a matter of faith but just of domestic arrangements. They are unconvincing. Episcopalian bishops have been as cavalier in their treatment of texts. They have generally disregarded the resolutions of the Lambeth Conference on sexual ethics and the treatment of those who cannot accept the ordination of women. The Lambeth Conference has decided that this innovation has not been received and that such ordinations are — unbelievably — provisional. The acceptance of homosexual marriages and the persecution of objectors to the ordination of women show that the Episcopalian bishops have ignored the resolutions of the Lambeth Conference.

It is clear that the one Church of Christ does have authority in controversies of faith and we shall examine this authority, its exercise and its nature, extensively below. The exercise of authority in the Church should only be concerned with the resolution of doctrinal disputes and the administration of the Church for the preservation of its vocation and the salvation of souls. It

---

[5] Dr Carey's speech in *The Ordination of Women to the Priesthood: The Synod Debate, 11 November 1992* (London: 1993). p. 22. The word, "Church," in Article 20 refers to the Universal Church in the opinion of most scholars. We have not found one who does not hold this view.

is, sadly, sometimes concerned with the exercise of political influence, with getting what one wants, of protecting one's dignity and concealing evidence of incompetence or sin. We are not seeking to defend that.

The problem of resolving doctrinal disputes so that the Church can be certain that its doctrine is the true Apostolic Doctrine is not new. The problem does not raise questions that have gone unanswered at earlier stages in the Church's life. We shall examine below one of the first and most influential examinations of this question, the Commonitorium of St Vincent of Lerins (434 AD),[6] and other, subsequent attempts to arrive at an answer to the question of how doctrinal disputes are to be resolved and the true doctrine discovered.

The fact that an Anglican theological teacher and college principal in England in 1998, (the Revd. Dr. David Holgate of the Southern Theological Education Training Scheme) found himself unfamiliar with the Vincentian Canon when asked about it in 1997 shows that such a study is necessary. His ignorance is one example of the blind spots to which we referred above. Bishop Jane Dixon, the Episcopalian suffragan bishop of Washington, is apparently ignorant of the teaching of the Gospels, the separation of church and state in the American Constitution and the terms of the canons of her own church as she seeks to remove a conservative priest she disapproves of by taking him to court.

---

[6] "The Commonitorium of St Vincent of Lerins" in Bettenson, *Documents of the Christian Church.* (London, 1963), p. 85. An examination of the teaching of St Vincent is to be found below.

Because of her ignorance of the canons she missed her chance to object to his appointment in time and has now resorted to the courts of law—in which she is not, at the time of writing, being very successful.

Fifty years ago Fr Georges Florovsky warned that the view that the heresies of the early years of the Church were no longer prevalent was seriously mistaken. He wrote, "It is an illusion that the Christological disputes of the past are irrelevant to the contemporary situation."[7] A study of Philip Lee's *Against the Protestant Gnostics* should convince anyone that the matters we are studying are urgently contemporary.[8]

---

[7] *Bible, Church and Tradition: An Eastern Orthodox View* (Belmont, MA, 1987), p. 14.

[8] (Oxford, 1989).

CHAPTER ONE

The Nature of Dogmatic Definitions

The faith of the Church is set out in doctrinal statements. While the faith of the Church is a lived reality it is possible to set out statements which have define the faith of the Church. We shall see how they do this in a moment. These statements set out the beliefs upon which upon which the following of Christ is built. They provide the essential doctrinal basis for that life. In this respect they are similar in character to the plans of a building. If the plans are sound the building, if correctly built, will be sound. Bad plans will cause an unsound building. In the same way a musical score provides the basis for the performance of music. If the score is bad the music will be bad. In this way doctrinal statements are related to the Christian life. The Christian life lived out, discipleship gives life to the doctrines.

The official doctrinal statements of the Apostolic Church are summed up in the Creeds of the Church. The Creeds are statements that define the limits of orthodox belief. These official doctrinal statements are called dogmatic definitions—dogmas—and we shall see, in due course, how they came about. We shall discover that they emerged over long periods of time.

They were usually defined after the most vigorous and sometimes acrimonious debate.

Dogmatic definitions have a particular character that makes them unlike almost any other statements. We need to understand their character clearly if we are to understand the strength and effect of dogmatic definitions. Their distinctive character is that they do not so much assert what must be believed as what must not be denied. Even when expressed in positive terms they have this negative purpose and effect. For example Christians believe in one God, who created all that is. The effect of that belief is that we may discuss and believe in God in any terms which do not deny His unity and that He made everything—and the terms of any other dogmatic definitions relating to the Godhead. We shall see this principle applied to other beliefs later.

This character of dogmatic definitions has a liberating effect on the consideration, discussion and expression of doctrine. Dogmas do not inhibit proper and fruitful speculation but set the boundaries of such speculation. The negative character of these definitions preserves us from what is sometimes called credal fundamentalism i.e. rigid adherence to dogmatic forms, the creeds, as the *only* permitted expression of a doctrine. Dogmatic definitions set negative limits to speculation but do not prevent it. This way of defining what must not be denied rather than what must be asserted—what is called an "apophatic" definition—also permits a degree of development of doctrine and its re–expression in new forms. We shall examine this below.

The negative or apophatic[1] character of dogmatic definitions we have just described has the following effect. A person may speak of a particular doctrine in many different ways, a new way if necessary, as long as he or she does not say something inconsistent with the terms of the dogmatic definition. That is the way that definitions that have this negative character work. Our blessed Lord is defined as being both God and man. The full definition of the councils of the Church is in Appendix 1. This means that one may speak of our Lord in any way that does not deny the dogmatic definitions of the Councils of the Church that He is both fully God and fully man.

The negative character of dogmatic definitions also means that they can be paradoxical — stating apparent contradictions, e.g. in defining the Blessed Trinity. This paradoxical character is inevitable since we cannot grasp the nature of the Godhead with our minds and so define the being of God in positive terms. A god who we could encompass with our minds so that we could define his nature in positive terms would not be God. If we could have tidy positive definitions of God He would not be God. We cannot comprehend and so cannot define God in positive terms; we can only do so negatively, only by saying what He is not.

In addition to the nature of the subject of dogmatic definitions — i.e. the being of God — which makes their negative character inevitable the negative character of dogma also springs, in part, from the circumstances

---

[1] See the glossary for an explanation of this word.

which give rise to the necessity of making dogmatic definitions. As we have seen in the letter of John Henry Newman to Bishop Ullathorne dogmatic definitions are only properly made in response to damaging doctrinal error. The definition is designed to exclude the doctrinal error by asserting, in the negative way that we have described, the Apostolic Faith that was held from the beginning. The definition is designed to set limits. We have noticed that definitions are like maps or plans from which can grow authentic Christian living. This characteristic is enhanced by their negative nature. Dogmatic definitions have a liberating rather than a restricting effect upon belief and discipleship. They preserve believers from dead ends and beliefs that lead away from authentic Christian living.

The Centrality of Doctrine

People find it difficult or almost impossible to see that dogmatic definitions are connected immediately with authentic Christian life. It is not easy to demonstrate that there is a direct connection between doctrine and conduct. The more obscure the doctrine the more difficult it is to show the connection. Orthodox have not included the words "and the Son" — *filioque* in Latin — in the Creed, for example, because they were not there from the beginning. The Roman Church has done so. The Orthodox believe that this is an error which has real effects in the life of the Church. An attempt to demonstrate the connection is in Appendix 2; it is not easy to do so briefly in this case. It is as hard to demonstrate briefly that any error in belief, that is a denial of some part of a dogmatic definition, makes the Christian life impossible but we must make the attempt. We shall suggest why it is hard to do so in a moment. It is clear that for most people doctrine is a trying obsession of theologians with no connection to living a good Christian life. That is a seriously mistaken view.

The most significant doctrinal error of the early years of the Church, one which we find opposed throughout the New Testament, e.g. 1 John 4:2-3, was gnosticism. Phillip Lee's book gives both a comprehensive account of historical gnosticism and also of the reappearance of the error in Western Christian life so that it is a modern as well as an ancient problem. In general terms gnosticism has two principal characteristics. The first is the belief that salvation is through the acquisition of spiritual knowledge — *gnosis*, the Greek word for knowledge. The second is the belief that the created universe is the creation of a lesser god and that the material creation is therefore debased and incapable of salvation. Only the spiritual is believed to be good and valuable.

Both these propositions are completely at odds with Christian belief. In the Church salvation is by repentance and faith in the saving work of Christ. The fullness of this saving work is the resurrection of the body, our union with Christ and the restoration of all things to the Father by the Son. However we find, both inside and outside the churches, people drawing away from the saving effect of the sacrifice of Christ and ignoring the essential place of repentance and faith in the way of salvation. They cannot see its centrality. Salvation, of some sort, is deemed possible without the sacrifice of Christ e.g. by knowledge and skill.

We see an Anglican bishop, for example, second a motion at a university union debate that "Jesus Christ is not necessary to eternal life."[2] He did not suggest where else salvation, is to be found or what constitutes salvation but by failing to assert the centrality and necessity of the Lord Jesus Christ he removed salvation and eternal life from being the result of the action of God's grace to being a human achievement. This has the effect, in the long run, of leading people to suppose that the ills of the Church and the world can be solved by better organisation and administration, more lively services, modern hymns and so on—anything but repentance and forgiveness. Each year brings a new translation of the Bible, a new liturgy, a new way of doing things—and all because last year's new solutions have not worked. The fact that the ills of the Church and the world are the result of sin and that the cure of sin is the sacrifice of Christ is not part of the consideration of the problem and its solution. The only real cure is ignored and none of the other attempted cures works.

Contemporary gnosticism can be found among feminist Episcopalian theologians in the United States,

---

[2] Bishop Christopher Mayfield, Anglican Bishop of Manchester in the Durham Union, November 1996. The same bishop was present as a crucified, naked, female figure, 'Christa", was carried around his cathedral at a service to celebrate the Ecumenical Decade of Solidarity with Women. Solidarity with the true Christ is a more urgent matter.

who want to "get rid of all this blood and sacrifice," i.e. the sacrifice of our Lord on the Cross. We refer to this view below as functional atheism, that is lip service to belief in the providential will of God while actually conducting one's affairs as though there were no God. Brightened up services and a new administrative structure are preferred to the grace of God—but they do not work. They do not heal the problems because the problems are not dull services and bad administration but sin. We can also see the effects of gnosticism in spirituality which is tested by the effect of emotional experience rather than by growth in love.

The effect of gnostic, New Age theology on personal morality can be seen in mainstream churches. The exponents of it, e.g. Bishop Richard Holloway, until recently the Primus of the Episcopal Church of Scotland, and many Episcopal bishops now teach that sexual promiscuity, homosexual genital activity and so on are no longer to be deemed sinful. This reflects and comes from the gnostic belief that the material is of no value and has no real significance. The body, therefore, and what one does with it—except experience pleasure—is of no moral significance. Experiencing pleasure is the only good. The concept of sin has, to a great extent disappeared, with the development of a new form of moral theology that we shall examine briefly below. It does not take long to discover that gnosticism is alive and well in Western churches. Its effects are everywhere. Lee's book gives a searching and extensive account of its effects on the life of churches.

Gnosticism is prevalent because there has been a falling away from orthodox belief. The true aim of human existence has been forgotten. The new doctrines that replace the orthodox beliefs are working themselves out in people's lives. If we find a distortion of the Christian life, some conduct or some strange worship, we can usually trace it to error in belief. This is the reason for the Church's passionate concern to remove doctrinal error from its life. This why, before all things, the Church seeks to preserve the Apostolic Faith in its purity, without distortions. The effect of doctrinal error is, in the end, a disaster. It keeps people from their salvation. That frustrates the whole Christian life, the purpose of God and the sacrifice of our Lord on the Cross.

It can be difficult for people unfamiliar with the process to see how doctrine has an immediate connection with living the Christian life. The line showing how one causes the other is not always obvious. To see it and to follow it through involves ways of thought which are unfamiliar and not often encountered. As if this was not bad enough there is another hazard.

The problem is made more complicated by confusion and error over what constitutes the Christian life. There seems to be no clear understanding of this among the leaders of many churches and so it is also often absent from the hearts and minds of members of those churches. We need to have a correct understanding of what it means to be a Christian, what the essential aim of the Christian life is if we are to understand the centrality of doctrine. We need to have a clear picture of the nature of authentic Christian life, its characteristics, its content. If we do not have that clearly in our hearts and our heads then we will be easily misled. We will not be able to see the connection between doctrine and authentic Christian living because we will not know what constitutes authentic Christian living and the state of salvation and we will follow a way that leads us from God into greater frustration and confusion. We will not know what the doctrine is supposed to lead us to. If we cannot see that then we shall not see the connection between orthodox dogma and the Christian life.

If we believe that we can sum up authentic Christian living as living a decent middle class life then we will not see the need for true doctrine. If that aim, or ones similar to it, are believed to be the functions of living a Christian life then correct belief does not matter. It does not matter, in general, what one believes if the purpose of life is to be a well-mannered member of the middle classes. The nature of our Lord's person or the nature of the Blessed Trinity or of God as Creator are irrelevant. Correct belief has no place in this understanding of the Christian life. Good and serious men have sometimes proposed that the rules of various games with their attention to fair play and so on represent the Christian ethic in a reasonably complete way. If this is the case then the truth of doctrine will have no importance. Doctrine is not relevant to being a well-mannered middle class person or a faithful follower of the rules of the game. What matters in that case is a belief that the Lord Jesus was a jolly good chap—a regular guy—who when playing a game would not cheat or argue with the umpire's decision. It would not matter whether He was God or not in this understanding. There is no real connection between the Apostolic Faith and these qualities of life. It is not surprising, if the vision of the Christian life is distorted, that people cannot see the importance of doctrine.

Another belief causing similar difficulty is the view that the function of living a Christian life is to experience a high degree of spiritual elation and comfort in time of difficulty. The singing of rousing hymns and the constant assurance that everything is all right bring us to that state of euphoria that is believed to constitute the full Christian life. Again the truth of doctrine plays no part in this. How can it? The distortions of the aim of the Christian life have many variations. Being continually happy is one variation.

If the aim of the Christian life is undisturbed happiness then the important thing about the Lord would be that He always wanted us to be happy on our own terms. A person who believed that this is the purpose of the Christian life will find it perverse to suggest that happiness on one's own terms is impossible. We would come to assume that we would be all right as long as we did not breach the normal ethical standards of the Church too often and too blatantly. In this case repentance and forgiveness would have no place in our lives—and we shall see below that it has disappeared from the moral systems of some churches.

Belief in Christian living as undisturbed happiness leads to a certain type of moral system and a particular sort of worship; we can see both of these in the life of churches. We see moral theology devoid of sin, repentance and forgiveness. We see worship designed to entertain the worshippers and bring them to an emotional and spiritual high. Life in Christ is not, however, being a nice, spiritually satisfied man or woman—middle class or anything else—who behaves himself or herself nicely and ignores the belief of the Church.

A moment's reflection—doctrinal reflection—would, however, soon show a person that the understandings of the function and nature of the Christian life that we have just outlined are unbiblical, totally inadequate and radically mistaken. They lead people from their true destiny. The Church holds before us a more exalted destiny. If we lose sight of the true destiny of the Christian life, or if we never see it, then doctrine has no place. Doctrine is not concerned with being nice but with being holy. It is not designed to bring us to contentment but to Heaven. The aim of the Christian life is union with the glory of the Risen Lord, not anaesthetized comfort.

It is frequently suggested that a person who points out that a particular act—usually a sexual sin—lacks compassion. To do so is likely to cause that person to be unhappy with guilt. That is deemed to be a cruel act. This is certainly how Dr Carey castigated those who criticised the Anglican Bishop of Birmingham in 1998 for marrying the divorced wife of one of his priests. (Many Episcopalian bishops have been married and divorced several times.)

It is very easy to characterize a person pointing out that sin is sin as judgmental and moralising. Both are terms of religious insult. It would take too long to distinguish between the person who is judgmental and moralising and the person who properly warns of the effects of sin. Any sensible person should be able to do so. The alternative, accepting sin and condoning it, is the cruellest thing in the world. It puts a person's salvation at risk, and there is nothing loving about that.

The New Testament commands the Church to preach repentance. Repentance is the essential first part of the proclamation of the Gospel but calling people to repentance is an empty exercise if sin is not to be rebuked. There is, in fact, no Gospel at all without repentance. If sin is not fatal because it separates from God then there is no Gospel of salvation because salvation is not necessary—and there is no need for the Church! Not surprisingly churches that follow this teaching die. There is no need for them, after all. All this distortion flows from an incorrect understanding of the aim of the Christian life.

Let us pursue this line of thought a little further and see its effects upon morals. Moral questions and moral decisions requiring a personal answer, such that a person sees that he should do or should not do something, are being replaced in the moral theology of many churches with the moral "issue." Issues such as unemployment or third world debt, about which individuals can do nothing, are replacing moral questions. A moral issue, about which one can do nothing, does not present one with a moral question. We cannot ask what we should do about third world debt because unless we are one of the world's political leaders we can do nothing. If we can do nothing we cannot have a moral responsibility in the matter.

The principle is very simple: "Ought implies can." That is, if we say a person ought to do something, has a moral responsibility in a matter, then that person must be able to do something. If he cannot do anything then he has no moral responsibility. The replacement of moral questions with moral issues produces a situation where the concept of sin as a morally significant act, for which an individual is personally responsible, disappears almost completely. Where there is no sin there is no redemption—and we are without hope. Where there is no sin or moral responsibility, to speak of, we do not need doctrines of the person of our Lord or of his saving work and so on. Nor do we need the Church. We do not need the saving work of Christ to worry about third world debt. Anyone can worry about moral issues but only governments can do anything about most of them. The moral issue makes doctrine irrelevant. What is tragic is that humanity is damned without any hope of salvation. The moral question leading to repentance and forgiveness gives sinners hope.[3] A moral issue does not.

---

[3] The final folly in this process is meaningless repentance for acts for which one is not responsible, e.g. the repentance of church leaders in England for religious wars and the Holocaust and so on or the repentance of Pope John Paul II for the Inquisition. None of those repenting actually sinned in the acts for which they are repenting, so their repentance is meaningless and debases to significance of true moral responsibility and true repentance.

The Lambeth Conference of Anglican Bishops of 1998 discussed a large number of moral issues. These included such matters as Third World Debt, past acts of racism, unemployment, etc. about which the Anglican bishops, or indeed any individual, could do nothing. For that reason, they were moral issues and not moral questions. At the same time the bishops of the Church of England confused and misunderstood the moral questions arising from homosexuality, divorce and other related questions. These are matters about which individuals can do something. The effective guidance given to Anglicans was inevitably derisory.[4] The

---

[4] "Issues in Human Sexuality," issued by the House of Bishops of the General Synod of the Church of England. 1996. Section 5.7, under the general heading, "The Homosexual in the life and fellowship of the Church," reads: "At the same time there are others who are conscientiously convinced that this way of abstinence is not the best for them (*this section follows one saying that abstinence from sexual activity is chosen by some homosexuals; that way is praised but not commended*) and that they have more hope of growing in love for God and neighbour with the help of a loving and faithful homophile partnership, in intention life long, where mutual self-giving includes the physical expression of their attachment. In responding to this conviction it is important to bear in mind the historic tension in Christian ethical teaching between the God given moral order and the freedom of the moral agent. While insisting that the conscience needs to be informed in the light of that order, Christian tradition (*which tradition?* —ed.) also contains an emphasis on respect for free conscientious judgement where the individual has seriously weighed the issues involved. The homophile is only one in a range of such cases...." This passage was rendered by the Anglican Bishop of Newcastle more crisply. He said, "homosexuality within a loving stable relationship is no sin." One of his clergy protested about this view to the

acceptance of sexual immorality by Episcopalians is now very widespread.

If bishops believe that a particular political party might act to resolve the moral issues they discern, and only governments can resolve most of them, then they are faced with a real and costly moral question. Do they urge the members of their church to vote for a particular party or not? It has not happened for a long time, if ever, in England or the U.S. It should if they wish to exercise their moral responsibility and do something effective. Moral questions requiring costly decisions and actions are avoided. The moral issue which gener-

---

Archbishop of York who delivered the judgement that the words of the Bishop were "not contrary to the worship, doctrine and practice of the Church of England." The Archbishop has, therefore, in a solemn judgement, endorsed the Bishop's view. That is now the teaching of the Church of England. It would be incorrect to assume that the words of the report given here reflect the Christian ethical tradition in any serious way. While one has the duty to obey one's conscience that conscience must be formed by the God-given moral order. That order persists whatever we think, feel or believe. Our consciences must be informed by the mind of the Church expressing the God -given moral order. The words of the report are seriously misleading and seem to propose that the individual conscience is of equal standing to the God-given moral order. This is reflected in the comments by the Anglican Bishop of Birmingham about "Christian reason/common sense" (page 26 n.7 below). An application of the principles of the report, inconsistent as they are with each other and the mainstream ethical teaching of the Church, would lead to moral anarchy; each one his own judge of what is right and wrong. This teaching is completely inconsistent with the Synod's 1988 decision on the matter that only 11 bishops endorsed when asked to do so a few years later.

ates much talk but discussion of which achieves nothing is preferred. It costs nothing to discuss a moral issue. Moral questions face us with costly decisions and action; repentance and seeking forgiveness.

When we accept that we are sinful and that our sins are the real problems then doctrine becomes central and the Church's function becomes clear. When we accept that sin ruins lives and is a distortion of the image of God in man, then we must start paying attention to doctrine. The healing of sin and the restoration of the Creation to the Father is spelt out in orthodox doctrine. The truth of doctrine must, therefore, be at the very centre of our concern. It is at the centre of the process of healing, redemption and restoration. If the fundamental human problem is understood to be sin, then doctrine is central. When we recognise that we cannot heal sin ourselves and cannot restore ourselves to the Father but, at the same time, must do something about our sin then doctrine is central.

If our Lord is not both God and man then His life and His death are not for our salvation as the Creed teaches and defines that it is. He cannot save sinners and we are without hope. We have no weapon against the sin that is behind racism and the others 'isms'. If we ignore the New Testament teaching that the destiny of man is union with the Son, divinization or theosis,[5] substituting one of the easier and more comfortable aims we have discussed then there is no point at all in the

---

[5] See the glossary for an explanation of this word.

doctrine of the person of our Lord. If the New Testament is correct then doctrine is central.

The true aim and fulfilment of our life is union with God in Heaven. That is a doctrinal statement. Our way to that is defined and shaped by orthodox doctrine. Coming to union with God in Christ and the effect of doctrine on that involves processes that are subtle in their operation and can only be discerned after careful reflection. Our actions spring from who and what we believe we are and what we believe our destiny to be. Without exploring fully the effect of symbolism[6] upon our beliefs and understanding of ourselves and our destiny it is not easy to show that an heretical belief about the person of our Lord is the cause of a person's sinful conduct. Nor is it simple to demonstrate that changing symbols changes, in time, our understanding of reality. Such an examination is beyond the scope of this study although the matter is touched on in Appendix 2. What is clear, upon reflection, is that this most fundamental element in the Christian life, i.e. the aim and destiny of the way of discipleship, is a matter which involves doctrine and that fundamental differences in doctrine will affect fundamentally the way to our destiny and its nature.

People have always observed that heresy and sin go together. That connection has been the dynamic behind the concern with opposing heresy and teaching true doctrine. It is more complicated and difficult to show that heresy leads to and causes sin. The difficulty

---

[6] See the glossary for an explanation of this word.

is the same, in substance, as the difficulty we encountered when seeking to demonstrate the opposite proposition, that is, that orthodox doctrine is necessary to live an authentic Christian life. An attempt to show that a particular innovation in order has led to a particular view about sexual ethics is to be found at Appendix 2. It may not be found to be persuasive. If the reader is not persuaded he or she would be unwise, all the same, to dismiss the general principle it is intended to illustrate. That principle is that doctrinal belief has a direct, causal relationship with conduct and the way of life that a person leads. One causes the other. We can even observe that a person may embrace a heresy in order to provide a justification for sin. The adoption of New Age theology seems to go hand in hand with sexual licence. It often seems that people seek the doctrine and worship that matches their life–style and then adopt it to provide a rationale for what they are doing. That way, of course, lies disaster.

Appendix 2 also points to one other characteristic of dogmatic definitions that we shall explore more fully below. This characteristic is that dogmatic definitions, and indeed every aspect of Christian discipleship—praying, morality, church order, worship, every aspect of Christian living—are all part of an integrated whole. Each one affects the other and is connected to each other.

If we believe that the Lord was not truly God and truly man then church order, our doctrine of salvation, worship and ethics, the sacraments and so on change. They change and cease to be part of an integrated whole. Doctrines are all related—and they disintegrate when the wholeness is broken. We can see the disintegration of morals, worship and church order in churches where the doctrinal integrity has been ignored or destroyed. This disintegration is a telling sign that doctrine is in error as the reverse, the integration of a doctrine into the corpus of the Apostolic Faith, is a sign of a doctrine's truth.

Part of the importance and effect of symbols in theology and Christian discipleship is that they point to this integrated quality. Indeed the word, "symbolic," means that which is thrown or held together and is integrated. The word, "diabolic," means the opposite; that which is thrown apart and is disintegrating. Creeds were originally referred to as symbols—and still are.[7]

---

[7] Symbols have the effect of making connections between absent realities and present realities. The absent realities are sometimes intangible. Symbols "throw together" two or more such realities so making the presence of one the effective presence of the other. Thus the monarch is the nation. In the monarch the nation, its concerns and power find a tangible locus. The Queen writes for us all when she sends a letter of condolence and sympathy in a disaster. Judges symbolize as well as administer the majesty of the Law. Very often the symbol is a symbol of grace. The monarch still functions as a symbol whether a good or bad person. In the same way the goodness or wickedness of the priest does not affect the sacraments which he administers specifically in the place of Christ. All sacraments are administered in place and name of Christ in his Body. If symbols are changed or abandoned then reality is effectively changed or we lose contact with some aspect of reality. This short note is not intended to do more than indicated some of the ways in which symbols "work."

Doctrinal truth and error are absolutely significant. To suppose that it does not matter what you believe but only what you do is both unbiblical and unhistorical. It fails to recognise the truth that what one does follows from what one believes. If you want to know the profound reason for a particular piece of conduct do not question so much the person's immediate motives but rather his basic beliefs. Belief and action are two inseparable parts of one whole. The one issues in the other. Belief, therefore, is not a private matter any more than conduct is a private matter.

The proper basis for the correct belief is not what a person finds himself comfortable with but the authoritative definition of the Church. The Church brings great experience and insight into the nature and effect of doctrine. It understands human destiny in its true context. The Church brings to the understanding and treatment of the question the whole of its life up to this point, i.e. the Tradition of the Church. To put what suits one as an individual or as a small group before the life and Tradition of the Church is the height of folly. It is to ignore proven wisdom. It is the function of authority in the Church, among other things, to discern true doctrine from false doctrine and to teach true doctrine. True doctrine provides the only sure basis for living the Christian life to the full. False doctrine makes it impossible.

There is a story of a driver of a staff car in the desert during the Second World War who did not realise that the car had four gears and so never drove above third gear. He never got the best out of the car and could not do his work properly. Ignorance of what is possible prevents growth. Not knowing the nature of the Christian destiny means we cannot direct our lives towards it, however feebly. Without a complete statement of true doctrine the Christian cannot see and so cannot come to the destiny for which he or she is created. That means the purpose of God and the sacrifice of Christ is frustrated.

The failure to understand the fullness of our calling renders the sacrifice of Christ meaningless. It leaves us as unfulfilled Christians. All the stratagems to warm up the life of the Church which are not concerned with teaching and living out the true Apostolic Doctrine of the Universal Church are doomed to failure. New and exciting services are not the solution. They are the result of a confusion about the purpose of the Christian life. They cost little and achieve nothing. Administrative reform is not the solution to a Christian community's ills because administrative inadequacy is not the cause of the ills. The cause is our sin. The solution is our repentance and forgiveness, and our union with Christ. In that exercise true doctrine is of central importance. It is the essential pre–condition for coming to one's salvation. There is nothing more important than that.

The Church, by the exercise of its authority, must discern, teach and live that doctrine. To fail to do so is to fail in its vocation. It is to the nature of authority itself and the way it works in the Church that we must now turn.

The Nature of Authority

Kinds of Authority

We need to have a clear idea of the nature of authority as such, of its basic characteristics. We need to understand what sort of thing authority is, how it works, what its natural limits are. We need to understand its fundamental nature. We can then see the way in which authority is exercised and works itself out in the Church. We can see the significance and importance of the sources of authority the Church exercises in the process of deciding if a doctrinal proposition is true or false. We can see, when faced with a new proposition, the inner workings of the way in which the Church decides whether it is true or false doctrine.

Authority is a relationship between an individual or group and another individual or group that has the effect of one obeying the other or accepting the judgements of the other and acting upon them. A person exercises his or her authority and others obey because that person has authority. One person obeys another because the parties are bound together in a relationship of authority. If a person does not have authority of some sort then he or she is not obeyed. Effective authority leads to obedience. Ineffective authority can hardly be understood to be authority at all. Authority can be defied but defiance of itself does not destroy authority although successful long-term defiance of an authority would, eventually, point to its lack of effectiveness. A person who removes himself from a voluntary relationship of authority, e.g. a priest from his bishop, is not an example of this however. He would have to remain as a priest subject to that bishop and yet defying his authority over a long period in order to render the bishop's authority ineffective.

The obedience that results from an exercise of authority is either obedience which can be enforced by the authoritative individual or group or is the voluntary response of the obedient individual or group. The person in authority can either force the other party to obey or the other party, group or individual, obeys voluntarily. An exercise of authority can, therefore, either be backed by sanctions against those who resist it or it can depend upon a voluntary response. We are considering, therefore, two different sorts of authority. We shall examine the differences in a moment. We can, however, see that both forms of authority have the common characteristic of being a relationship that issues in the obedience of one party.

We shall see when we come to consider the nature of authority in the Church that these two types of authority have many other characteristics in common. That is not surprising. All authority in the Church — and, St Paul says, authority of any kind[1] — is ultimately the authority of the Blessed Trinity. We are concerned, in this study, with how that single authority of the

---

[1] Romans 13:1 ff.

Blessed Trinity is mediated to the Church and the world and where it can be discerned with the greatest degree of certainty. We are concerned, therefore, firstly, with the relationship of authority which exists between the Blessed Trinity and the created order and secondly, with the discernment and exercise of that authority by the Church. The relationship between the Blessed Trinity and everything else — all creation — is one of loving authority in which God wills our salvation and the Church discerns the saving will of God.

We shall see below that both the discernment of the will of God and his authority and the communication of that will and the exercise of that authority are properly part, and a major part, of the Church's vocation and function.[2] The Church's failure to discern and exercise the authority of the Blessed Trinity, where it occurs, is a failure of vocation and function. The Church fails in the most serious way when it fails in this. It is not doing what God created it to do. We should add that this vocation is among the most costly Christian

---

[2] A function is best described as what will not happen when the functioning object is absent. For example the function of an electric light bulb is to provide light rather than to be decorative. How do we know that? We take the light bulb away. What is missing? The light is missing. The function of the electric light bulb is, therefore, to provide light. This understanding of the function of something concentrates our minds on the precise function and effect, preserving us from being confused by effects that are not essential i.e. not functions. It is a valuable definition. The Church exercises the authority of God in, for example, remitting sin (c.f. John 20:21-23). That is one of the Church's functions. If the Church were not there this ministry would go unexercised.

vocations. Not a few patriarchs and bishops of the Church have gone to their martyrdom because they were faithful to the vocation of discerning and exercising the authority of the Blessed Trinity on behalf of the whole Church.

There are several ways of distinguishing between the two different forms of authority. We can distinguish them most simply by observing that there is, firstly, an authority that is conferred externally by a structure, an organisation. The exercise of authority of this kind may result in either enforced obedience or voluntary obedience. The authority of the state, exercised in various different ways — the police, tax collection and so on — is an example of structural authority, conferred from outside, which can be enforced. The state can act to enforce the payment of taxes or act to stop people committing offences. These are examples of authority in a structure where obedience can be enforced.

The authority of a church or school, on the other hand, is obeyed voluntarily to some degree. If a person does not wish to obey the authority of a church then he or she leaves it. If a parent does not like the authority of a school in some particular then he removes his child and finds somewhere else that suits the child better. These are examples of authority in a structure that is obeyed voluntarily. When a person leaves the structure he breaks off his relationship with the structure and an element in that relationship was the relationship of authority.

There is a second type of authority, personal authority. This evokes voluntary obedience. This authority resides with the person and is not exercised by him on behalf of a structure. He or she is obeyed because of the personal authority he or she bears not because his or her authority is a manifestation of the authority of a structure. He or she does not act on behalf of an organisation or structure.

Personal authority can be either charismatic authority, to which we shall refer below, or the authority of experience and expertise. A compelling preacher may evoke obedience to his words. He speaks as a minister of a church that gives him authority to preach. The compulsion to obey him that people experience comes, however, from him rather than the structure. If he is not a charlatan, he is exercising the authority of God. He exercises it, in some sense, personally, not simply as the representative of a structure, in this case, a church. We can call this charismatic authority. The authority of expertise is different. We obey the doctor when he prescribes a course of treatment because we believe that he knows what he is talking about. We follow a lawyer's advice on the same principle. If we do not trust his expertise we do not obey him. His authority stems from his expertise.

We can call these two broad types of authority (a) structural, and (b) personal/charismatic. The use of the word "structural" points to the fact that this form of authority is only properly used within the law-giving structure. This structure, e.g. church or state, confers authority on a particular person, usually the holder of an office. The office represents the authority. The office holder acts for the structure or organisation. The

authority of a bishop, for example, is primarily structural since it is conferred on him by the structure that
appoints him, the church. He does not act on his personal authority but for the church, which authorizes
him. In the case of an established church the government is the structure which appoints bishops. A
bishop's authority can only be exercised, therefore,
within the laws and canons of the structure, church or
state, which appoints him. He ceases to have structural
authority when he ceases to hold office. He may, incidentally, have personal and charismatic authority as
well. That authority would survive his departure from
office.

Structural authority can only be exercised within
the laws of the structure, e.g. a church, a state or a company. The authority of the office holder is the authority
of the structure. He can only give effect to the authority
of the structure as expressed in it rules and laws. The
structure speaks and acts through its appointee who, in
that activity, acts for the whole structure. An office
holder who seeks to exercise structural authority as
though it is personal authority will very soon act
beyond the authority he has been given. This is called
acting *ultra vires* — beyond powers. He is attempting to
exercise powers beyond those given to him by the
structure or organisation.

Personal and charismatic authority is that authority which evokes voluntary obedience by the expertise
or charismatic nature of an individual. It is self–
authenticating. We do not need to ask about the origins
of charismatic authority. The origin is self– evident. We

experience it. We would not know such authority existed unless we experienced it; see, e.g. Luke 4:2. It is unenforceable as such. The possessor of charismatic authority does not have the power, because of the nature of his authority, to enforce obedience as a further stage in the exercise of authority. The idea of enforcement does not make sense since the power of charismatic authority is precisely experienced as a desire to obey voluntarily. If we did not feel the compulsion to obey we would not know ourselves to be in the presence of an authoritative person. We would not be in a relationship of authority.

Many who exercise charismatic authority may also possess structural authority. Some elements of both types of authority may be found in any particular exercise of authority. The police officer is more readily obeyed if he has gifts of personality which ease the exercise of his authority on behalf of the state. A politician, for example, would not last long in a democratic society if he depended wholly upon structural authority. The President of the United States possesses enormous structural authority. He comes to that office and exercises it effectively because he also possesses personal, charismatic authority. A parent may exercise a form of structural authority with such charisma that children have little sense of having their obedience forced. Charismatic authority may evoke a high degree of obedience without much real reliance upon an existing structural authority. It would be a very restless and unhappy ship that was commanded only by structural authority, that is, only by the operation of Naval Law.

Gifts of management—a form of charismatic authority—must be present for a really effective exercise of structural authority.

Structural authority can, however, be effective in causing obedience without any dependence upon the personal qualities of the person exercising the authority. A police officer can arrest someone according to the terms of the law without any dependence upon his or her personal qualities although in human terms he will experience some difficulty in exercising authority without some charismatic gifts. By an extension of that principle, Article 26 of the 39 Articles of Religion of the Church of England teaches that "the unworthiness of the ministers... hinders not the effect of the sacrament." The sacrament is the act of the Church of England through its minister. The sacrament does not depend for its effect upon the personal qualities of the minister. Most churches teach that principle. But as we have seen structural authority is almost always more effective when accompanied by charismatic authority. It is important also to note that "unworthiness" means moral unworthiness and not doctrinal error. A person who is in heresy has separated himself from the Church and cannot purport to act on its behalf. Neither this article nor the principle it enshrines applies in the case of heresy.

One further aspect of the exercise of structural authority, upon which we have already briefly touched, needs further consideration. Structural authority is the authority of the whole structure. It is expressed and exercised in the actions of authorised groups and individuals within that structure. To take a secular example—a corporation, e.g. a company or a city council, may have the right to do certain things because that right is contained in its charter. The governors of that corporation can delegate to individuals, employees or members of the corporation, authority to perform certain actions which will carry the authority of the whole corporation. If the individual goes beyond the powers granted in the charter which sets out the constitution of the corporation, its powers and authority, with or without the approval of his superiors, then he is said to act *ultra vires* or beyond powers.

As we saw above, the ecclesiastical application of this principle is obvious. The structural authority of a minister ceases when he ceases to hold office. It also does not apply to matters outside the canons of the church of which he is a member. In some churches a minister deposed from holy orders has the structural authority, the church's authority, to minister in emergencies when no other minister is present but even then he does not exercise a personal authority but the church's authority.

More significantly the expression of a doctrinal opinion by a minister derives its authority only from his office and the fact that the doctrinal opinion is consistent with the dogma of the Universal Church. It is this alone that gives authority to doctrinal teaching. If an archbishop or even a patriarch makes a doctrinal pronouncement which is inconsistent with the dogma of the Universal Church then he speaks without authority.

We have seen so far that authority is a relationship that issues in effective action or obedience. It can be either structural or personal and charismatic or a mixture of both. Structural authority can only properly be exercised within the structure and within the powers conferred by the structure within its laws. It is, in fact, the authority of the whole structure itself exercised by an individual given authority by the structure. The individual represents the structure.

Most writers on authority observe that authority has the function of serving the freedom of the individual. We shall see that authority is essentially the exercise of love to bring people to a full life. If it is not this there is something in the exercise of the authority which is distorted. We shall examine some of the further implications of this when we consider the fundamental source of authority, the Blessed Trinity. If St Paul is correct, and it would be a bold person who said he is not, then as we have seen, all authority is from God. This gives authority its loving and creative quality (cf. Romans 13:1 ff.).

What is the relationship between authority and power? This relationship principally concerns the enforcement of structural authority. Clearly there is a difficulty in exercising coercive power lovingly but it is a mistake to suppose that it is impossible or that it is always wrong to exercise authority in a coercive way, even in the Church. Just as we require children to do things out of love and act to prevent criminals injuring others out of love so it is loving to act against heresy and doctrinal error.

Some people make a sharp distinction between authority and power e.g. Dr Runcie in *Authority in Crisis*.[3] The distinction is, however, misleading. Structural authority has power to command and enforce obedience by the laws of the structure. The authority of a police officer to arrest someone and his lawful power to do so look very much like the same thing unless we are speaking of the officer's physical powers, and we are not.

Of course, power can operate without authority. In this case it is exercised *ultra vires* and ultimately it is subject to the authority of a structure e.g. the United Nations or the state. It is not really possible to speak of personal charismatic authority as lacking power. It is precisely power — that is, that the authority cannot properly be resisted — which makes us aware that most charismatic authority is, in fact, authoritative. The exercise of charismatic authority and its power generally go together. The two seem to be the same thing in effect. We know we are in the presence of an exercise of charismatic authority because we experience the power of that authority even if we defy it. Unless we had experienced it we would not know that it existed. The experience of charismatic power is evidence of the existence of charismatic authority. We know we are in the presence of authority because of its power to bring us to obedience. We see this in the reaction of people to the words and actions of Jesus that, in any worldly

---

[3] (London, 1988).

sense that we can understand, lacked structural authority.[4]

The Roots of the Word, "Authority"

If we examine the roots from which our English word authority comes we can find out more about its nature. The Greek word for authority, which is used in the New Testament, is the word, *exousia*, which comes from a verb meaning "it is lawful"; "it is within one's power", "it is allowed", "it is possible". The verb is *exesti*. It is, therefore, in its origin concerned principally with structural authority, that is, it is concerned with whether an action, for example, is against the law of a state or organisation. We ask, "Is it lawful?" The answer is that it is or is not lawful. In the New Testament, however, it is almost always used to describe personal and charismatic authority.

In due course we shall see that the Orthodox principle of describing things negatively or apophatically rather than describing things positively (kataphatically) is consistent with this understanding of authority. It is lawful because it is not inconsistent with a law. We came across this understanding when we looked at the basic characteristics of dogmatic definitions earlier. We noticed then that dogmatic definitions do not so much set out what is to be believed as what is not to be denied. This is a fundamental principle. If governed by this principle, that is, that we must not deny the defini-

---

[4] See Matthew 7:29, Mark 2:10, and Luke 4:32.

tion of a dogma or teach anything inconsistent with it, then speculation about doctrine is valuable and will not stray into heresy. The Creeds are essentially apophatic in nature. They provide boundaries for belief. They do not tell us so much what we must believe as what we must not deny. We can speculate in any terms not inconsistent with the Creeds.

There never has been, for example, a dogmatic definition of *how* the life, death and resurrection of the Lord Jesus is for us men and for our salvation. That it *is* for our salvation is defined. *How* it is for our salvation, the way in which our salvation is achieved by the life, death and resurrection of our Lord, is not defined. Theories of the atonement abound. They often have the intriguing characteristic of reflecting the world-view and political order of the time and place in which they are generated but that is not relevant to our discussion. They are only heretical if they say that the life, death and resurrection of the Lord is *not* for us men and for our salvation as defined in the Creed; i.e. if the theories suggest that salvation is possible for men and women without His life, death and resurrection they are heretical. In the same way the debate about the person of Jesus will continue and should do so, but the fact that our Lord was very God and very man in the terms of the Chalcedonian definition[5] and subsequent defini-

---

[5] The definition of the person of Christ of the council of Chalcedon is reproduced in Appendix 1. Some elucidation of this definition was made at subsequent councils but, in general, the major part of the dogma of the person of Christ was completed at this council.

tions must not be denied. To deny the dogma would be unlawful and without authority. A statement that contains a belief inconsistent with the dogma of the Church would lack authority, it would lack *exousia*.

The Latin word for authority is *auctoritas* and derives from the verb *augere*—to increase or enrich. Authority in the Church (indeed, all authority as we have suggested above) has the function of bringing men to fullness of life in Christ. Authority should be exercised for this purpose. The high doctrine of civil authority in Romans 13:1 ff. is clearly based on this understanding. The civil authorities derive their authority from God. They exercise it for the benefit of those under the authority of the particular government. It was upon this principle that Dietrich Bonhoeffer, the German Lutheran martyr, for example, criticised and sought to bring down the government of Hitler. That government was *ultra vires* at a profound level. It is this principle which lies behind the morality of seeking to overthrow a tyrannical government or of conducting a just war. If it is true that civil authority must be exercised for the ultimate benefit of the ruled then it is even more obviously true of those exercising authority in the Church. The title assumed by one of the great Bishops of Rome, St Gregory the Dialogist (540–604), was "servant of the servants of God." Indeed, the title, "pope," simply means "father."

Plainly ecclesiastical authority can be used in ways that do not bring the subjects of that authority to fullness of life in Christ. Bishops can be sinners and behave in ways that do not bring people to salvation if only by behaving scandalously. Since all authority comes from God it cannot, however, if properly administered, be oppressive to those who are doing good. If it is oppressive and destructive of growth in Christ then there is some sense in which it is *ultra vires* even if not strictly so in terms of the particular structure. Even a church structure can have laws which distort the will and authority of God. State authorities certainly can do so e.g. the South African law, now long repealed, which forbade interracial marriages. The Nazi anti-Jewish laws are another example. It is worth adding that no authority can destroy Christian freedom which is the freedom of our Lord on the Cross, absolute freedom within worldly constraint. The suffering love of Christ seen on Calvary and in His Body, the Church, is the highest authority in Heaven and Earth and cannot be defeated.

Discerning the authority of God

All authority, rightly exercised, is an expression of the authority of God. At this point we will briefly examine where that authority can be discerned and how it can be discerned. We shall examine later the means we use to ensure that we have discerned it correctly and also, what are called, the "sources" of authority. It is necessary at this point to clear up a serious confusion that exists over the sources of authority, i.e. the places in which we can expect to discern the authority and will of God with authenticity.

Liberal Protestants teach that there are three sources of authority—Scripture, Tradition and Reason within which the authority of God can be discerned. This teaching seems a confusing and inadequate understanding of the significance of Scripture, Tradition and Reason in the process of discerning the authority of God. Indeed talk of sources of authority is itself confusing. There is one source of authority, the Blessed Trinity as there is one God. This authority is communicated to men in divine self–disclosure, revelation; God reveals his will and purpose to us. The Scriptures are a record of that revelation, of God's self-disclosure to his people. In them the Church can discern, by grace and faith and guided by the Holy Spirit, the authority and will of God.

The Tradition of the Church is the non-scriptural record of God's continuing self-disclosure in the life of the Church to the People of God and the Church's discernment of it. It is the life of Christ in the Church. Scripture is canonical. It provides the standard, the rule, by which all revelation is measured. The authority of Scripture and Tradition is discerned by the consensus of the Faithful, the whole People of God. The canon of Scripture—"canon" means rule—is the standard against which the developing Tradition, the life of the Church, is measured.

Scripture and Tradition are not, therefore, sources of authority They are records—using that word broadly, in the Bible, in the sacraments and orders and life of the Church, within which the Church discerns, by faith and grace, the authoritative revelation of God. The

People of God find, by prayerful and faithful study, the authoritative will of God in the Scriptures and the Tradition of the Church. Scripture and Tradition are the records of God's self-disclosure. (In referring to the Tradition as a record we do not mean a written record but a locus of revelation, a living reality in which revelation, the life of the Holy Spirit in the Church, can be discerned.) In view of this the proposition that Reason, i.e. human reason, is a source of authority on an equal standing with Scripture and Tradition seems nonsensical at several levels.

Human reason, as such, cannot be a source of authority since reason is simply a means by which the human mind processes data and forms conclusions from that data. A detective gathers clues and deduces from them that the butler did it. The preacher reads the Scriptures and by faith and prayer discerns the word of God that he must preach. In neither case does the power to reason, of itself, provide any fundamental data. It works upon data provided from other sources. It could be argued that *the fact that humans can reason* is itself a revelation of God equal to Scripture and the life of the Church expressed in the Tradition. We shall examine, in a moment, the significance of the fact that humans and perhaps some primates, alone among the created order, can reason but this is a different point from suggesting that human reason, as such, rather than the fact that humans can reason, is a source of revelation. The one is the working of the human mind and the other is the observation that the species *homo sapiens* has a brain that functions in this distinct way.

A good example of using the fact that humans can reason to deduce a profound theological truth is the way that Descartes argued from the fact that he could think to the fact that he existed and from his own existence argued the existence of God—the famous aphorism *cogito ergo sum*—"I think, therefore I am." To suggest, however, that human reason, as such, is a substantive source of revelation is, as we shall see, untenable. We must distinguish between the existence of a particular natural phenomenon i.e that humans can reason and the exercise of that phenomenon.

We can see that it makes sense to say that the human capacity to reason is itself a datum or evidence from which conclusions can be derived by reason. That does not mean that human reason, as such, is a source of authority any more than any other human faculty such as sight or the imagination. Human sight, human imagination or human reason are not records of God's revelation in the way that the Bible is. Nor does one find in human reason or in any other human attributes the continued life of Christ in the People of God, which is the Tradition of the Church.

The capacity to reason itself is, of course, part of the natural order of creation. We shall suggest in a moment that the natural order may properly be understood as a reality within which we can discern the authoritative revelation of God. Giving more weight and significance to human reason, as such, than it can properly bear and seeing it as more than a means by which data is processed, can, however, lead to some very strange statements. Dr Mark Santer, the Anglican

Bishop of Birmingham suggested to the Anglican Synod that there is a source of authority, Christian reason, that looks mightily like a form of human reason. He further suggested that this Christian reason took precedence over, and was to be preferred to, Scripture and Tradition.

If human reason or Christian common sense — they are much the same — is a source of authority to stand with Scripture and Tradition then there is an urgent need to explore its nature as a source of data as thoroughly as possible. It should be examined as thoroughly as Scripture and Tradition have been examined. We should know the way in which its supreme authoritative status came about. Scripture and Tradition have a history of becoming authoritative. Is there such a history for Christian common sense/reason? It seems not.[6]

---

[6] Dr Santer's comments reported in the verbatim report: "The Ordination of Women to the Priesthood." The Synod Debate. (London, 1993), p. 31. This is what Dr Santer said in the relevant passage: "For me the key issue is the credibility of the Gospel. What kind of Good News is it that only men may represent Christ in the priesthood of the Church? Arguments from authority are indeed indispensable, but in the tradition to which we belong, not only as Anglicans but as Christians of the West, arguments from Scripture and tradition must in the long run also commend themselves to the Christian reason. One cannot argue forever from the letter of Scripture or from precedent alone. We have to ask ourselves if it makes sense to the Christian mind. We must also ask if it makes sense to unbelievers. I have to say this: I cannot see any way in which the liberating power of the Gospel of Christ is commended to an unbelieving world by the assertion that only men may be priests. That for me is the conclusive argument."

If we do accept that Reason is a source of authority we finish up with an odd proposition. There are, it is proposed, three sources of authority—Scripture, Tradition and Reason—which are discerned and pondered by Faith and Reason. At some point human reason can be supposed to operate on human reason to discern, within itself, the authoritative revelation of God; that is an odd proposition.

Finally, if human reason is a source of revelation which can override the authoritative revelation discerned in Scripture, Tradition and the created order then a very strange circumstance is possible. A person ought to be able to discern the revelation of God sitting with his eyes closed and just thinking, with no other data. This should be possible without any reference to Scripture and Tradition. That proposition also does not seem to make sense. Even Descartes reflected upon his capacity to think within the context of the revelation of God in Scripture and Tradition, and he reflected upon an aspect of the created order, i.e. his capacity to think. The revelation of God did not just bubble up in his empty mind.

For these reasons we do not believe that we can sensibly regard human reason as a source of authoritative revelation. There is, however, such a source that is frequently ignored and might be mistaken for human reason. That is the created, natural order. The created order is the speech of God. It is, in a true sense, the word of God. It finds its fulfilment and most perfect form in the Word of God, the Logos, Jesus the Lord.

God spoke the creation.[7] It is in the speech of God, the Created Order, that faith and human reason, now in its proper place, can discern the self–disclosure of God. The spoken created order exists now because of the continued speech of God. As the continued speech of an honest and truthful man bears witness both to his continued existence and activity and to his mind and will so too the created natural order reveals the continued activity and loving will of God. The Scriptures and the Fathers witness to this truth.

"The heavens declare the glory of God and the firmament proclaim the work of his hands" (Ps. 19:1). This doctrine is widely taught by the Fathers:

> The creation is beautiful and harmonious, and God has made it all for your sake. He has made it beautiful, grand, rich and varied. He has made it capable of satisfying all your needs, to nourish your body and *so to develop the life of your soul leading it towards knowledge of Himself*— all this for your sake. (St John Chrysostom, *On Providence*, 7.2.)

> If you observe the heavens, says Scripture, their order will guide you towards faith. They do in fact reveal the artist who made them. If you then observe the beauty of the earth, it will help you to increase your faith. (St Basil the Great, *On Psalm* 32.3.)

---

[7] Genesis 1.

For everyone who sees a beautifully made lute and considers the skill with which it has been fitted together and arranged, or who hears its melody, will think of none other than the lute maker or the lute player and would recur to him in mind though he might not know him by sight. *And thus to us also is manifested That who made, moves and sustains all things although He be not comprehended by the mind.* (St Gregory Nazianzus, *Oration* 28.6.)

The italics are ours. They highlight the part of the passage that teaches most clearly of the revelatory nature of the created order. In the words immediately following the passage just quoted, St Gregory Nazianzus speaks of the place of reason correctly understood.

At the simplest level we can see, in these passages, human reason, in its proper place and informed by faith, operating upon nature to discern the truth. We do this, for example, when we judge an act to be against the natural order and, therefore, wrong. There are some philosophical problems and problems of definition in using the concept of "the natural order" but they go beyond the bounds of our study. They do not, however, invalidate the understanding of the natural order as a source of authority together with Scripture and Tradition in the way we have described. As we shall see the "together" is vital.

It is important to realise that the exploration, cataloguing, predicting and description of the natural order — science — is not opposed to revelation. Science is, rather, one of the means by which God's revelation in the created order is discerned. It is a good example of human reason operating on data. This conclusion clearly follows from the acceptance of the natural order as one of the means by which God reveals Himself to us. There is no fundamental conflict between faith in our Lord Jesus Christ and the researches of science. Too many good scientists have also been profound theologians, e.g. Fr Georges Florovsky, for that thesis to be sustained for long. That, of course, is not all there is to it but the understanding of the created, natural order as being a record of revelation is theologically creative, utterly orthodox and consistent with Biblical revelation, e.g. Romans 1:18 and Ps.19.

Biblical Authority

The Nature of Biblical Authority

There is one fundamental principle we have to understand before we can make any progress in understanding the authority of the Bible. If we do not understand this principle it is unlikely that we shall ever truly understand the nature of Biblical authority. The failure to understand and apply this principle is the chief cause in making serious mistakes about the authority of the Bible—either by overstating it and getting oneself into fruitless arguments or underestimating its authority or giving it no real authority. The way to avoid these dangers is to apply a very simple principle: Getting the correct answers comes from asking the correct questions. Conversly, asking an incorrect question leads us to an incorrect answer. Nowhere is this general principle more valuable and more properly applied than in understanding and discerning the relationship of the Scriptures to the authority of God. That is the central issue we are exploring in this chapter: what is the relationship of the Scripture to the authority of God?

In the definition of authority which we suggested in the previous chapter we spoke of a relationship in which the party with authority is able to command, in some sense, the obedience of the other party. However

it is achieved the exercise of authority is designed to result in obedience. That is its fundamental nature. That is
what authority is. In exploring the relationship of the
Bible to the authority of God it follows that however we
discern the authority of the Bible what we discern, in
faith and reason, will be that which commands our
obedience not something which interests us or makes
us better informed about science or history. Our obedience will be the obedience necessary for our salvation;
this is because the authority we are concerned with is
God's authority. He exercises this freely to bring about
the loving purpose of his saving work to bring men to
salvation. This fact gives the subject its central importance to us. We are concerned with coming face to face
with the saving revelation of God not with being informed. We are concerned with his self-giving for our
salvation, the mighty acts by which He works to restore
the created order to Himself. Jesus Christ is the ultimate
and perfect revelation of God and that revelation is "for
us men and our salvation" as the Creed tells us. Our
concern with Biblical authority is, therefore, a concern
with the record of God's self-disclosure—his revelation
for our salvation—and with nothing else.

The discernment of the authority of God is obviously, therefore, never simply a matter of curiosity. We
cannot take it or leave it as we can take or leave historical or scientific information. We would be taking or
leaving our salvation if we did. It is always a critical
and urgent matter. The authority of God is never a
matter of indifference to the person to whom it is revealed. If a person is indifferent then he has not dis-

cerned the revelation. He has not heard or seen the Word of God spoken for his salvation. We cannot properly, therefore, be concerned with matters that a true disciple does not find urgently necessary to his salvation. The "flora and fauna of the Holy Land" school of Bible study is seriously misguided. It confuses salvation with an interest in the geography, wildlife or botany of the Holy Land.

That God created me out of nothing is a belief that is necessary to my salvation. It has the authority to command my obedience. Other matters related to the Creation also concern my salvation. It may, however, be possible to ask questions of the Creation narratives that do not have this quality. For that reason they do not have any authority that I must obey for my salvation. If we address questions to the Bible that are unrelated to our salvation, questions concerning history, geology and so on we will not receive an authoritative answer. The authority of God mediated and revealed in Scripture is for our salvation. It is not there to satisfy our curiosity or to inform us of matters unrelated to our salvation. It speaks directly to us for our salvation and for nothing else. It is not interesting. It is vital, essential and urgent.

Let us follow this line of thought a little further and see where it leads us. If the authority of God revealed and mediated in the Scriptures commands our obedience for salvation then it does so because the Bible is a record of God's self–disclosure in history. It is an account of the action of God in history for our salvation discerned and recorded by the people of God. God reveals Himself to bring us to our salvation not to entertain and to inform us. For this reason teaching about the Bible that concentrates on its value as a source of information about the life of Israel, and so on, has missed the point of Scripture. Indeed it fails to understand the reason why Scripture is Scripture. The Bible brings us an account of the saving activity of God. It is saving history. That is its authority. Anything that distracts us from that is misleading and mistaken, if not seriously damaging and dangerous. God's revelation of Himself is never merely interesting. It breaks our world, shaking the foundations (cf. Isaiah 6). Revelation is always of urgent concern because salvation is always of urgent concern.

The revelation of God is in the events and thought recorded in Scripture. Because the record of revelation brings us face to face with God's authority the text of the record itself — the text of the Bible — shares, in a secondary and derived way, the revelatory quality of the events, thought and so on that it records. A person reading the text — the record of God's action in history — in faith comes face to face with that revelation mediated through the text. The revelation of God in history becomes present to the people of God in the text when it is read and expounded with faith and grace.

We avoid some needlessly distracting and damaging problems if we stick to the definition of the Bible as the record of revelation bearing in mind that the text itself has a secondary and derived revelatory quality. The text is the channel of the record of revelation. It is valuable because it is the only way in which we know of the acts of God, His saving revelation, in the history of the people of God. In the Bible we have a set of texts which are records of divine revelation. For this reason the documents themselves have the authority to command our obedience to salvation for the reasons we have just set out. Because they are a record of revelation their authority concerns, and only concerns, questions of our salvation. Their authority does not necessarily extend to matters unconnected with our salvation and their authority in these matters is irrelevant to us. We do not study the Bible to answer questions about physics and astronomy or even history. There is plainly a solid historical background too much of the Biblical narrative or it would be nothing but fantasy but that is not our concern when considering the authority of the Bible.

It is worth noting, in any case, that there is a fundamental problem in coming to an objective account of what happened in any particular event recorded in the Bible, an event in which God discloses Himself to us. There is a simple way of demonstrating this problem. Consider the description given to you by a thoroughly honest and trustworthy young man of a young lady whom he loves. She is loved by him precisely because, at some level, she brings something home to him that other girls do not. Meeting her and coming to know her has a revelatory quality for him. That is one of the elements in honest love between a man and a woman. His description of her, if true, must contain that revelatory "plus" that he discerns; in this case it comes from "being in love." The fact that she reveals something to him is, and must be, woven into his account of her.

If he introduced you to her you might wonder, as we sometimes do, what he sees in her. The objective reality, the simple historic account of the girl, if there ever was such a thing (5'1", brown hair, brown eyes, clear skin etc.), cannot, of itself, convey to you the revelatory "plus." It cannot convey a truth about the girl that is of any real significance and value. If you never met the young lady you could not penetrate through the account that contains the revelatory "plus" to an objective and simple statistical account of that girl. You could not encounter, in some way, the girl as she is to someone who is not in love with her precisely because the account you have is from someone who loves her. The love is in the report as an integral part of it. That is a fact we have to accept. If someone asks us if the young man's account is the truth, what can we say? We might observe that only a person who loves someone can truly know that person and that only an account of a person written with love is a true account. The truth of a person is the truth as seen by someone who loves that person. The absolute truth of a person is the truth as seen by God who loves us absolutely.

We cannot penetrate behind the description of a young man who truly loves a young woman to come to an objective, historical account of what she is like. In the same way we cannot penetrate behind the record of revelation to the event as it might have been seen by someone who did not look at it with the eyes of faith or to whom God did not disclose Himself. The famous question of Professor Leonard Hodgson—"What must the truth have been and be if people who thought and believed like that wrote in those terms?"—cannot be answered.[1] Why can it not be sensibly applied to a Biblical text? Because it will give an answer which purports to be the objective case, the simple facts. The simple facts, as such, however, cannot be for our salvation because it is the simple facts *grasped in faith and discerned as revelation* which constitute the authoritative revelation which commands our obedience to salvation. The revelatory "plus" communicates the revelation. The simple objective record, if recoverable, would be of no interest lacking, as it does, the revelatory "plus." As we have seen in the example in the last paragraph: a) we cannot separate out the revelatory "plus" to leave an objective account of what happened, and b) even if we could such an objective account would be of no value. It would be like trying to show that the Holy Communion is the Body and Blood of Christ by scientific examination. God's revelatory acts in history are sacramental in the same way that sacraments are sacramental, that is, the truth of them is only discerned by faith. Only God's revelation grasped in faith, and with that revelation communicated, can be for our salvation.

The record we have in Scripture is of events and facts grasped in faith and discerned as revelation,

---

[1] That fairly represents the question although it has not been possible to verify its precise terms. We have been in contact with several scholars who are familiar with the question but could not trace the original. Their memories confirmed that this version contained the substance of it.

events which brought home profound truths to the people who witnessed them and took part in them. We cannot go behind the text to a position where we can read objective records of events and facts uninterpreted by the faith of the observer and recorder of the events. We do not have an account of these events from someone to whom *they did not bring home* profound truths. Digging around in the text, trying to come to such an objective account is a futile exercise. The question about the objective nature of the events cannot be reliably or even seriously answered except to say that in some events God acted to reveal Himself and someone who discerned these events in faith as revelation recorded them as we have them.

I cannot seriously ask, "What happened?" and expect a simple and unadorned answer just as I cannot ask, "What sort of girl is she if a boy who loves her describes her like that?" and get a simple and unadorned answer. It is the same sort of futile and unanswerable question.[2] One is simply whistling for the moon if one asks it and the answer will tell us nothing of value. The

---

[2] This constitutes the fundamental weakness of many schools of Biblical criticism. An interesting observation by John Mortimer about the nature of opera—narrative with the emotions on the outside—provides some parallel to the nature of the record of revelation. The truth of the opera is to be seen in the showing of emotions outside the person, in words and music, which are normally kept inside. In a sense this is one way in which the truth of divine revelation is communicated. How else but by hyperbole does one convey the experience of divine revelation? Such an experience cannot be contained within ordinary language any more than the being of God can be spoken of exceptapophatically.

failure to apply this principle of asking the correct question constitutes the basic weakness of many schools of Biblical criticism. They exercise themselves over matters that are of no fundamental concern to the recorder of revelation, the Biblical writer, or to the believer. They are ultimately playing an irrelevant intellectual game; very clever but with no concern for salvation.

The Biblical account of the event or the expression of thought or of some other type of material to be found in the Biblical writings always contains the revelatory "plus." That is why it is revelation. That revelatory "plus" is what makes it authoritative revelation. The revelatory "plus" cannot be separated out by us to leave an objective account. The truth of the revelation of God is in the event. If we could, by some means or another, separate out from the record of revelation an account of "what really happened" it would have no value. The objective account, the objective report of the facts as they were seen, without faith, the history without interpretation, would not bring the revelation of God to us. It would not bring the non–believer to belief because it would lack a central element of the truth of the event. It would not be the whole story. The whole story is the record of the event with the revelatory "plus." This alone is the whole truth and it is only the whole truth which can bring a person face to face with the revelation of God. It is precisely this whole truth which constitutes the authority of the Bible. Simple accounts of events without the revelatory "plus" have no value for the believer or the non-believer. They are not the whole truth. They have no more value than an objective account of the beloved. That objective account will not bring people who never meet her to love her or understand why she is beloved. The truth is in the poetry; the poetry is the truth. An objective account will not bring people to love the girl because it is not the truth of the girl. The truth is the account given in love and faith in which the reporter is part of the event, bound into the event or the person by faith and love.

All that the "Bible as History" school will tell us is that our record of revelation is a record of real events grasped in faith and that they are not fantasy. This, at a preliminary level, is important but incomplete. It is worthwhile reflecting, in view of the above discussion, that no serious secular historian supposes that a secular account of an event is objective, "as it happened" history. All history, even a newspaper account of a football match, is record plus interpretation.

Plainly the Bible contains many different sorts of writing; myth, legend, history, philosophical reflection, poetry, letters, apocalyptic and other sorts of material. All classifications are, to some degree, arbitrary and definitions can vary. This study is not the place in which to describe fully the many different sorts of writing that we find in the Bible. It is important, however, to make a point about the way in which we understand mythological writing. Myth is often taken to be synonymous with untruth. A person may say that something is a myth when he means that it is a fanciful untruth. That is a very serious misunderstanding. Mythological writing is serious writing intended to convey profound truth. It can, briefly, be described as the presentation of a present and immediate truth about man's standing before God in the form of an historical narrative. It is distinct from interpreted history or any other form of material which, with others, constitutes the record of revelation that commands our obedience. It is obviously the case that the various forms of writing have become intermingled in the Bible so that myth and legend and so on are sometimes intermingled and so confused but this does not affect either their authority or the way in which we discern that authority.

We shall examine later the various ways in which the authority of Scripture has been understood. It is appropriate, however, to deal with one important and central aspect of this teaching now. Later definitions, in the Roman Church particularly but also more generally, have stressed what has always a central characteristic of the revelation recorded in the Bible. This is a doctrine that has always been held by the Apostolic Church. It is the rejection of the proposition that only those parts of Scripture which deal with spiritual matters are inspired and bring us the revelation of God. To distinguish between parts of Scripture in this way makes a false and arbitrary division in the Bible. It introduces into our interpretation of Scripture and our understanding of its authority a highly subjective standard of what is and what is not inspired Scripture. By what criteria does one decide what is spiritual and what is not? Attempting to do so opens the door to highly subjective judgements about what is and what is not revelation. A person may decide — we do not know by what criteria — that an account of part of Israel's history is not spiritual; some of it is fairly gory. In doing so he or she may ignore the revelation of God. It is precisely in the "unspiritual" events of history that God acts. "Spiritual" and "disembodied" writing frequently does no more than make us comfortable in our sin. At the same time it introduces a concept which, in line with heretical, gnostic teaching, largely limits the activity of God to the spiritual. It also demonstrates a serious misunderstanding of the nature of revelation.

The universal witness of Scripture and the belief of the Apostolic Church is that God acts in human history to bring His people to obedience to salvation. He acts in *all human history* not just the history of the people of God. That is where the activity of God is most surely discerned but God's revelation is not even confined to the history of the people of God (cf. Isaiah 45:1).

The belief that God only acts in spiritual matters and not in real events is responsible for what might best be called functional atheism. Functional atheism is seen when a person or group proclaim belief in God but do not act as though God rules and acts in loving providence in the contemporary world.

Functional atheism underlies many reforms of church administration. An administrative problem or some other sort of problem is discerned, a shortage of priests or a shortage of money or something like that. It is analyzed and reforms are suggested which, it is hoped, will remedy it. The reforms never do solve the problem because they are based upon the supposition that God is not active in human history to bring his people to salvation. They presume that the Church is a human organisation that can be managed and administered like any other human organisation. That is a very serious error in understanding. The Church is the Body of Christ, the People of God living by every word which proceeds from the mouth of God. It is not, most definitely, as described in Bishop Richard Holloway's phrase, "the expression, often unacknowledged, of an obsolete, though still powerful structuralist paradigm."[3]

The problems which administrative reforms are designed to remedy are believed to be the result of administrative failure or a failure in public relations. That cannot be correct. Failure in the Church is the loving and effective judgement of God. It cannot be cured by administrative reform but by conviction of sin, repentance and forgiveness. To ignore this truth is functional atheism.

The following extract from a consecration sermon of Metropolitan Anthony Khrapovitsky of Kiev and then of the Russian Church Outside Russia puts the point simply and well:

> It always pained me when I heard it said that a certain bishop was indifferent to the services and was not very prayerful, but "at least he's a good administrator." Such administrative skill is not necessary in a hierarch. If he would see prayer as his primary duty, the administration

---

[3] *Dancing on the Edge* (London, 1997), p. 182.

would take care of itself, and everything around him would improve on its own.[4]

That is the diametric opposite of functional atheism. Metropolitan Anthony recognised that the life of the Church is to be found in the loving providence of God not in man's skill. Compare his words with an example of functional atheism.[5]

The understanding that God acts to reveal Himself in history forms the basis for our rejection, in due course, of belief in Biblical literal inerrancy. This is the belief that the text of the Old and New Testament, as it

---

[4] Metropolitan Anthony Khrapovitsky of Kiev and ROCOR, quoted in *Man of God: St John of Shanghai and San Francisco* (San Francisco, 1994), p. 22.

[5] A good and apparently harmless example of functional atheism in the writing of an Anglican bishop is the following from Dr Stevenson of Portsmouth in a visitation charge given in 1996. It is the second paragraph of four and does not refer to or depend upon other paragraphs. It is complete in itself. "Secondly, I want to talk about *partnership*. It is a word that is as old as the hills but is being used much more today, as so many different structures in society are altered in order to express the different ways that people are learning to co-operate with each other, *to create quite simply a new and better world*. All this presents fresh challenges for partnership building in ministry itself. So the partnerships that exists among the whole people of God, are vital for the future of the Christian gospel." In other words the Kingdom of God does not come down from Heaven as a bride adorned for husband but is built up by people like the Tower of Babel. The inherent functional atheism of these words is concealed by several "good" words and phrases like "partnership"', "an new and better world", "fresh challenges" and "ministry" but in the end it speaks of a graceless game in which we, not God, create the new world.

stands, is simply an unadorned account of events as they occurred dictated by God. The stars in their courses fought against Sisera and so on. This is normally, and inaccurately, called "Biblical fundamentalism." God acts and reveals, however, Himself in human history not in infallible texts. There is a nonsensical book that proposes that God dictated the Bible to Moses and in doing so built in certain precise predictions so that the future can be foretold from the decoding of these predictions. This is another example, similar to the view of the literary inerricists, of a belief that God does not act in history but in dictating words. If these theories are correct then His revelation ceases to be the Word and becomes words. We do not seek, in this view, his revelation in history, including our own history, but in words. It is enough to say that the whole record of God's dealings with men is a record of revelation, a record of God's self-revelation in history. This is the relationship of the revelation of God to the text. The text is not a source of information about geography or archaeology and so on.

To conclude this part of this chapter it is worth observing that we must be quite rigid in our understanding of the Bible as a record of revelation rather than an infallible textbook. It is no more an ethical textbook, for example, than it is an archaeological or geographical textbook. A study of the reign of Henry VIII (1509–1547) in England which precipitated the English Protestant Reformation (although that was, of course, a very complex process) reveals the danger of using the Bible as an ethical textbook. By applying texts from the Old Testament to the complex process of his brother's and his own betrothal to the same woman, as though the texts yielded simple answers to a complex problem, he seriously misled himself.

Of course, the discernment of the authority of God in revelation has an ethical dimension and content. That does not, however, make the Bible an ethical textbook any more than it is a textbook of anything else. Textbooks present us with simple answers to simply defined questions. Revelation meets us in our sin and brings us to repentance. We cannot use revelation to solve problems except insofar as the fact of human sin and the need for redemption is treated as a problem. Using revelation to solve an ethical problem was Henry VIII's mistake. That is not the function of revelation. Textbooks leave us knowing more of a subject, an intellectual condition. Revelation leaves us flat on our face in repentance before the mystery of God; a moral and spiritual condition.

Since we come in sin to meet the revelation of God we shall, of course, encounter an ethical and moral dimension in true revelation. The fact of our sin makes that obvious but the function of revelation is not to answer ethical questions. It is to lead us to salvation. A person might address an ethical question to the text of the Bible out of interest and suppose that an answer can be found. An answer may be found or it may not be. A question about the punishment of adulterers or murderers might be asked, for example. Are they to be stoned or executed, or forgiven? Having received an answer is the person either better informed or brought before the revelation of God, which brings us to our knees and the confession of sin, perhaps only if an adulterer or murderer? If he is better informed but is not brought to his knees then the exercise has been a waste of time. It is in this context that we suggest that the Bible is not a textbook, even an ethical textbook, but a record of revelation.

The Reasons for Biblical Authority

As God acts to bring us to salvation we can take it that He acts effectively and efficiently because it is most loving to do so. His acts are enough to bring us to salvation. If we accept that the Bible is a record of God's revelation in history then we have no difficulty in accepting that what it contains is necessary to our salvation. The revelation recorded in Scripture is sufficient for our salvation. We cannot suppose that God is so incompetent as not to act effectively to bring about the end which He desires, that is the salvation of man.

The revelation of God is complete and perfect in the person of the Lord Jesus Christ, Who is the Word of God, the second Person of the Trinity, very God of very God. The Lord Jesus Christ is the Incarnation of God the Son and He is necessary to our salvation—He is our salvation and nothing and nobody else is. The record of revelation which is summed up in the life, death and resurrection of the Lord Jesus Christ therefore contains everything necessary to our salvation.

For the Anglican bishop of Manchester who, together with many Episcopalian bishops and the Anglican Archbishop of Perth in Australia, does not believe that Christ is necessary to eternal life, and for those who share his views, our salvation may be in someone else other than Christ. This will distort the understanding of Scripture as containing all things necessary to salvation and belief in the Bible's unique authority will be diminished. The distortion of the understanding of the nature and function of the Church, the Sacraments and worship is the inevitable result and can be witnessed in the contemporary churches. Those who believe that our Lord Jesus Christ is not necessary to salvation do not indicate how we come to salvation—or even what constitutes salvation. It seems, in this package of belief, that we come to salvation by "being nice" and that being saved consists of "being comfortable." We do not need the saving work of the Lord Jesus in order to be spiritually comfortable.

The only question that receives an authoritative answer in the Bible, commanding our obedience, concerns our salvation. It is in seeking our salvation that we understand the authority of Scripture and only then. It is odd to speak of addressing questions to the record of revelation but insofar as we come to the text, prayerful and receptive, seeking our salvation then this rather inadequate way of speaking will do. There is, in truth, a question implied in the very nature of human existence: "What is man and why is he what he is and is there a remedy for him?" It is this question, however expressed, which lies behind man's search for God and for salvation. It is vital to understand that God does not disclose Himself in Scripture in order to answer our questions. He does not reveal Himself at our initiative, in response to our questions but rather to meet the fundamental question implied by our human condition. He acts in love to bring us from sin to holiness. He reveals Himself to save us. He exercises his authority to fulfil His purpose of bringing us to union with Him.

Why are we correct to attribute divine authority to the present books of the Bible? Why are we correct to believe that they are a record of God's revelation? The answer is simple; because the Apostolic Church discerned that the present books of the Bible were authentic records of revelation. By what right did the Apostolic Church make this discernment? By what process does this discernment take place?

The promise given to the Apostolic Church by the Lord is that it will never completely fall away and that it will be guided into all truth. The Apostolic Church was promised indefectability and infallibility. Part of that gift of indefectability and infallibility is the gift of discernment. The nature of this infallibility and indefectability is easily set out. The Church is indefectible in that it will never fail in a succession of members. The natural body of the Lord Jesus was incorruptible but before the Resurrection was liable to human infirmities — tiredness and thirst and so on. In the same way, in the Mystical Body of the Lord Jesus, the Church yet to be glorified, each of its many members is liable to sin and fall away from the grace of God. Nothing, however, can touch the life of the Mystical Body itself. The fullness of the Spirit dwells in the Lord Jesus and He is the Truth. So too the Spirit, by virtue of whose indwelling the Body is one and united to its Head, guides the Church into all truth.

The mystery of the Church's life is necessarily connected to the saving purposes of God. We would have to assume that the saving purposes of God could fail if it is assumed that the Church can, ultimately, defect or fall from the Truth. The Church could not defect or fall from the Truth without a failure of God's loving mercy. This, briefly, is the basis for belief in the indefectability and infallibility of the Church, the steadfastness of the Church in the Apostolic Doctrine. The Church's ultimate infallibility in conflicts of doctrine is an aspect of this. The Church is guided, and must be guided in the end, in discerning the authenticity of revelation. The proposition that it is not so guided falls by the same argument that demonstrates the Church's general infallibility and indefectability.

The experience of the people of God is the acid test in discerning the authenticity of revelation. This is demonstrated in a powerful way in a particular Pauline line of argument about the Resurrection in 1 Corinthians 15:11–12. St Paul is dealing with the question of the truth of the Resurrection of the Lord. He appears, on a quick reading, to base his claim to apostleship solely on the similarity of his experience to that of earlier witnesses of the Resurrection. His use of certain words[6]

---

[6] He uses the word, *opthe*, a form of the verb *horao*, which means to see or appear and in the passive - to be seen. He uses it to describe the appearance to him of the risen Lord. It is a very rare word in the Pauline literature being only used twice by him (1Cor. 15:5–8 and 1 Cor. 9). This makes it likely that he saw his experience

gives weight to understanding his argument in this way. If we read the passage carefully, however, we find something else is also happening; in fact the argument also works the other way round. He does not argue from his experience to the truth of the Resurrection nor from the truth of the Resurrection to his experience. It is more subtle than that. He begins with the fact of his preaching and its effect in bringing the Corinthians to new life in Christ. He then concludes that since his preaching has had this effect the Resurrection must be true. A falsehood would not have had this effect. What matters is that he preached the same Gospel as the others and that the Corinthians believed and were saved. The new life in Christ which has been experienced by the people of God certifies the truth of the preaching that Jesus has been raised from the dead.[7]

A similar process certified the canon of Scripture. It was in canonical Scripture that the Church discerned the revelation of God to salvation. This was the experience of the people of God. Professor C. F. D. Moule, the distinguished New Testament scholar, pointed out that even if a new work was discovered and on the grounds of linguistic analysis and so on was believed to be authentically Pauline it would not, for that reason, become canonical Scripture.[8] In the same way a Biblical

---

as the same sort of experience as other witnesses where this verb is used and used it precisely to stress the similarity.

[7] 1 Corinthians 15.

[8] This point was made by Professor Moule at a lecture to an Anglican clergy school in Hereford, which the present writer attended.

work which scholars argue, using linguistic analysis, is unlikely to be from the pen of the purported author does not, for that reason, cease to be canonical Scripture.[9] It is the discernment and experience of the Church that is the acid test. We do not, as we shall see, depend upon the researches of scholars for the authentication of the sources of authority. The whole Church decides such matters. It is just conceivable that a truly universal council of the whole Church might add a work to canonical Scripture but it would be both practically impossible and theologically suspect to do so. The important point, which will be expanded below, is that the discernment of revelation is not given to scholars but to the whole Church. The experience of the Church that the text is an authentic record of revelation bringing men to salvation is the test. Discernment of the present texts as Scripture is believed to have finished with the early patristic era i.e. by about 200 A.D.[10]

The process of discernment leading to the present canon was lengthy. That is to be expected. The texts had to be experienced. The Canon of Scripture could only be discerned slowly and over a period. The Old Testament

---

[9] Some scholars who have applied linguistic analysis to work attributed to St. Paul have concluded that linguistic differences make it unlikely that some works so attributed actually come from the pen of St. Paul. The point is, however, that whether they are right or wrong is irrelevant. The books are canonical scripture accepted as such by the Church. Nothing else really matters.

[10] This is also about the date at which, in the opinion of Candido Pozo, the authentic apostolic developmental interpretation of the message and works of Jesus ceased. *Encyclopaedia of Theology* (London, 1975), p. 357.

canon, despite legends to the contrary in 4 Esdras, was closed sometime during the first Century AD. The oldest list is that of Melito of Sardis, (c. 190 AD). The Old Testament for Protestants consists of the Hebrew Bible in the order found in the Vulgate (an early Latin translation). There existed, in use by Jews dispersed throughout the world, a set of what became referred to as deutero–canonical works or the Apocrypha. These are, in general, accepted by the Orthodox Church and the Roman Catholic Church as canonical but not by Protestants. A council at Rome in 382 produced the earliest complete list of Biblical books and this list appears in the decree of Pope Gelasius (496). The list is repeated in the councils of Florence (1442) and Trent (1546). An earlier conciliar decision, Canon 60 of the Council of Laodicea (a provincial council c. 350 AD), excludes Tobit, Judith, Wisdom, Sirach, 1 and 2 Maccabees and the Revelation of St John the Divine all of which were subsequently included.

The earliest list of New Testament books containing all those in our present New Testament is to be found in the Thirty-ninth Festal Letter of St Athanasius in 367. This list appears again in the decree of Pope Gelasius, although the attribution to this pope is questioned, and in subsequent conciliar decisions. Some points need to be made about this process:

a) The effect of canonising a written tradition is to create a standard and canon against which a purported element in the Tradition of the Church can be measured. Collections of non–

canonical scriptures are available.[11] They are worth examining. It soon becomes clear why they are not canonical.

b) It is important to realise that we have a Tradition, part of which has been canonised, the Bible. This grows out of the whole Tradition of the Church, i.e. its life lived in the presence of God under the guidance of the Holy Spirit. The Tradition of the Church is one reality.

c) The spur for canonising certain books comes from the emergence of what we have come to call apocryphal books and the need to know the limit of the canonical record of revelation. Some books have been omitted which were subsequently accepted as canonical and some books, like Barnabas, the Shepherd of Hermas and 1 and 2 Clement, were accepted which, in the long run, were deemed not to be canonical by the Universal Church. There are readily available translations in modern English of these books.

d) The process, as we have observed, was lengthy but the principal parts of the canon were settled quite early. The only differences

---

[11] The fullest collection of this material in an easily available form is to be found in Vol.8 of the translation of the *Ante Nicene Fathers* (Grand Rapids, 1978).

and uncertainties concerned a limited number of books.

Modern Theories

There are many theories about the nature of Biblical authority. Different Christian groups at different times have understood the Bible's authority in different ways. That is to be expected. It is not possible, in a short compass, to explore all the variations and different theories of Biblical authority that have been and are still held. It is necessary to apply a fairly broad brush to this question. We will, therefore, only examine the principal theories.

One characteristic of some of these theories, both in recent evangelical thought (say the last 150 years) and the teaching of the Roman Church during the same period, has been their reactionary nature. Reactionary does not, in this context, mean ultra–conservative. It simply means that the theory has been developed in reaction to someone else's thesis. That is not a bad thing since doctrine is usually defined in reaction to novelty as we have seen. The novelty, in this case, has been the Biblical criticism of the nineteenth and twentieth Centuries. The Orthodox Church, which from the beginning had a more creative and rich understanding of the Bible as revelation has never developed such reactionary theories because it has never had to do so. It has not been subject to the corrosive effects of some forms of Biblical criticism and has not, therefore, developed misleading doctrines of Biblical authority in response to them. The Orthodox have developed a method of Biblical interpretation which makes criticism irrelevant and so the theories developed in reaction to criticism are also irrelevant. The Orthodox method of Biblical interpretation is called typology and this method, together with a superficially similar but fundamentally different method which has some popularity, allegory, will be discussed below. The Orthodox never, therefore, found themselves in the interpretative dead ends into which some Western theories have led; dead-ends which have led, in some cases, to the abandonment of any belief in Biblical authority.

The most extreme reaction to Biblical criticism in the understanding of Biblical authority developed in the Princeton School in the nineteenth-century to form the ideological basis of the modern phenomenon of fundamentalism. Because this phenomenon is so misleading and so widespread we must examine the arguments for and against it on its own terms and demonstrate its fallacies. We shall refer back to the observation we made above about the basic misconception that underlies fundamentalism.

We need to define some terms. It is necessary first to distinguish between Biblical inerrancy and Biblical fundamentalism. The latter is a crude distortion of inerrancy. In fundamentalism it is assumed that every word of the text is true in a simple way and should be taken at face value. As we observed above, fundamentalists would propose that the stars in their courses came down and fought against Sisera and so on.

Biblical inerrancy is subtler. It has been defined thus:

> [It is] the view that when all the facts become known they will demonstrate that the Bible in its original autographs and correctly interpreted is entirely true and never false in what it affirms whether that is related to doctrine or ethics or to the social, physical or life sciences.[12]

The framer of this definition, Dr P. D. Feinberg, goes on to observe that inerrancy is not at present demonstrable and that no present text can be deemed inerrant because it is not known if it is an original autograph. Inerrancy also depends, in Feinberg's definition, upon correct interpretation. His view can be more crisply expressed as, that in the end, there will be no conflicts between the truth conveyed in the Bible and that conveyed in any other way. Feinberg avoids the difficulty of the belief in an inerrant Biblical text by defining it out. He sets conditions to the inerrant nature of the Bible that cannot be fulfilled. In doing so he merely raises the problem in another form. He also falls into errors that are fatal to his proposition. Firstly, he places the discernment of the authority of the Bible with the scholars not with the whole Church. It is scholars who can best come to conclusions about the originality and authenticity of texts but as we have already seen the discernment of *the authenticity of the revelation* lies

---

[12] Art Feinberg, "The Inerrancy and Infallibility of the Bible" in Elwell, ed., *The Evangelical Dictionary of Theology* (London, 1985).

with the whole Church, not just with scholars. We shall develop this point below.

Secondly, Feinberg raises the whole question of correct interpretation — "correctly interpreted." This, however, is the problem which belief in inerrancy is assumed to solve. Inerrancy *is* an interpretive theory. It is supposed to release us from problems of interpretation. To place the condition "correctly interpreted" into a definition of inerrancy is simply to raise the original problem of interpretation in another form. Thirdly, he relates this matter of interpretation to the End Times, "when all the facts become known." All things will only become known at the consummation of all things, at the End. Doctrines and beliefs which are related to and concerned with the final consummation of all things are called eschatological from the Greek word for "last" — *eschatos.*

The difference between this version of inerrancy and what we have called fundamentalism — the belief that every word in the text of the Bible, usually the King James Version, is a correct literal record in every particular--is obvious. Inerrancy is subtler and is concerned with the true nature of the Bible's authority rather than seeking to give the Bible a character that is wholly misconceived. By giving the Bible an incorrect character the fundamentalists destroy it as a record of revelation. We shall examine this further below. The view Feinberg describes is more acceptable but still has some serious weaknesses. We need to examine these now.

The first thing, as we have seen, is that the doctrine of inerrancy puts questions of authority of the Bible into the hands of scholars rather than into the hands of the Universal Church. This is a fundamental weakness. Scholars have an obvious function in such matters as translating Greek and Hebrew texts. This is important enough in some cases, e.g. in Romans 8:18, where the Greek (*eis hemas*) is sometimes translated as "to us" and sometimes as "in us." In the context that is a substantial difference with weighty implications for the understanding of the nature of salvation and our part in it. (The context seems to point to "in us," but see the glossary entry, "variant texts"). Scholars also have an important function in settling the authenticity of variant texts on scholarly grounds, i.e. which texts are most reliable as to origin and translation. They do not, however, have a central place in deciding how the text is to be interpreted or how the text is to be applied and preached. That is the task of the whole Church. Scholars employ different criteria in coming to their conclusions and have a different task from the task of the whole Church.

The function of interpretation, of discerning authoritative revelation, lies with the whole people of God. Scholars proceed from scholarly criteria to arrive at authentic texts and correct translations. The whole people of God use, seeking those things that are necessary to salvation, different criteria and methods. They start where the scholars finish, with a settled text. They are seeking something other than the scholarly verification of texts. They are seeking their salvation. It can, further, be observed that the fundamental work on the closing of the canon of Scripture has long been completed and therefore the text is, but for variants and translation, settled. Scholars are concerned with the provision of the best text and the translation of that text. The whole Church has the responsibility so to interpret that text and to preach it so that people encounter the revelation of God.

This characteristic of belief in Biblical inerrancy, i.e. its dependence on the researches and opinions of scholars, gives it a fundamental irrelevance in the consideration of Biblical authority. It is precisely the text before us, with questions of translation and authenticity already settled, that demands of us a view of its authority. To say that a text is inerrant in the sense that there will be no final conflicts in the text and no final conflicts between the authority of the text and all other sources of authority does not answer the one important question. What is the authority of this text now? That question is not answered by telling us that at some time in the future texts which cannot be recovered will be found to be consistent with and not in conflict with other sources of knowledge. In the End we shall not need the Biblical record of revelation for we shall know as we are known.

The silliness of the fundamentalist view simply does not merit serious attention. It is a kind of idolatry. It gives the text an absolute quality which can only properly be attributed to God. It concerns itself with questions unconcerned with salvation. By asking the wrong questions it comes up with wrong and irrelevant answers.

So deeply has some form of inerrancy dug its way into the general understanding of most Christians and unbelievers—most non-Christians believe that Christians are fundamentalists and many Christians who are not believe that they should be—that its foundations and weaknesses need to be set out. This is necessary because the theory is usually held in an undigested form. For that reason it is even more dangerous. The text of the Bible is misunderstood and either rejected or misapplied. The task of bringing the revelation to bear on the life of contemporary people becomes almost impossible. So much energy is spent defending an indefensible and incorrect theory that the task of true interpretation is forgotten.

The problems that doctrines of inerrancy face are not new. They seek to deal with problems which have been dealt with much better by the Fathers of the Church. They struggled with questions that the simplest criticism raises for those for whom verbal inerrancy in its simplest form is the accepted doctrine. St John Chrysostom, for example, was not alone in puzzling how hills could skip and hop in Psalm 114. The development of the allegorical and typological schools of interpretation was, to some degree, a response to concerns like these.

There are four elements in the argument for inerrancy. An examination of them highlights its weaknesses. The first is that the Bible teaches its own authority and inspiration and that this justifies belief in inerrancy. It is argued that if its teaching is inspired and commands obedience then it must be inerrant. Scripture's own principles of interpretation, its hermeneutics, proceed, so it is argued, from the basis of its own inerrancy.

It is further argued that since God cannot lie His revelation cannot lie either; perhaps "not be true" would be better than "lie." This argument has two serious weaknesses. The first is that it jumps past questions of interpretation, jumping from God who is Truth to the truth, in a literal sense in every circumstance, of the record of His revelation. That God is the Truth is a clear article of belief; God cannot be untrue. That does not mean that the record of an event discerned as revelation cannot contain errors in matters not related to salvation or that the form in which the revelation is presented need be taken literally. Such errors are not material untruths. An error over a place name or a date would not, in most cases, affect the capacity of the text to bear true revelation for example. It is unjustifiable to jump from a correct belief about God to attribute the same divine characteristic to the text of the Bible. It deifies, to some degree, the text. That will surely lead, as it does lead, to error. In any case the way the Truth of God is discerned is precisely the question at issue. Jumping past the question of interpretation in this way is a mistake. It begs the very questions one is seeking to settle, i.e. in what sense is the Bible authoritative and how do we discern authoritative revelation? By saying that the Bible teaches its own authority we a) beg the question of its authority (it seems to be self-certifying), and b) it infers that there is no need for interpretation. We can just read it off.

Secondly, inerrancy confuses God's revelation in history with the record of that revelation which is Scripture. This brings us near to the dangerous view that God dictated a text rather than acts, then and now, in history. If that is true then revelation finds its principal locus in the text and not in history. It requires a belief that God does not act in history but dictates a text. This opens up the way for all the misleading games with the text that lead to misinterpretation. The idea that God dictated a text containing codes to be unravelled later—the Bible Code nonsense—is one of the possible results that we mentioned above of locating the revelation of God in the text rather than in history. At one further step along the process it leads to a reduction in the importance of the course of human history and the history of the people of God. The developing life and Tradition of the Church comes to lack significance and immediacy. It is not too big a step from this to ignoring the life of the Church completely, with schism and bizarre apocalyptic sects on one hand and an unhistorical, spiritual religion very much like gnosticism on the other.

There is, further, a history of belief in inerrancy. We know its roots and it is not clear that it is correct to discern a continuum of belief in inerrancy in the faith of the Universal Church. Inerrancy, as we experience it now, was only developed and expounded in the face of the relatively modern phenomenon of Biblical criticism, as we have observed above. Biblical criticism is a nineteenth-century phenomenon. The Fathers were aware of very simple critical questions but were always concerned to ask questions about salvation not about geology and other matters. The terms in which Feinberg defines inerrancy, in its refined form, were not present in the minds of those who, earlier in the Church's life, held a belief in inerrancy. They did not have to react to a theory of Biblical criticism. They did not, therefore, develop theories of inerrancy, which were similar to the modern theories conditioned by criticism. The question was not a serious issue for them. Their response to critical problems, insofar as they experienced them, was typological and allegorical interpretation that we shall examine with below.

The argument that all knowledge revealed by the Bible must be undoubted, inerrant and incorrigible, that the knowledge obtained from the Bible must be rooted in absolute certainty seems to fall at two points. The first is that it is knowledge to salvation not simple knowledge as such that is brought to us in the Bible. We are not concerned with matters other than our salvation. The second is that it is precisely knowledge born of faith, rather than inerrant and incorrigible knowledge, that discerns the revelation to salvation in the Bible. Revelation is only discerned by faith. We do not come to saving knowledge on the basis of a cast iron guarantee. We encounter God in faith. That is sure and certain enough but with a different quality of sureness and certainty than that which fundamentalists propose.

Finally there is the argument that denial of general inerrancy to one piece of material in one part of the Bible raises questions about all other parts of the Bible and all the other revelation in the Bible. This, it is argued, leads to doctrinal collapse. It is, however, precisely this argument that makes belief in general inerrancy so dangerous. If we hold that the Bible is inerrant in all matters rather than in matters of salvation then we place honest men in an intolerable dilemma. They discover, with complete integrity and honesty, that some element in the Biblical text, when examined for material other than that concerned with our salvation, is incorrect. In the face of assertions as to the absolute inerrancy of the Bible in all things they conclude that it is in error over all matters. One error in a matter not related to salvation destroys the authority of the Bible in matters of salvation if a person is told that the Church believes the Bible is inerrant. That the Bible contains all things necessary to our salvation is the Church's faith. That in matters related to our salvation the Bible is inerrant is, of course, a central and ineradicable belief of the Universal Church. We have seen how the structure of orthodox belief has collapsed into gnosticism in the wake of the collapse of belief in Biblical authority. This is, however, a million miles and quite different from the belief that the Bible is in all respects inerrant i.e. that it answers *all* questions with absolute correctness. The danger of belief in general inerrancy is that it often erects a barrier between the explorations of science and religious belief. That is not just foolish. It is a tragedy.

The argument is extended to suggest that to admit that one aspect of the Biblical text, an aspect not related to salvation and interpreted literally, may not be authoritative will lead to a collapse of Biblical authority generally. This might be called the slippery slope argument. It cannot be sustained either logically or in experience. It seems persuasive until we examine it. In order for it to be a valid argument we should be able to see two things. First, we should be able to see a connection between the cause and the effect. We should be able to see that denying an authoritative quality to the text in a question of geography must mean that we deny its authoritative quality in matters of salvation. We cannot do so and if we could it raises the danger we have just discussed, i.e. that authority in regard to salvation will be rejected because authority in respect of geography and so on cannot be sustained. This is the converse of the slippery slope argument.

It can also be observed that the necessary connection between this aspect of the doctrine of inerrancy and the other doctrines of the Church cannot be demonstrated and that, in itself, makes it a highly questionable doctrine. The capacity of one doctrine to integrate with all other doctrines is, as we shall see and as we would expect, a strong indication of its truth. We should expect to see a doctrine of biblical inerrancy necessarily integrated with all other doctrines e.g. the Doctrine of God, of Creation and the Atonement and we do not do so. Since doctrine is the reflection and codification of the revelation of the one God we should expect to see this integrated quality. We do not. Inerrancy does not integrate with the body of the Apostolic Faith.

Second, the experience of the Church suggest that the slippery slope argument is unsustainable. It is not the case that those who do not accept the doctrine of inerrancy in some form or another necessarily abandon other doctrines. Many believers are quite capable of distinguishing between different areas of authority and can understand that the Bible contains all things necessary to our salvation but not everything necessary to our skill as a geographer or archaeologist. It is well understood and is the general experience of Christians that an error in a matter not concerning salvation does not invalidate the authority of the Bible in respect of matters concerning salvation. They are different areas of concern and reality.

One can, however, observe a reverse effect, that is that some people who do hold simple fundamentalist views of Biblical authority, e.g. the Jehovah's Witnesses, hold doctrines that contain serious errors about the person of the Lord Jesus. Jehovah's Witnesses do not believe in the divinity of the Lord Jesus. They have a belief very similar to the heresy of Arius condemned in 325 at the Council of Nicaea; that is that the Lord Jesus was not from the beginning and not of one substance with the Father. Biblical fundamentalism is no guarantee of doctrinal purity. Some Biblical fundamentalists are in serious error over central doctrines. As we shall see the fact that the Bible must be interpreted according to orthodox principles of interpretation preserves us from these dangers. Historically inerrancy, in its sophisticated and in its crude forms, developed in reaction to liberal criticism. It often deals with matters which were essentially of no concern to earlier believers. The Church did not use the Bible as a source book to answer questions not related to salvation. It is not correct to say either, as it is suggested, that Bible teaches its own inerrancy. It teaches its own inspiration, that is that it is a record of true revelation authentically discerned and recorded and nobody has problems with that. That is a quite different proposition from the proposition that it teaches its own inerrancy. That is the doctrine of the Church.

Inerrancy in both its forms falls on three grounds. Firstly, the point that we have labored, that Scripture brings us a record of revelation to our salvation, not a text book on the natural sciences and so on.

Secondly, the doctrine is not falsifiable. We cannot disprove inerrancy in the terms in which Feinberg has defined it because the original autographs to which he refers almost certainly no longer exist. By bringing the authenticity of the whole text as revelation into the area of matters which can be tested practically—and the authenticity of revelation cannot be so tested—Feinberg makes a fatal mistake. His theory purports to be provable, in the end, by scholarly means but as we have seen those means are not available to us. The means he puts before us are valueless. The original manuscripts almost certainly no longer exist. The theory depends on the success of tests but the tests cannot be carried out. The theory is not falsifiable and so not provable. We cannot test the proposition that the Bible is inerrant in all matters by the means in which propositions are either proved false or true by evidence because the evidence is no longer in existence. We cannot answer the question about the authority of the Bible on this basis. As soon as we go beyond belief in the truth of matters related to our salvation into dealing with the truth of matters which are unrelated to salvation we meet this problem. Feinberg is confusing two types of knowledge; that acquired by examining evidence and that which comes from faith. That confusion is fatal to his argument. Acceptance of biblical authority is an act of faith.

Thirdly, the belief renders the Incarnation of the Lord, in some sense, irrelevant by overriding the freedom of man. All revelation partakes of the basic nature of the revelation of God in the Lord Jesus. The Lord Jesus is the final revelation of God and all revelation is christological. The Lord Jesus is both God and man. The duality of the Incarnation is to be found in all events in which God reveals Himself. God acts and man responds and the response is in the record of revelation. This duality is to be found in the Church, in the Tradition and life of the Church and in the Scriptures. If the Scriptures came into being by a process which bypasses this human involvement then they are not revelation. The involvement of the people of God discerning revelation in their history and recording it is a central and necessary element in the process. God works through men and women as, ultimately, God is in Christ reconciling the world to Himself. The theory that the Scriptures by-pass this process is unchristological because it ignores the human element in revelation and so destroys the nature of revelation itself. Revelation is God's self-disclosure in history *to His people* and the apprehension of that revelation in faith by those people. The whole event, the disclosure and the apprehension of it, is the revelation. Revelation does not take place in empty rooms in a dictated form. It is not a literary process but the action of God in history. It is a living encounter with God in history. The people of God encounter God in their history and are brought to their knees by the glory and wonder of the meeting. They see the work of God in their history, both their personal history and their national and corporate history. It is this encounter and the discernment of its nature that is brought to us in with authority in the Scriptures. Jesus Christ, truly God and truly man, is the final and complete revelation of God to man. Excluding human freedom from the act of revelation ultimately denies that our Lord is the final revelation.

It would be beyond the scope of this study to give a comprehensive account of the many principles of Biblical interpretation; the technical name for such principles is hermeneutics. It is, however, necessary to give an indication of these principles in order to show how the revelation is discerned from the text. We cannot speak seriously of the authority of the Bible if we stop at the very point at which the revelation of God recorded in the Bible is brought to the people of God i.e. in its interpretation. The Bible must be preached and preaching involves the interpretation of the Bible. It is central to a real experience of the Bible's power that the authority of the Bible is discerned in response to certain questions and that those questions concern our salvation. We have examined the fatal weakness in the theories of Biblical interpretation of those who hold that the Bible is inerrant in all matters. There are, of course, other principles of Biblical interpretation, other means by which the revelation of the Bible is believed to be brought to the people of God. How other theories propose that this is done is what, in broad terms, we shall examine now.

Allegory and Typology

We shall, in this section, examine briefly two major principles of interpretation, allegory and typology; one is an authentic method of interpretation, the other inauthentic. We shall then later examine liberal approaches to Biblical interpretation. We will not examine some of the more obscure Jewish means of Biblical interpretation which are based on arbitrary number and letter codes. They have no place in any orthodox interpretation of the Bible nor are they applied seriously by anyone in the mainstream churches. Of the two we examine now one was very popular and appears to have New Testament authority — at one point St Paul uses the word "allegory" to describe a typological interpretation in Galatians 4:24 — that is interpreting the text by assuming that it is an allegory. The other principle seems to be very similar but is in fact very different, that is typology.

The great Biblical theologian of the third century, Origen of Alexandria, following the example of the Jewish theologian, Philo of Alexandria, developed a very sophisticated system of semi-allegorical interpretation. It combined elements of both principles. While it is rarely used in modern Biblical interpretation Origen was so influential a scholar that it is worthwhile briefly examining the principle upon which he worked. He was, in every sense, a remarkable man and a remarkable scholar. Although he was condemned for heresy much of what he taught was orthodox and valuable. He was not the only theologian of the early Church who was judged heretical in some respects but much of whose work is deemed of value. The great Latin theologian Tertullian finished his days in an heretical sect and the writer Tatian spent only a short time in the Church.

Origen's principle of interpreting and drawing the teaching from the text—exegesis—grew from his understanding of the nature of the saving work of Christ. This he understood to be the redemptive restoration of the fallen creation from the material to the spiritual (hints of gnosticism!)[13] That sounds as if it is, and it may have been, born of a belief in the division between the spiritual and the material and soon led to trouble with orthodox understandings of the nature of reality. Certainly Origen was condemned as a heretic, as we observed. In an age before many dogmatic definitions were fully formed, he speculated more widely and adventurously than subsequently proved wise. Many modern theologians value his work very highly and the distinguished Roman Catholic writer Fr. Hans Urs von Balthasar prayed for Origen's acceptance and canonization.

---

[13] This doctrine is called the doctrine of *anakephalaiosis*. There is an explanation of it in the glossary.

Origen applied the principle that the spiritual was more real than the material to interpreting the text of the Bible and to his teaching on the sacraments. He taught that the reality of the Bible and the sacraments could be discerned at two levels; one of the image i.e. the external appearance and another of the reality. The inward spirit of the revelation is contained within and under the letter of the text. He understood the text to be an allegory, although whether he understood that definition in precisely the way in which it is understood now is questionable. The task of the interpreter of the Bible — the exegete — is, for Origen, to penetrate the allegory so as to perceive, within its material body, the soul and spirit of scripture. The spirit and soul of Scripture is its relevant application to the immediate, personal, moral and religious concerns of Christians now. It is the answer it gives to our question about salvation. The ability to make such a correct interpretation is a gift of grace. It is by faith and grace that the truth of the text is discerned in the same way that the truth of the Church and the sacraments is discerned by faith and grace. If we approach the externals alone we shall not see the truth. The grace of God and our faith reveal the truth concealed in the externals.

This last insight is vital to all authentic Biblical interpretation. It is clear that the correct interpretation of Scripture is a gift of grace — the point Origen made. The Bible does not yield its truth except to the faithful. The belief that one can simply pick up the text of Scripture and read off answers to questions is likely to lead to serious errors. St Hilary of Poitiers wrote, "For Scripture is not in the reading but in the understanding" (*To Constantius Augustus,* 3:9). Many orthodox theologians have observed that heresies can usually be sustained by misapplied and misunderstood Biblical references as we saw with the Jehovah's Witnesses. Origen teaches that only those who read and expound the text in grace and faith do so authentically and with authority. This means that authentic Biblical interpretation can only take place within the Church within the context of right belief. Tertullian, to whom we referred above, would not discuss the Bible with those outside the Church. There would be no point in doing so. The truth of the Bible can only be discerned by faith and within the community of faith and grace. It is the Church, alone, which provides the necessary doctrinal basis for interpreting the Bible. Florovsky goes so far as to say that one should preach the Creeds.[14] In this, as in almost all else, he is correct.

The Creeds are the encapsulation, in the forms we have discussed above, of those saving truths discerned in the record of revelation by the Church. They are, therefore, obviously the proper basis for the preaching since they provide the correct doctrinal basis for discerning the revelation of God. The revelation cannot be discerned by those in doctrinal error. Those who depend upon the principle of *sola scriptura*—scripture alone—ignore the dogmatic definitions of the Church at their peril. The doctrines of the Universal Church prevent us from being carried away by heretical interpre-

---

[14] op.cit.p.11.

tations of Biblical texts, of which there are very many. The record of revelation and the doctrines developed from the experience of the Church together constitute the basis of the true apostolic life of the Church so that the doctrines are not inconsistent with biblical revelation and grow from the logic of salvation. By the term "logic of salvation" we mean the controlling effect of the fact of God's action to save us upon our reasoning e.g. in the Incarnation. Since we experience the Lord Jesus as our salvation He must be both God and man. If He were not He could not save us. The full argument is in the appendices. This fact conditions our interpretation of biblical texts and is consistent with biblical revelation. Some have argued, on the basis of biblical texts, that the Lord Jesus is either not fully God or not fully man. The logic of salvation tells us that those interpretations are incorrect. If they were correct then our Lord's saving work could not save us and we know that it does.

It is, of course, precisely in the authentic interpretation of Scripture and its preaching within the boundaries of the doctrines of the Creeds, and only within those boundaries, that Biblical authority becomes clear. To understand preaching as a sacramental act revealing the authority of the Bible roots that authority in the life and worship of the people of God. That is its only proper context. Preaching makes explicit and contemporary the revelation of God in the Bible that is the Church's record of God's revelation. Preaching enables the Bible to speak in a contemporary environment and shows the Church the nature of the treasure it possesses in biblical revelation. Only within the ongoing life of the Church and its Tradition can the Bible be authentically interpreted and brought to the contemporary world.

This is an essential principle to hold onto and it is central to Origen's thinking. Origen used the method of allegorisation, broadly defined, and in the hands of such a great Biblical scholar it works, to a very large degree, but allegory has its dangers despite its occurrence in the Gospels and elsewhere in the New Testament.

What are the dangers of allegorization? We can see them if we remind ourselves of what an allegory is. It is defined by R. P. C. Hanson as a "method of interpreting Scripture whereby the text is made to yield a meaning which is other than its literal or surface or historical meaning."[15] The most frequent means by which this achieved is the application of a code to a narrative such that the narrative is interpreted by means of the code. This person represents this, this group that, this place something else and so on. When the original narrative is a fictional parable told by the Lord there is no problem, e.g. Mark 4 and 12. The fiction and the code applied to it are designed to illustrate a point. With a fictional parable allegorization is no problem. The fiction has been written, as an allegory, for the purpose. It is a perfectly acceptable teaching technique. We know where we are when a story is told and then allegorised.

---

[15] R. P. C. Hanson, "Allegory" in *Dictionary of Christian Theology* (London, 1982).

The two examples of allegorisation in the Gospels we have just referred to are both obviously fictional parables, that is, stories told by our Lord to make a point. There is no suggestion that they are real events. The drawing of a moral, by the Lord Jesus, by means of allegorisation, from a story told precisely to make that point presents, of course, no problem. The telling of the story and its use are the revelation. The danger comes when allegorization is applied to the Biblical revelation, parable or event, from outside, i.e. by someone other than the Lord Jesus, to interpret it, e.g. seeing the two coins left by the good Samaritan with the injured man as the two major sacraments of the Church. (A similar typological exegesis of this passage may be possible but an allegory of a parable will not be authentic exegesis.)

If we use allegory on the record of the revelation of God, parable or event, in history then the Bible ceases to be a record of revelation. It becomes a book of parables devised by us and separated from the historical concreteness of God's action in history. It becomes a set of examples or principles rather than a record of God's action in the world in which He reveals Himself for our salvation. It is precisely in its historical concreteness that the Bible speaks with authority. It is in history that God reveals Himself, not in a text the meaning of which is discerned by use of an arbitrary code. Allegorisation produces edifying moral examples not a real, living encounter with the self-disclosure of God. The Bible is, if it has any authority, the living, immediately and directly relevant word of God—His speech to us now, for our salvation. Allegory produces generalised principles not an encounter with God. It removes the immediacy from the record of revelation. The generalised principles do not speak to us with urgency to bring us to our salvation. In allegory we substitute our ideas, our understanding of Christian principles and so on for the revelation of God. We may, by chance, get it right from time to time. More often than not we shall get it wrong.

The arbitrary nature of the code in an allegory means that the interpretation of the text and its authority depend upon the selection of the code. The choice of which roles and functions shall be applied to the actors in the revelation depend upon us. We can choose whatever code we like, and so, it must be obvious, we can choose whatever might pass for the word of God. The content of the interpretation—what should be our encounter with the revelation of God—depends upon a fallible, sinful human selection of a code. It does not spring from the reception of revelation in grace and faith. The selection of a code will, almost certainly, be conditioned by considerations external to the text. The interpreter can pick the code to get the revelation he wants. Without reference to the record of revelation he decides what it is that he wants to say and designs the code to achieve that result. By applying the code he selects to the text he can get the message he wants. If he wants a different message he can change the code.

Further to this, allegory is the interpretation of a text and that is not good enough. The authentic interpreter must penetrate through the text to the act of God in history. It is the act of revelation, not a set of words, that must be interpreted. He must encounter the God who is revealed in the events and the text and preach God's revelation. As St Augustine, a frequent allegorizer as it happens, put it, "We ought to seek the mystery not just in the word but in the fact itself."[16] It is even an error to allegorise material that is fictional in the Gospels, e.g. the Parable of the Good Samaritan. While our Lord can allegorise his own story it is a mistake to suppose that we can properly allegorise one of his parables which he did not Himself allegorize. This will probably lead to misinterpretation.

The method of interpretation used by St Paul and the Fathers was typology. The typological method of interpreting the Bible proceeds from the belief that the text is a record of God's revelation in history. Hanson, in the same article referred to above defines typology as "the comparison of an event or series of events in the past and an event or series of events in the present or immediate future." To invent a word we might call it an "analogization" since the analogy or correspondence between past and present events and persons acting in those events lies at the heart of the process of typological interpretation. The past person and event is said to be a "type" of the present person or event. Alternatively the present person and event is seen to be a "type" of the past person and event.

Because the events recorded reveal the one and only God there is an inner coherence between all such revelatory events and our own standing before God now. There are fundamental similarities between the

---

[16] *Sermon on Ps. 68*, 2:6.

standing of one person before God at one moment in history and another at a later stage in history. There are many examples in the New Testament—in Pauline writings in particular—of the use of typology. In Hebrews 3:1ff Moses is seen as a type of Christ; in Romans 5:12-21 Adam is seen as a counter type of the Lord Jesus. There are other examples at 1 Cor. 5:6-8, 10:1-11, 15:45-49. We can see the use of typological analogy in the careful description of the clothes and person of John the Baptist in the Gospels who is clearly a type of Elijah (cf. Malachi 3:1 and 4:5-6). The whole setting of the story of the feeding of the multitude is so rich in typology that we can discern several layers of meaning, e.g. the Messiah was expected to feed his people in the desert as Moses fed his people in the desert and Elijah fed his. The Lord Jesus is the Messiah who sums up Moses—the Law—and Elijah—the prophets. It clearly looks forward to the Eucharist. The Jewish understanding of Heaven was of a Messianic feast. The whole context is a typological interpretation of the Eucharist even to the offering of the people that in the hands of the Lord is made enough to feed the crowd.

In a more modern context typology can work in two directions; either from the contemporary situation to the biblical type or analogy; or from the biblical revelation to a contemporary type or analogy. In the first case we might have a reference to Ruth's adherence to the God and people of Naomi referring forward to the situation of converts to a church, the former being a type of the latter. For the second case the text is read and prayed over until the inner coherence between the revelation of God and the response of the people of God in the record of revelation becomes clear. It is then expounded and set out. The Lucan story of the widow who gave her farthing (Luke 21:1–4) is, for example, a rich passage for understanding the way in which the least gifted Christian can further the work of God. The most clear distinction between allegory and typology is to be found in the nature of the interpretation. In allegory we finish up with generalised moral and religious principles. In typology we finish up with an immediately applicable moral and personal demand, the answer given by the text to our question about our salvation.

It will be useful at this point to remind ourselves of the nature of the Bible, which is the basis of typological interpretation:

1. That it is a sacred book addressed to believers i.e. those who come before God seeking their salvation.

2. That is it the creation of the community of the people of God.

3. That its meaning can only be discerned by grace and faith.

4. That it is the story of God's dealings with his people i.e. the history of salvation.

5. That is contains the record of God's acts and the response of the people of God — good and bad responses.

6. That it is one basic reality because it is the record of the acts of the one God.

7. That it is consummated in Christ and this means, among other things, that He is the centre of history. There is a consummation to come but it will be the realisation — the making present — of his consummation in his saving work. His cry from the cross is "It is fulfilled" (John 19:30).

8. The word of God, his message, the encounter of the people of God with his revelation, is not a set of proof texts or Christian principles.

9. The reality of the revelation is re-enacted in the life and sacraments of the Church. The Church is part of the revelation or as Fr. Florovsky has put it "salvation is the Church".[17]

This is why passages from 2,000 and 3,000 years ago speak to us with immediacy. This is why the psalms for example, are always relevant to the human condition.

Authentic typological interpretation of a passage of Scripture involves firstly the discernment of the inner coherence, the fundamental analogy between the reve-

---

[17] Florovsky, op.cit. p.38.

lation recorded in the text and the contemporary situation of those being addressed. This is why it is a prayerful act of grace. Having discerned the revelation the expositor, the preacher, must then set out the inner coherence and analogy to be found between the event in which the revelation of God is discerned and situation of those being addressed. He must do it in such a way that the immediate questions implied in the existence of the hearer or reader are answered to that person's salvation.

The word and revelation of God recorded in the Bible thus speaks directly to the contemporary situation of the people of God. The inner coherence and analogy between the events recorded in the Bible and the contemporary events speaks to the Church now. Sermons are, for this reason, generally ephemeral. Unless they are the words of a truly great preacher they very rarely speak to situations other than those originally addressed. They essentially apply to the time and the situation in which they are preached. Great sermons convey the revelation of God so faithfully that they can transcend the conditions of history.

When we come to the biblical text we must see it as speaking directly to our condition. We must discern the action of God recorded in the text as showing us our contemporary relationship to God such that we are brought to obedience to salvation. The Bible is the "living oracle of God." It is a sacramental reality in which God is present to us now and discloses Himself to us now for our salvation. Typology does not hinder and distort the freedom of God to act as does allegory. Allegory is under our control because we choose the code by which the text is interpreted. Typology lets loose upon us the revelation of God for our salvation.

Fr Georges Florovsky writes of the nature of typology as rooted in the event in which God reveals Himself.[18] He refers to the tradition of exposition of the Suffering Servant Songs in the prophecy of Isaiah. This is a classical example of typological interpretation. The passages have been understood, for centuries, to set out the suffering of the one called to be the servant of God. They have been applied most obviously to the Lord Jesus Christ but have also provided an insight into the nature and effect of suffering for God throughout history. His book, in which this reference is made and the details of which are in the book list, contains the most profound examination of biblical interpretation and its relationship to the Tradition of the Church.

This brief examination of the two major principles of interpretation was necessary in order to give substance to the proposition that the Bible contains all things necessary to our salvation. There are two major ways in which it is believed the authority of the Bible can be discerned. Typology is the principal method used by the Fathers of the Church and those who follow their methods.

It is in the authentic interpretation of Scripture that the Church and the individual Christian are brought to that obedience in which lies our salvation. It is the real, urgent, existential, immediately relevant engagement

---

[18] Florovsky, op.cit. p.31.

between the revelation of God in Scripture and the precise situation of the hearer that constitutes the essential environment for apprehending the authority of Scripture. This, says St Hilary of Poitiers, "is in not in the reading but in the understanding," as we have seen. The Bible speaks in answer to our need for salvation. Within the record of God's self disclosure in history, which constitutes the Bible, we encounter the saving acts of God. Our salvation lies in our obedience to his Word. That is why the authority of the Bible is a matter of central concern and is why correct principles of interpretation are equally of central concern. The various, slightly bizarre, techniques of interpretation that are sometimes popular lead us away from the authority of the Bible and away from our salvation.

Liberal and Critical Interpretation

There is another understanding of Biblical authority, which we can call "liberal/critical" — although "liberal" and "critical" are not synonymous. The critical fallacy is that because the authenticity of the text comes from scholarly research so too does its authority. We have examined this in substance above. It may sound perverse to some but the recognition of the authority of the Bible, and so of the texts that comprise it, does not come from a scholarly authentication of texts. We do not accept the authority of a text because scholars authenticate it but because the Church recognises its authority. It comes from the Church's acceptance of those texts as an authentic record of revelation. Critical scholarship cannot invalidate the authority of a text accepted as inspired scripture by the Church. As we have noticed a Biblical book or an apostolic letter would not cease to be inspired scripture because scholars were able to demonstrate that the author of it was not the author after which it is named. The recognition of the authority of the books of the Bible depends upon the discernment of that authority by the Church not their authentication or otherwise by scholars. By the same reasoning, as we have observed above, a newly discovered letter of, say, undoubted Pauline authorship, would have no more authority than that, apostolic authorship. It would not be canonical scripture. The gift of discernment that revelatory authority lies with the whole people of God not with the scholars.

The first function of scholarship as we have seen, is to verify the best texts among the many variants in Scripture. The Hebrew and Greek texts have many variants which are listed at the foot of most texts. Few of the variants have a significance in doctrinal matters. Where they do it is the job of the scholars to guide the whole people of God in deciding which of the variants is the most secure. The second function of the scholar is to provide the best translation from Hebrew and Greek into modern language. They must ensure that as far as possible the modern translation reflects the best texts and the meaning of the original most accurately. There are also contemporary references in some texts that need elucidation, e.g. heaping coals of fire on someone's head sounds like a hostile act.[19] Its meaning could be misunderstood. It is in fact a kindly act and the scholars can explain why. Scholars, as such, have no special function in interpreting the texts. That is a gift of grace not of the intellect. Since scholars are more familiar with the texts than most people they are likely to feature more among the interpreters than others – but not necessarily so. Scholars are not always the best preachers. They do not always or mostly provide the most authentic interpretation so that people are brought to encounter the revelation of God and come to their salvation.

The position of liberals in respect of Biblical authority presents a different problem from that of the critical approach. It is important to observe that there is not one species of Christian called a liberal who shares with all others, so named, the same views. "Liberal" is an untidy and in some ways misleading adjective. Our definition will be an operational definition, that is, we will say what we mean by "liberal" accepting that it is not a general definition.

The principal characteristic of liberal interpretation of the Bible is that the inspiration of the text takes second place to other considerations in particular the culture and mores of contemporary society. The position has been classically stated—albeit probably unconsciously—by the Anglican Bishop of Birmingham, Dr

---

[19] Romans 12:20. Heaping coals of fire on a person's head had something to do with a primitive central heating system, not with burning a person's head!

Mark Santer. In the Church of England Synod's debate on the Ordination of Women to the priesthood he observed that Scripture and Tradition, which indicated that the ordination of women to the priesthood was incorrect, must give way to Christian reason/common sense. Christian reason/common sense, undefined, with no clear character or boundaries, indicated that they should be ordained. The exaltation of Christian reason/common sense above the authority of Scripture and Tradition constitutes the distinctive mark of Liberal secularism. The crucial question for them and for us is, "What constitutes Christian reason/common sense?" What its sources are and the nature of its authority are nowhere defined. We do not know what it is except what someone might rather think is acceptable to modern society. Its seems to consist of an attitude to ethics and doctrine which is a composite of contemporary human desires and aspirations, and the mores of the society and time in which one is living. It is more "common sense" than "Christian" and often ignores reason.

If a Gospel demand seems unreasonable or if some aspect of Church order or ethical teaching seems to be inconsistent with Christian reason/common sense then it must be abandoned. Christian reason/common sense seems to be what the man on the city bus or more likely the young lady on the subway feels—and perhaps thinks—is reasonable. If a doctrine or practice fails the test of Christian reason/common sense it is no good. Is this a caricature of the liberal position? Very slightly but wide experience suggests that it is only slightly so. This form of liberalism, which is widespread in some churches, is, in fact, grossly illiberal in its effects. It depends upon feelings, emotions and untested perceptions. It is, in its effects, a sort of pink fascism in which euthanasia, unmarried sexual activity, abortion and irresponsible social ethics create a hellish society. It leads to the exaltation of feelings above faith and reason. When the feelings turn nasty it becomes hellish. This road to hell is paved with good intentions. Its error is to set up man as the ultimate standard against which we test the word of God. People forget that it is the will of God the Creator, which it is man's duty and joy to obey, that is the best for us. It is in the service of God that we find our perfect freedom.

The fundamental illusion lying behind much liberal thought, to which we have referred briefly above, is that sin and happiness are ultimately consistent with each other. They are not. Sin leads to unhappiness both in the short and the long term. To suppose that we ought to accept sin because it produces short term happiness is the most cruel of errors. The liberal point is made again and again as a person in open sin is seen to be happy at one level in that state. Bishop Richard Holloway sets up human happiness and well being as the ideal to be achieved. He complains about the best being the enemy of the good. This is the silliest fallacy to emanate from the lips of an intelligent man that one can imagine. The best is Heaven, union with God. To opt for something else than Heaven or to encourage people to go for something less than Heaven is to condemn them to perpetual frustration. It is to blind them to their destiny. St Augustine is a better guide: "Our souls are restless until they rest in thee."

Those who point out the ultimate incompatibility of sin and happiness are often accused of lacking compassion. If this liberal principle is applied to Biblical interpretation, as it is, together with Christian reason/common sense, of which it seems to be one manifestation, then the revelation of God cannot be discerned.

Apart from wrenching Biblical texts out of their context to support a view that they have come to on other grounds, liberals of this sort give no real authority to the Bible at all. The Bible is, for them, not the living oracle of God, a record of revelation, but rather a record of the history of Israel and the early Church and so on. It has no significance for most liberals beyond its value as an historical source and is subordinate in authority, as we have seen, to Christian reason/common sense, whatever that is. For the liberal, Biblical ethical teaching obviously has no ultimate authority. It refers only to the period in which it was written. In general it has only historical value. There is, therefore, no liberal (as we have defined the word) doctrine of Biblical authority which has any real significance. The fact that many liberals find hard to accept is that, for them, the Bible has no authority.

CHAPTER FOUR

Tradition and The Church

Tradition and "traditions"

How does the Church discern the authority of God within its own Tradition? That is the next question and we need to define both the word, "Tradition," and the word, "Church." These words are not quickly defined and it will take some time to come to moderately adequate definitions. The Tradition is the life of the Church. This must be remembered. Any definition which deals with Tradition and Church as separate entities will be misleading if this fact is not stressed. The Tradition and the Church are not separate realities. The Tradition is the life of Christ in the Church, God's continuing revelation in the life of the people of God.

First we need to distinguish between ecclesiastical traditions and the Tradition of the Church. The Orthodox and Anglican tradition of married clergy and the Roman tradition of clerical celibacy or the Methodist tradition of abstinence from alcohol—never a disciplinary matter—are not, for example, simply to be identified with the Tradition of the Church. They are ecclesiastical traditions. While they may be important at a practical level in some cases they are, in the end, peripheral to the being of the Church. They do not touch the essential nature of the Church or the way of salvation. It is, however, wise to proceed very cautiously at this point. It is very often the case that almost every element in the life of the Orthodox Church is understood to be an aspect of the Tradition of the Church. In almost all cases this understanding is correct. Often what appears to be an ecclesiastical tradition in the life of the Orthodox Church can be seen, on reflection, to be an expression of the Tradition of the Church. It can be seen to derive directly or indirectly from a central doctrine or can be seen to be symbolic of such a doctrine or a central part of the Church's life. It would be unwise, therefore, simply to identify any aspect of the Church's life as an ecclesiastical tradition rather than as an element of the Tradition of the Church. By making this mistake central elements in the Church's life can be changed when change is a mistake. This has happened and the results have almost always been damaging. There is a tendency among some Orthodox to see everything in the Church's life as integral to the Tradition and this can be confusing and amusing. Bearing all these things in mind we can see that there are elements in the life of any church or part of a church which persist over time until they become the accustomed way of doing things. There will obviously be many elements in these accustomed ways which are not necessarily linked to or expressive of the Tradition of the Church.

Ecclesiastical traditions frequently develop in response to historic conditions and persist when those conditions have changed as a means by which a church asserts its identity. This is probably true of the Methodist tradition of abstinence from alcohol for example.

We need to be able to discern these ecclesiastical traditions from elements of the Tradition of the Church. If we are not successful in doing so we shall finish up with some serious confusions. We must be careful to discern between what is part of the Tradition of the Church and what is an ecclesiastical tradition. If the structure of the ministry of the Church is a manifestation of the Gospel and the Tradition of the Universal Church[1] then that must be demonstrated.

The definition of Tradition has a history. We can discern three broad schools of understanding, each of which has some variations within it. First there is the Protestant view that Tradition does not exist as a source of authority. That is simply unrealistic. It is not true to the facts of Protestant history. The Word of God is not preached in a cultural and ecclesiastical vacuum outside the experience of the continuing life of a community. It is preached within a life of faith and worship, within a church's life. The whole worship and life of a church together are related to the progress to salvation of the members of that church. A group of Christians with a distinct ecclesiastical identity may discern that a certain belief or practice is binding upon Christians because it is derived from Scripture. If it is understood to be related in an essential way to salvation and if a succession of others follow that belief and practice then an element in the Tradition not hitherto recognised may

---

[1] Cf. "The structure of Catholicism is an utterance of the Gospel," in Ramsey, *The Gospel and the Catholic Church* (London, 1956), p. 54.

be made explicit. Some elements in the life of a church bear upon salvation and are essential to salvation. They are authentically part of the Tradition. Without them the Church fails in its function. Those that are not integral to salvation are not part of the Tradition. They are ecclesiastical traditions.

Some of the traditions of Protestant churches, while not part of the Tradition of the Universal Church, have enormous authority in those churches. This is even the case when, as with the tradition of abstention from alcohol in the Methodist Church, there is not only no Biblical foundation for the tradition but contrary Biblical authority. We have to distinguish, as we have just observed, between traditions and the Tradition. This Methodist tradition is not part of the Tradition. In general, though not in the case we have just mentioned, traditions in the Protestant churches are tested against the Tradition of Scripture. Those that are deemed to be consistent with the Tradition of Scripture become part of the tradition of that church. They are handed on by the preaching of the Word of God and by teaching. They become more than ecclesiastical traditions. In many cases these traditions are consistent with the Tradition of the Universal Church.

The Protestant understanding of the Tradition can be impoverished by a failure to grasp its significance and nature. It can, in the Protestant understanding, be concerned principally with the transmission of truths that are guiding principles for life in Christ, passed on by preaching. It is obvious that the Tradition of the Universal Church, seen in dogmatic definitions, for example, has authority in Protestant churches. The dogmas of the person of Christ and of the Blessed Trinity, for example, are held by many Protestants. These beliefs are derived from the Bible by the use of orthodox principles of Biblical interpretation. The very fact that Protestants hold to dogmatic definitions from the Councils of the Church indicates acceptance of an authoritative Tradition however attenuated. That they interpret Scripture in a way consistent with these dogmatic definitions means that although they do not recognise it they hold, in some measure, to the Tradition of the Church. This is particularly the case over matters such as the nature of the Blessed Trinity, the nature of the Lord Jesus, his saving work and the work of the Holy Spirit as we have just observed. Dogmatic definitions are, as we have seen, simply the belief of the Apostolic Church based upon the record of revelation. Protestants have an authoritative tradition which is related to the Tradition of the Universal Church and partly reflects it. It would be flying in the face of the facts to deny that. There is, of course, in many churches a tendency to regard doctrines of the Faith as intellectual phenomena and so to regard the Tradition as a collection of doctrines rather than the full life of the Church in which those doctrines are lived out.

John Calvin, the French reformer, taught that the Spirit interacted with the Word of God to illuminate the believer (note the parallel with Origen's views). He believed that the work of the Spirit was to be discerned in the building up of the Tradition.[2] This teaching is consistent to some degree with the definition of Tradition in Orthodoxy that we shall examine below. Where there is, in Protestant churches, an authoritative tradition of Biblical exegesis which together with the order and liturgy of the church constitutes the life of that church then there is an authoritative tradition. It is foolish to deny it. It is not always identical to or consistent with the Tradition as understood in the Universal Church but it exists. Part of the reason why the reformers gave a very limited significance in their thought to Tradition was the development of the understanding of Tradition in the Roman Church. As Tradition came to play a more significant part in the thought of the Western Church so the reformers, distancing themselves from Rome, gave it less and less significance. Each reaction fed upon the other and so as reformers came to reject, or more correctly, thought they were rejecting, the place of Tradition in the life of the Church in reaction to developments in the Roman Church so the Roman Church in turn reacted. It developed its own understanding of Tradition. This was on the opposite extreme to the reformers.

The Roman development was conditioned by two things in addition to the developments among reformers; here we are speaking of reformers in the West before the Reformation. The first conditioning factor was the growing dependence, for various reasons, on the centralised papacy as a source of authority in the West.

---

[2] John Calvin, *Institutes of the Christian Religion*, 1.9.3.

Gradual separation from the rest of the Church and the breakdown of the unity of the Empire gave the Bishop of Rome a position of unequalled influence. This led to the second development, which was the gradual diminution in the West of the significance of councils of the Church. The initial effect of this development was an increase in dependence on the authority of Scripture. There was, however, a problem with this. By about the fourteenth century, doctrines such as that of Christ's absolute poverty and the Immaculate Conception of the Blessed Virgin came to be widely accepted. Neither of these, with other doctrines, could be shown to have a Biblical foundation or to be consistent with Biblical revelation or, in the case of the Immaculate Conception, with the body of Apostolic Doctrine. This led to the development of belief in an unwritten tradition of parallel authority to the tradition of Scripture. The doctrine of an unwritten tradition became more strongly held in the Roman Church as Protestants came to reject, incorrectly as we saw, the concept of any authoritative tradition other than Scripture.

The view of Tradition as an unwritten body of dogma parallel and equal to Scripture held firm in the Roman Church, in general, until the nineteenth century. In the later nineteenth century Newman, together with Mohler and others from Tubingen, influenced by the Romantic movement, taught that Tradition was a developing reality growing from the seeds of Scripture over the years. The accepted view by the time of the Second Vatican Council was that Scripture was materially sufficient for salvation. It was believed to contain the whole deposit of the faith in seed; a belief implied by the theories of Newman and others. Fr Yves Congar's teaching is that the Tradition is one reality. It is to be found partly in the teaching, liturgy and discipline of the Church and partly in the canons of the Church. This represents the mainstream, post—Vatican 2 belief about Tradition in the Roman Church and we shall see, again, that this is largely consistent with the Orthodox doctrine of Tradition. It is a richer concept than the earlier one and is rooted in the life of the Church. It is preserved and can be discerned in the life of the Church.

Rather like the Irishman who when asked the way to Cork said that he would not have started out from here, the Orthodox do not start out from the same conceptual basis as the West. Just as the Orthodox did not have to face any Biblical criticism so too they did not face attempts to demolish the authority and reality of the Tradition; the Tradition for the Orthodox was and is never an idea but the whole life of the Church. There was, therefore, no belief in Tradition as a parallel code to the Biblical tradition. The tendency of both Western Catholicism and Protestantism to see tradition as a more or less authoritative code to be affirmed or denied is, therefore, completely alien to the Orthodox Church. For the Orthodox the Holy Tradition is the apostolic witness to the Lord Jesus in Scripture and in the whole life of the Church, an expression of the presence of God in the New Israel. It is, in essence, the full life of the Church, the life of the Church lived to the full. At first sight St Basil of Caesarea seems, incorrectly as we shall explain, to be speaking in the voice of a Tridentine Roman Catholic when he writes:

> ... among the doctrines and teachings preserved by the Church we hold some from written sources and we have others transmitted in an inexplicit (*mustikos*)[3] form from the apostolic tradition. They have all the same value... For if we were to try to put aside the unwritten customs as having no great force, we should, unknown to ourselves, be weakening the Gospel in its very essence, we should be turning *kerygma* (i.e. the proclamation of the Gospel) into a mere word.[4]

By this he means that the Tradition is expressed in the very life of the Church, not in a code, written or unwritten, but in every aspect of the Church's life. That is the force of inexplicit or *mustikos*. St Basil continues, in this passage and later, with particular reference to details of the Sacraments of Baptism and the Eucharist and e.g. of the custom of standing at prayer and so on. Much of this cannot be found in Scripture but grows out of the life of the Church and is symbolic of and enshrines dogmatic truths. The life of the Church gives life to and lives out the dogmas of the Church. The Orthodox doctrine of the Trinity, for example, gives a par-

---

[3] This means that the Tradition is not explicitly handed down in a codified form as the Roman Church might have taught at one time but that the Tradition is the life of the Church, its sacraments, its continual sustenance by the Holy Spirit and the life of Christ.

[4] St Basil, *On the Holy Spirit*, 27.

ticular quality to the membership of each member of the Church. The Church is an icon of the Blessed Trinity. We shall discuss this below. This life is the Tradition and is one with the Scriptural Tradition. The Tradition is therefore the Scriptures *and* the living sacramental presence of the Lord in the Church in one whole continuing life.

Fr John Meyendorff expresses the unity of the Tradition in this way:

> There cannot be, therefore, any question about "two sources" of revelation. It is not, in fact, a formal dictation of certain formally definable truths to the human mind. Revelation in Jesus Christ is a new fellowship between God and man, established once and for all. It is a participation of man in divine life. Scripture does not create this participation; it witnesses, in a final and complete form, to the acts of God which realised it. In order to be fully understood, the Bible requires the reality of the fellowship which exists in the Church. Tradition is the sacramental continuity in history of the communion of the saints; in a way, it is the Church itself.[5]

In this passage Meyendorff draws attention to a point which we shall examine later, i.e. that one central manifestation of the Tradition is an Orthodox Tradition of interpreting the Bible: "In order to be fully under-

---

[5] Meyendorff, *Living Tradition*, p. 16.

stood, the Bible requires the reality of the fellowship which exists in the Church." The life of the Church is, therefore, the truth of the Biblical revelation given life. It is realised revelation, and it is, therefore, revelation itself. St John can say that "we know that we have passed from death to life because we love the brethren" (1 John 3.14.) because living in the love of the brethren, in the full life of the Church, i.e. the Tradition, is precisely living the risen life of the Lord Jesus; thus we know that we have passed from death to life in the life of the Church. The communion of the Church is the revelation of the Resurrection. As Florovsky puts it "salvation is the Church."[6]

Compare the words of Meyendorff, which we have just quoted, with the words of St Irenaeus: "Where the Church is there is the Spirit of God and where the Spirit of God is there is the Church and every kind of grace; but the Spirit is the Truth."[7]

Fr Georges Florovsky concurs with these descriptions of the nature of the Tradition and the life of The Lord in the Church:

> Tradition is the witness of the Spirit; the Spirit's unceasing revelation and preaching of good tidings... To accept and understand the Tradition we must live within the Church, we must be conscious of the grace-giving presence of the Lord in it; we must feel the breath of the Holy Ghost in it... Tradition is not a protective, con-

---

[6] *The Bible, Church and Tradition*, p. 38.
[7] *Against the Heretics*, 3.24.1.

servative principle; it is, primarily, the principle of growth and regeneration.... Tradition is the constant abiding of the Spirit and not only the memory of the words.[8]

Elsewhere Florovsky writes, "The truth of the book is revealed and vindicated by the growth of the Body."[9] Thus the two revelations are one, the revelation of the Bible appearing, coming to life in, being realised in the life of the Church. The Church is precisely a sacred and wonderful mystery because it is the living revelation of God and in this one revelation of the one God the revelation of the Bible and the revelation of the Tradition are united and become one.

The final observation of Florovsky points to two truths implicit in the Orthodox understanding of the Tradition. The first we have examined when we observed that the Church discerned the record of revelation of God in certain texts. The life of the Body certifies the authenticity of that discernment as Florovsky points out. The life of the Church, the Tradition, is the living out of the revelation of the Bible. It is in the life of the Church that the revelation of the Bible is made real for contemporary man. We know the texts are authentic records of revelation because we observe new life in Christ in the Church just as St Paul reports in 1 Corinthians 15, a passage we have referred to above. The life of the Church is the reality in which we experience the

---

[8] Florovsky, as quoted in Ware, *The Orthodox Church* (London, 1963), p. 206.

[9] *The Bible, Church and Tradition*, p. 26.

truth of our salvation—salvation is the Church. The Church is a revelation itself of the saving work of God. "We know that we have passed from death to life because we love the brethren." The Church is the authentic continuum and arena of the saving work of God. That is why Meyendorff says that the Tradition is the Church itself. That is why the sacraments of the Church are necessary to salvation because they are the effective and active signs of full life in the Church. They are signs in the sense that the great signs and miracles of St John's Gospel are signs. They reveal the truth of Christ and his Church.

The second truth which is implicit in the Orthodox understanding of the Tradition is that within the Tradition, as part of what composes it, there is an Orthodox tradition of Biblical interpretation. This point is implied in Florovsky's comment that "the truth of the book is revealed and vindicated by the growth of the Body". The Tradition is experienced, in part, as an Orthodox tradition of expounding the Scriptural Tradition. We become part of the living Tradition, the life of the Church, when we expound and interpret the Bible in ways consistent with the Tradition of the Church. The authentic interpretation of the Tradition of Revelation contained in Scripture will build up the Body. The growth shows its authenticity and that it is an expression of the Tradition. There is, therefore, an Orthodox tradition of Biblical interpretation that is implicit in and an essential part of the whole Tradition. It is the effective and living word of God in the life of the Church. It is a line of life, of lived new life, so to speak, from the revelation of God in history to his revelation now in the Church. Thus it is—or, more properly, Christ is—the life of the Church. When we speak of "building up" the body we do not simply mean—or even necessarily mean at all—growth in numbers but rather conformity to the life of Christ. This may or may not lead to numerical growth in the short and medium term.

The growth of the authentic Tradition of the Church is the expression of and comes from the meeting of the Apostolic witness with new geographical and historical environments. New conditions cause the life of the Church to develop in certain ways. Where these ways touch the essential life of the Church they may, from time to time, be authentic and essential expressions of the life of Christ in the Church. They must be tested for their consistency with the whole Tradition and with the body of Apostolic Dogma. Those who deny any authority to Tradition, ignoring the existence of their own traditions, have made this authentic development of life impossible. The authentic life of Christ is absent and so cannot guide and enliven the development. It is in this sense, in part, that Newman spoke of the development of doctrine.

The *sola scriptura*—scripture alone—school has hampered the development of authentic tradition by detaching interpretation of the Bible from the orthodox Tradition of interpretation. We have seen that heretics throughout history have been found among the strongest adherents of *sola scriptura*. The list quoted by St Vincent in his "Commonitorium" is enough evidence of this as are the Jehovah's Witnesses in our own time. The word, *homoousios*,[10] opposed by the Arian heretics, for example, translated as "of one substance/essence" in the Creed of Nicaea and Constantinople, is not scriptural. The Fathers of Nicaea could, however, find no other word to describe the relationship of the Logos to the Father. This was an authentic development in the expression of the Apostolic Faith and of the Tradition. It was not, however, only dependent on Scripture but was consistent with the Bible and grew from the faith of the people of God and the logic of salvation.

Those liberals who deny effective orthodox authority to the Bible have inauthentic developments of doctrine that do not bring men to new life in Christ in the Church. Those who have a defective tradition of exegesis have a defective church life so that it does not bring people to Christ. We can see the authentic Tradition of interpreting the Bible at work in what we have referred to as the logic of salvation; we shall explore that concept more now.

When we examine dogmatic definitions in the context of the life of the people of God we can see that there is a fundamental dynamic behind such definitions. It is a dynamic which does not always surface and it is absent in inauthentic definitions. We bring this dynamic into operation by asking the simple question: Which definition and which interpretation leads to man's salvation and the fulfilment of God's purpose? The interpretation of Scripture and the defining of dogma, if authentic, must be concerned with this one thing: the

---

[10] See the glossary for an explanation of this word.

fulfillment of God's purpose of bringing man to salvation or, in other words, the logic of salvation. They are never matters of speculation or interest. When interpreting a passage from the Bible we are constrained by the fact that only that interpretation which leads us to our salvation is authentic. It might be possible to interpret a particular passage in such a way that it is deemed to show that our Lord is not truly God or not truly a man. Many have done so and still do. An open ended principle of interpretation might conclude that the passage points one way or another or is uncertain in its meaning. The logic of salvation leads us to interpret the passage in a way consistent with the way of salvation. If a person concluded that the Bible pointed away from the divinity and humanity of Jesus it would make salvation impossible and would therefore be inauthentic.

Any theological speculation that does not have this dynamic—the dynamic of the logic of salvation—is doomed to failure. If the concern and purpose behind the speculation is to be reasonable or to appeal to the modern mind it will inevitably be an error. If it is designed to be consistent with contemporary standards and mores or with the contemporary understanding of the ordering of society and the Church and so on it is doomed to be inauthentic. It will lead to the disintegration—in every sense of the word—of the Church and the frustration of the purpose of God. It creates a state where people are shut off from salvation. This is why Biblical interpretation and dogmatic definition is the work of the whole Church rather than of scholars alone.

The encounter of the Apostolic witness and life with new cultural environments may require the re-expression of the Apostolic Faith and witness in its living, immediate, existential, urgent, saving reality. This, inevitably, means the possibility of the use of new language that is not found in the Scriptures. It does not and cannot mean a change of substance. The fundamental elements of man's relationship with God do not change. They persist through changes in culture and language. The fundamentals of human existence, of virtue and sin, of joy and guilt are to be found in every age and culture. That is why, at a secular level, great literature and great drama continue to affect us. Greek drama and Shakespeare still "work." They work because the fundamentals of human existence persist. The words and the understanding of human existence that gave rise to the words are consistent with all human experience regardless of culture or age. Human beings are not fundamentally different from their forebears because they can travel at 1,000 m.p.h or use a computer. The basics of human nature do not change simply because, at the time, sexual licence or sexual repression or something else is the cultural fashion. The language changes and the culture changes. The underlying realities of human existence do not; because they do not neither do the dogmas of the Church. The dogmas of the Church do not change because they are the answer of the one true, unchanging and loving God to the human condition, which does not, in its essence, change either.

We can define the Tradition of the Church as the continuation of God's self- disclosure in the life of the people of God, the new Israel, discerned by them. It is the continuing life of God in Christ in the Church. The Bible is the canonical tradition against which all subsequent expressions of the Tradition are measured and tested.

The Church

We must now attempt to define the second major element in this part of this study, that is the Church. Careful definition is a central requirement but it is also a central problem. At every point, the discernment of revelation by the Church, both in Scripture and Tradition, is crucial. The act of discernment is not made by any other group but the Church. The definition of the Church will affect the authoritative discernment of revelation. If any definition of the Church will do then any group will be deemed to be the Church that authoritatively discerns the revelation of God. We will have to choose between conflicting groups, each of which claims to be the Church with the power to discern true revelation. Any doctrine at all may be deemed an authentic doctrine of the Church if the Church is undefined and can be any group. The definition of the Church is, therefore, a central issue for without the correct definition we shall finish up choosing our own doctrine. That is the way to confusion and chaos as we can see in the life of some churches and chaos and confusion are the marks of Hell. What and who, therefore, constitute the Church? To whom do we point when we point to the Church and upon what grounds do we point to one group rather than another? Which group does the discerning authentically? We need to know this because although the Bible does not derive its authority from the Church but from God's acts of self-revelation that it records it is the Church which discerned which books are and which are not records of that revelation. We examined this process briefly in the last chapter. The authority of the Church is, in a sense, primary for it is the Church which did and which does the discerning. The authority of the Church is not, however, superior to the Scriptures for the authority of Scriptures is the authority of the authentic self-revelation of God that they record.

The function of the Church in discerning which books authentically record the revelation of God makes the questions we have just set out about the definition of the Church very urgent. To which group shall we attend? When we reflect that the authority of the Church creates, as does all authority, a relationship of obedience to salvation then the questions become even more urgent. Our salvation is concerned in all this. Which group, therefore, must we obey for our salvation? As we have seen the definition of the Church is central to our understanding of the way of salvation.

As soon as one starts to attempt a definition of the Church three characteristics of such a definition become clear. First, it is clear that from time to time the Church's definition will have a negative element to it; it will be apophatic[11]; that is we shall in part define the Church by what it is not. That is not surprising since the Church and its nature is an article of the Apostolic Faith as expressed in the Creeds. Such definitions are negative, concerned with what we must not deny rather than what we must affirm, i.e. apophatic, as we have seen above. The credal definition of the Church, and the Church itself, is part of the dogmatic corpus of the Apostolic Church, integral to the Apostolic Faith. This means that we must understand the dogmatic definitions of the Church in the same way as other dogmatic definitions, that is as making assertions that we must not deny rather than stating what we must affirm. The Church ministers the power of God in e.g. ministering forgiveness (e.g. Mk 2:1–6 and Jn 20:23) and in other ways. It is not surprising, therefore, that the dogmatic definition of the Church shares certain characteristics with the ways we speak of God. The definitions, like other dogmatic definitions, are negatively shaped, relate to the End and will only be fully realised at the End. This leads us to the second characteristic of definitions of the Church.

It soon becomes clear that the definition of the Church must be understood to refer to the relationship of the Church to the End. When considering this characteristic we must bear in mind that when we speak of the End we speak at one and the same time of that which comes at the End of Time, when all things will be revealed and the purpose of God consummated and

---

[11] See the glossary for an explanation of this word.

also of another reality. This other reality is the existence of all things in the presence of God at the present moment. The End, the consummation of all things, is always present as well as always being a future reality at the same time. St Paul makes this clear in 2 Cor. 6:2 and such a belief lies behind the passage at Romans 13:11. The parable in St Matthew 25:31–46 also teaches the same. In the fullness of time we shall see the fullness of the Church and that fullness is a present and a future reality. The Church is as near the End now as at any time. The End, the Kingdom of God, is a present reality as well as a final reality. Although that answer does not give us a simple answer if we want to know where to find the one Church of Christ now that the earlier unity is broken it must be clear that any consideration of the Church's unity, holiness, catholicity and apostolicity must be done in the knowledge of the "now and not yet-ness" of the Church's being, its relationship to the End now and yet to come. We must include an eschatological element in the definition of the Church because it is an eschatological reality.

Time and space are part of the created order and so will, like all created things, pass. There will be an End of time as there will be a passing of all created reality, even if we cannot get our heads around it. If that seems a trying evasion of the issues involved in defining the Church simply we will put it another way. The qualities of the Church and all the many things we can say about the Church are at once true now in the calling of God and as seen with God's eye in the End. This is because God is in the same relationship to each moment of time as to each other so we can say that we meet the End now. Because the Church lives in the presence of the End it is complete when seen with the eyes of faith and the definitions cannot be denied and yet, in a sense, they are still to be fulfilled. The reality is only visible at the End and in the face of the End and it is seen now if the Endness of now is understood and discerned.

The fact that the truth of the Church is a matter of faith as well as of experience should surprise nobody since the Church is a Christological reality, a sacramental mystery. The divine and human exist in the Church as they are to be seen in our Lord. The Church is the Body of Christ. The Church is, in a clumsy word, theandric, (*theos* = God, *aner* = man, theandric = being both divine and human), that is it is human and divine as the Lord is human and divine. The humanity of the Church, imperfect as it is, is yet to be fulfilled.

The Hebraic understanding of reality is that the significance and truth of things lies not in what they appear to be but what they are in the calling of God. Any definition of the Church which grows from the New Testament, with its strong Hebraic roots, will be a definition of what the Church is in the calling of God, i.e. an eschatological definition. What the Church is cannot be completely or adequately defined by a definition of what we see and experience. The truth of the Church is not simply an empirical and experienced reality. We have not seen all the truth of it when we look at a particular group of people who, in that place and at that time, constitute the Church.

The Church is a reality of faith as all other experiences of the Body of Christ are or were realities of faith. The term, "Body of Christ," has several meanings, e.g. the presence of our Lord as the Body of Christ which we receive in Holy Communion, the Church and the Lord who would have been seen walking in the Holy Land. The truth of each of these realities is only seen by faith. Holy Communion looks like bread and wine and Jesus looked like an ordinary man so that without faith he could do no mighty works (Mark 6). What was and is observed was and is not the whole truth of the Lord Jesus or of the sacrament of Holy Communion. The same is true of the Church. What is observed is not the whole truth of it or the most significant truth of it. The Church as the Body of Christ must be defined against the truth of what the Church is called to be, what it is in the calling of God and so what it is to the eyes of faith. In any way in which we use the phrase, "Body of Christ" we must understand that we only see the truth of the Body of Christ by love and faith — as we only see the truth of any person by looking with love and faith. Love and acceptance transfigure all things and reveal the truth of all things.

The third characteristic of any definition of the Church is that we have to live with two classes of definitional problem. There is a theological problem, the nature of which we have been considering in part in the preceding paragraphs. There is also the more simple and pragmatic one of which of two or more groups claiming to be the Church and yet saying different things is in fact the Church. Which group can properly claim to be the one Church of Christ discerning the truth of the Tradition? The very reality of having to make a choice and of dealing with particularities makes the second question, in a sense, the more urgent. If St Cyprian is right and there is no salvation outside the Church, which body is the Church to which a person must belong in order to be saved? This body, and this body alone, will be the bearer of the Tradition and the Apostolic Body able to discern the truth of the Scriptural Tradition authentically. It alone will show the Apostolic life completely in its life. It alone will completely authentically expound and interpret the Scriptures.

Plainly the theological definition of the Church is the fundamental definition. The problem of which group we point to when we speak of the Apostolic Church has, however, to be resolved in some way and to a large degree simply because choices have to be made. How do we decide to accept the claims of a particular body when there are several different bodies making the same claims? We must try to find an external definition that is consistent with the most adequate criteria possible and with the theological definition. We need then to see which group matches the criteria and to which we must, therefore, adhere. We must also accept that a list of criteria will not be completely adequate for the reasons we have discussed. The truth is that all concise, readily framed definitions of the Church are inadequate. Some communions identify the Church with themselves. A significant number of Orthodox Christians do so and the Roman Communion has done so in the past and nearly seems to do so now. Which is correct?

This definition of the Church from the catechism of Cardinal Pietro Gasparri[12] represents the classical Roman position. Gasparri was the Papal Secretary of State until 1929, immediately preceding Cardinal Eugenio Pacelli, later Pius XII. He was responsible for the revision of Roman Canon Law:

> The Catholic Church instituted by Jesus Christ is a visible society composed of men who have received baptism and who, united amongst themselves by the profession of the same faith and bonds of mutual communion, strive for the same supernatural end, under the authority of the Roman pontiff and the bishops in communion with him.

This definition, in general, held sway until the Second Vatican Council at which a slightly more subtle definition was agreed:

> This Church (referring to the one Church of Christ) founded and organised in the world as a society, subsists in (*subsistit in*) the Catholic Church...although outside its framework there are found many elements of holiness and truth, and they give an impetus to universal unity, in-

---

[12] Guillou, "The Church," in *Encyclopaedia of Theology*, ed. Rahner (London, 1975).

asmuch as they are gifts which belong to Christ's Church.[13]

It seems, despite the acknowledgement of the work of the Spirit outside the Roman Communion, that the final answer is very nearly the same as earlier definitions of which Cardinal Gasparri's is characteristic.

We shall explore one Orthodox understanding of the location of the Church below — and there are several. We need at this stage, however, to make one objection to a possible interpretation of St Cyprian's dictum, "outside the Church there is no salvation", which assumes that "the Church" means the Roman Church. This objection, together with some observations from a more conservative part of the Orthodox Church, might have the effect of putting St Cyprian's dictum in a different light.

The objection is this. If we take our salvation to depend upon membership of one particular communion capable of empirical definition e.g. all those in communion with the Bishop of Rome or all those in communion with the Ecumenical Patriarch, then we have salvation by jurisdiction. Our salvation on these terms depends upon which jurisdiction we enter. That cannot be the case. Our salvation is by faith through grace. We receive salvation as we come penitent to receive the forgiveness of God mediated through the saving work of Christ and His Church. (Even a person in a community outside the Apostolic Church hears of the saving work of Christ through the Church.) It is Christ's work

---

[13] *Lumen Gentium*, 8.

and our free participation in it by repentance and participation in the life of the Church that saves us. We cannot be saved by our decision to be a member of one jurisdiction rather than another unless that process involves repentance and full participation in the life of the Church that is impossible elsewhere. There are, of course, churches that do not require this of their members and churches that have abandoned part or all of the Apostolic Faith. These churches exclude themselves from consideration. It is clear that the doctrine, discipline and order of some particular churches are more likely than others to bring individuals to the saving state we have described. It is just that our salvation cannot depend solely upon our adherence, as such, to one jurisdiction rather than another. Our salvation depends upon our penitent reception of God's forgiveness in Christ and our growth in grace by a full life in the Church and our continued repentance.

We can try to escape from the jurisdictional dilemma by adopting the now discredited proposition that there are several branches in the Apostolic Church. That theory never had wide acceptance. It was a brave but hopeless attempt by Anglicans, for example, to include themselves in a jurisdictional definition of the one Church of Christ. Fatally for many Anglicans it led to reliance upon a doubtful claim to adequate jurisdictional criteria at the cost of repentance and a full sacramental life.

We cannot deny that the Church is one, holy, catholic and apostolic. That is a dogmatic definition that cannot be avoided. This is a statement of the Church's essential character and a statement of faith. But where, empirically, can we find the one Church of Christ? Which of the many groups which claim either to be the one Church of Christ or to be part of the one Church of Christ is correct in its claims?

It is hard to accept that churches with unbroken lines of bishops from the Apostles and formally holding the Apostolic Faith are, for those reasons alone, the only authentic parts of the Church which seems, within our experience, to be fractured. How can the Church be one if there are parts not in communion with each other? Talk of being part of a body in which the bonds of communion are broken is problematic. A church is, at least, a community sharing a common faith and with bonds of communion stemming from an apostolic patriarch or synod. The absence of that is fatal. That is the Anglican problem. There are no longer in that communion any ministerial, doctrinal or sacramental bonds. It lacks the fundamental elements of a church. The possession of the forms rather than the substance of Catholic Order, bishops, priests and deacons, does not, of itself, guarantee that to some degree the church, with Catholic Order, will not fall away from the Catholic Faith.

While Catholic Order is a sign of the Gospel,[14] the presence of it does not guarantee the presence of the Gospel nor does its absence mean that the preaching and living of the Gospel is absent. In any case reliance on this approach can, in the end, put us into the hands

---

[14] Ramsey, *The Gospel and the Catholic Church*, p. 47, n. 1.

of the scholars again. If a church is a church because of an unbroken succession of bishops from the apostles then we have to wait for the scholars to demonstrate which church or churches possess this line. The Roman Catholic scholar Peter Anson, in a private letter to the present writer in 1964, observed that it was quite impossible to assert with absolute confidence that there had been an unbroken line of bishops in the Roman Church from St Peter to the present Bishop of Rome. In any case, Antioch has a strong claim to be the first Petrine see. Is Patriarch Ignatius IV of Antioch the true successor of Peter rather than John Paul II of Rome? A claim of unbroken succession is subject to the research of scholars and if such an unbroken line is a necessary element in the authenticity of a church's claim to be the Catholic Church then we are in an even stranger case than that of salvation by jurisdiction. We will have salvation by research. We will wait upon the decision of the scholars to tell us which church to join. That does not make sense. Too many definitions of the Church depend upon empirical tests, which put us into the hands of researchers and scholars. This dependence puts us in an impossible situation. We do not know what the scholars will find next nor have we the resources to test their findings. When those findings bear on our salvation such a degree of uncertainty in matters not subject to faith but to knowledge is not acceptable. We cannot depend upon the scholars for those decisions.

One further necessary observation is that historically the definitions of the Faith made by the Universal

Church were often made at a time in which there were serious schisms. Schisms, in fact, often triggered the calling of a council. St Cyprian himself and some of his fellow African bishops were out of communion with Bishop Stephen of Rome for a significant period during his time as Bishop of Carthage (248-258). It seems that whatever he meant by "outside the Church there is no salvation", he did not mean that being out of communion with the Bishop of Rome was a hazard to his salvation. He did not believe himself to be outside the Church when he was out of communion with Rome.

St Cyprian's dispute with Rome was not the only serious schism in the early centuries of the Church. The Church in Antioch, for example, was broken by the Melitian Schism (c.362-381) with two rival patriarchs for much of St Melitius' time as patriarch. It would be hard to say where the Catholic Church was for some of the time preceding the Council of Nicaea. Almost all but Athanasius of Alexandria and a few adherents, in flight up the Nile, held to a heretical doctrine of the person of Christ and so of the Blessed Trinity, i.e. the Arian heresy. In time, for a period between about 325 AD and 1054 AD, when the schism between East and West became permanent, Catholicism was to be seen in a large, fairly easily definable body called the Catholic Church with few major divisions. It consisted of those Christians in communion with the five patriarchates of Rome, Constantinople, Antioch, Jerusalem and Alexandria. That is almost certainly what St Cyprian meant by the Church despite his dispute with the Bishop of Rome.

The Articles of Religion of the Church of England point to one solution to the problem of defining the Church. Article 19 says that the visible Church of Christ is a congregation of the Faithful in which the pure word of God is preached and the sacraments duly administered. As with all definitions, however, in a subject in which there is no agreement on basic concepts there are some questions begged here. Is it not precisely the Church that decides *if the word preached is the pure word of God* and what does "duly" mean? Those questions are not, however, that difficult to answer. The pure word of God calls men and women to repentance and sanctification and, over time, results in conversions, the growth of the Church, sanctity and Christ-like life. (cf. Florovsky's observation, "The truth of the book is revealed and vindicated by the growth of the body," and 1 Corinthians 15:11-12).[15] The purity of the Word preached is a self-authenticating reality. It proves itself by the effects it produces. There may be some argument about specific examples and about details but in general we know sanctity when we see it and it is the product of the pure preaching of the Word of God.

"Duly" means according to historical forms and as an expression of the Apostolic Faith. Archbishop William Temple, however, suggested that when a godly non–episcopal minister breaks bread and offers wine in obedience to our Lord with the intention of offering the Eucharist and uniting himself and the people he serves with the life death and resurrection of our Lord and

---

[15] Florovsky, *op.cit.*, p. 26.

with his saving work it is nonsense to say that nothing happens.[16] It is not clear how far one can go with that view as a definition of "duly", especially in the light of Archimandrite Constantine's thesis. In general, however, there is much weight in what Temple says. Since there are Protestant saints it is likely that something rather than nothing is done. When a convert to Orthodoxy was told that the Holy Spirit was not to be found outside the Orthodox Church he asked, very pertinently, "Who, then, brought me to conversion?"

How can we draw some satisfactory conclusions from this disorder? First it must be admitted that simple, practical criteria, e.g. all those in communion with a particular bishop prove, on examination, to be inadequate. Let us rather say what the Catholic Church must be, what must be true of it. Let us then describe the minimum characteristics that we ought to be able to discern in a community that claims to be the One, Holy, Catholic and Apostolic Church.

The members of the One Church of Christ must together hold to the Apostolic Faith as expressed in the Creeds of the Apostolic Church and as defined in those Councils which were undoubtedly ecumenical. Catechumens of the Orthodox Church do not, in so many words, undertake to hold the faith of a particular church but rather the Catholic Orthodox faith. This is the Apostolic Faith. It is enshrined in the Creeds and the decisions of ecumenical Councils. A church can only

---

[16] Temple, *Thoughts on the Problems of the Day* (London, 1931), p. 110.

claim to be the one Church of Christ if it holds no more and no less than the faith defined by the Church through councils which were judged to be councils of the whole Church. This would exclude additions made to the Apostolic Faith under circumstances other than definition by an ecumenical council. It would avoid statements of faith that excluded elements of the Apostolic Faith approved in the same way. The details of the additions to the Apostolic Faith that are to be found in the Roman Church are at Appendix 4. They are the addition of 'and the Son' to the Creed of Nicaea and Constantinople, the dogmas of the Immaculate Conception of the Blessed Virgin, the Infallibility of the Pope and the Assumption of the Blessed Virgin. The first is common in the Western churches that derived from Roman Catholicism. In addition most Western churches have also either lost Apostolic Order as it developed in the Apostolic Church or hold to doctrines which are inconsistent with the Apostolic Doctrine as set out in the Creeds and the decisions of councils. Because of the dogmatic additions of the Roman Church serious questions have to be raised about her claims to be the one Church of Christ. The claims of the Bishop of Rome to universal ordinary jurisdiction and infallibility in faith and morals in the terms of the definition have, in addition, destroyed the patristic basis for the unity of the Church as set out by St Cyprian. This was that the unity of the Church is preserved in the fraternal love and concord of the bishops themselves established by the Holy Spirit and evidenced in sacramental communion.[17]

The members of the one Church of Christ must be in sacramental communion with each other although that communion may be broken from time to time, as it is, by non-dogmatic considerations. The Church of England, for example, is no longer united by bonds of sacramental communion. Not all its priests are recognised as priests by all its members and the right to refuse such recognition is written into the law of the church. It is also divided on the basis of dogmatic considerations. Talk of having impaired communion is not, logically, unlike talk of being slightly pregnant or a little bit dead. It cannot conceal the radical nature of the divisions. The issues that divide members of the Anglican Communion go to the very roots of Christian dogma. There are differences of a profound nature on the doctrine of God, on the person of Christ, on order, on the sacraments, on authority. These lead to differences on ethical teaching. The ordination of women to the episcopate and the priesthood in a minority of Anglican provinces has destroyed the claims of Anglicans to have retained the historic orders of the Catholic Church. While there are divisions in the Orthodox Church they are not based, in general, upon differences of dogma i.e differences over fundamental belief.

The one Church of Christ must have a continuous ministerial and sacramental history back to the Apostles and must express the Apostolic Faith in Catholic Order

---

[17] Cyprian of Carthage, *Letters* 17,25, and 75.

and in the Catholic Sacraments even if there were times and places where that continuity broke down to some degree. We cannot really be sure of a continuous line of Bishops of Rome from St Peter to the present Bishop of Rome. There were however successions of bishops throughout the whole Church in the years when the history is unsure. The Apostolic Ministry developed under the Holy Spirit so that quite clearly by the second century the Church had the ministry of bishops, priests and deacons. At the same time the sacramental life of the Church developed. The full sacramental life was to be seen in the life of the Church from earliest times. A continuous sacramental life is the mark and expression of the Tradition. Even if it is argued that there were gaps in the succession in the earliest years of the Church that does not justify innovations at a more developed stage in the Church's life. The Church is the vessel of the Holy Spirit under the Spirit's continuous guidance.

Developments which became settled very early in the Church's life, like the orders of the Church, cannot properly be changed or abandoned at a later, supposedly more developed stage. We must ask the question, "Developed towards what?" We must examine the principles upon which changes are made and test their consistency with the Apostolic Faith. Changes of a radical nature must have the acceptance of the whole Church. The bishops of the Church of England recognised this when they said in 1988 in paragraph 177 of their report of that year that the ordination of women must be accepted by the Universal Church if it was to be deemed the mind of Christ for his Church. The Church is a living organism. We cannot expect it to stay constantly in the same state. Elements will develop. Those elements of the life of the Church in the Apostolic age which are necessary in order to live the Apostolic life now must however be preserved. These questions must be judged by the whole Church.

The one Church of Christ must live constantly under the Word of God and the truth of that Word must be vindicated by the growth in numbers and holiness of the members of the Church, by the continued life of the Church. External conditions can cause an ebb and flow in the life of any church spread over the face of the world. The continual resurgence of the life of the Church under the Word of God is, however, a sign of the authenticity of the preaching and living of the Word of God.

Only one Church meets all these criteria in full; that is the Orthodox Church. The Church of Rome, by the adoption of the clause in the Creed, "and the Son", without authority and by nineteenth and twentieth-century dogmatic definitions, made without the authority of the Universal Church, has lost its secure hold on the Apostolic Faith in its fullness and its claim to be the One Church of Christ. Other churches have abandoned, to a greater or lesser degree, the Apostolic Faith and Apostolic Order. Only the Orthodox Church fully meets the criteria set out in above paragraphs. It can be argued that these criteria have been selected by an Orthodox precisely to fit the Orthodox Church. That evokes the response, "What other criteria are there?"

Are some superfluous or are there missing criteria? If so that must be demonstrated. The debate will continue — as it most assuredly will — on the basis of differences over the criteria which define the Church, pragmatic and empirical criteria as opposed to theological criteria. These are the criteria designed to answer the questions, "Where is the Catholic Church?" and "Which group of Christians is the One Church of Christ?" It is hard to see what other criteria can be used to define the Church than those we have set out. They have been held for a long time and even those who will not agree with our application of them — e.g. Roman Catholics and Anglicans for example — do not seriously question them.

If a church outside the Orthodox Church believes that it holds the Apostolic Faith and has preserved the ministerial and sacramental life of the Apostolic Church then it is incumbent upon it to seek union with the Orthodox Church. Not to do so for political or historical reasons is understandable but ill-advised. Union with the Orthodox Church is not similar to submission to papal authority and jurisdiction but is rather entry into the bonds of apostolic faith and love that mark the life of the Church.[18] So are all those who are not Orthodox not members of the Church and thus doomed to be lost? That, of course, depends upon just what St Cyprian meant by "outside the Church there is no salvation" and how we interpret his words. That is dealt with in Appendix 3.

---

[18] See note 17.

An interesting thesis on this subject comes from a more conservative part of the Orthodox Church, the Russian Orthodox Church Outside of Russia. It is in an article published originally in 1970 in *Orthodox Life* by Archimandrite Constantine (Zaitseff) of Holy Trinity Monastery, Jordanville, USA. It has recently been re-published.[19] As the editor observes, Fr Constantine's thesis caused something of a stir when first published and those who wish to read it will find "his sentence structure difficult." Fr Constantine observes two types of ecumenism. The first is that of the official churches. This he calls the ecumenism of Anti–Christ. It is the ecumenism referred to above in which doctrinal negotiation takes place leading to a dilution or abandonment of the Apostolic Faith. He discerns another ecumenism which he calls 'the natural, mutual, attraction to one another of those who want to remain in Christ.

> Thus there appears a certain contrasting analogy to the ecumenism of the Antichrist—in the spiritual kinship of all the appearances of faithfulness to Christ, wherever they are found, even if in the manifestation of heterodoxy far from the fullness of Truth. Be it the colossus of Catholicism or some crumb of an ecclesiastical body on the most distant periphery of heterodoxy, if there arises a reaction to the ecumenism of Antichrist in the form of the defence of a minimal bit of the genuine Christ which re-

---

[19] *The Shepherd* (July 1999), Ed. The Brotherhood of St Edward, Brookwood, p. 2.

mains in that ecclesiastical body, then this cannot but arouse the sympathy of the "faithful", regardless to the degree to which they are "orthodox". And here, of course, is not excluded any formulation of such a unity in faithfulness to Christ. Moreover, if this unity embraces all the "faithful", regardless of the fullness of their faithfulness, then does there not quite naturally arise a striving for the *general* possession of the fullness of the Truth.

Fr Constantine concludes his essay with these words:

To define the Orthodox point of view more precisely in this process of thickening apostasy, it can be said that all, in the eyes of Orthodoxy, are her own, if only they manifest a faithfulness to even a little bit of genuine Christianity which they receive in their denomination. But, on the part of Orthodoxy, more than ever before, a missionary effort must be directed to these heterodox in the name of forming, before the face of the Antichrist, one fold following one shepherd.[20]

As we have indicated above the Orthodox Church alone retains both the fullness of the Apostolic Faith and the Apostolic Order and Sacraments of the Universal Church. Fr Constantine's thesis proceeds from that belief. The faith and order of the Orthodox Church is

---

[20] *The Shepherd* (July, 1999), page 5.

the standard by which all is tested. Yet Father Constantine provides not so much a liberalisation of it as a recognition that historical circumstances have led to the existence of groups within other churches which hold to the Apostolic Faith and life. This can be discerned by their opposition to what he calls the ecumenism of the Anti-Christ. He asserts salvation by repentance and faith in the saving work of Christ rather than by jurisdiction. At the same time, he asserts the claim of the Orthodox Church to be the true Universal Church of today. His use of a negative criterion—opposition to the ecumenism of the Anti-Christ—has the same liberating effect that we find in dogmatic definitions. They are negative and apophatic, i.e. defining what must not be denied rather than what must be asserted. Popular ecumenism has not led and will not lead to unity because it does not lead to unity rooted in the Apostolic Faith or, in other words, dogmatic unity. It is not, therefore, unity in Christ but unity on the basis of the most limited doctrinal statement that everyone will swallow. This is not the Apostolic Faith. The resulting community cannot, therefore, be the one Church of Christ—or even a group outside the Church but holding to the truth, as contemplated by Father Constantine, since it has come into being precisely by abandoning the Faith of the Apostolic Church.

As we can see in our discussion of St Cyprian's letters even in the early third century of the Church's life there were divisions over significant matters of discipline that took a long time to resolve. It was possible, however, to travel from one end of the Roman Empire to the other — and beyond — and still find the Church of the land to be in communion with the Church of one's home. They were, in fact, one Church.[21] The Church was one and it was this Church, rather than heretical schisms, that discerned the revelation of God in Scripture and the Tradition. There have been no universally accepted dogmatic definitions since long before the schism of East and West. The Seventh Ecumenical Council (787) was the last universally accepted general council. This does not, however, make the question of which church is the one Church of Christ irrelevant.

Questions do arise that must be faced by the whole Church, however it is defined. The ordination of women to the priesthood is one such since ordination touches vitally on the ministerial and sacramental life of a church. It also has dogmatic implications since the innovation grows from a defective Christology. The churches which have maintained either in their fullness or a very great degree of the fullness of those elements which we have suggested are the mark of the one Church of Christ i.e. the Roman Church and the Orthodox Church, have discerned that this is an inauthentic development. Interestingly, in the case of the Bishop of Rome he rejects the innovation because he believes he lacks authority to make such changes alone (24).[22]

---

[21] M. Deanesly, *The Pre-Conquest Church of England* (London, 1963), p. 1.

[22] Pope John Paul II. Encyclical, *Ordinatio Sacerdotalis*, English translation (London, 1994), p. 10. "I declare that the Church (i.e. the Roman Church) has no authority whatsoever to confer priestly

When we examine the history and beliefs of the churches we can reasonably conclude that the church which is the true successor to the Church of the Apostles and the Church of St Cyprian is the Orthodox Church which has retained without diminution or addition the Faith of the Apostles. When we wish to know which is the One Church of Christ we can, with confidence therefore, say that it is the Orthodox Church and it is this Church which authentically discerns the true revelation of God within its Tradition.

---

ordination on women and that this judgement is to be definitely held by all the Church's Faithful." Unrelated but of interest in the light of subsequent discussion is the question of the status of this document. Is it infallible? It certainly looks like it.

Discerning the Truth within the Tradition

Preliminary Considerations

It might be appropriate to preface this chapter with a health warning—a mental health warning. We enter now an area of study in which it is easy to become confused. The confusion is caused by highly flexible definitions, that is definitions with a "Humpty Dumpty" quality. The words often mean what people choose them to mean. No doubt the present writer will not escape that condemnation. We will try to be as precise as possible and to warn the reader when a definition is rather wobbly. If we use a word in a particular way that might not be a general definition we will say what we mean by it.

There is also a problem with presentation we have mentioned before. It is the way of theology that every topic touches on every other. What one believes about the Lord Jesus has connections with how one prays and what one believes about the Church and the Sacraments. Topics inevitably connect up with each other. For this reason a discussion of the reception of doctrine will, for example, refer back to a discussion on the Church and forward to discussions on the nature of councils. This study is, therefore, not tidy. The compartments are not watertight and this is sometimes confusing. But despite all that we encourage brave souls who have come so far to brace themselves for a rough ride and stick with it. The issues are important, and they are issues that every disciple of the Lord Jesus should try to understand, if possible. With those warnings we proceed.

We now have a reasonably clear understanding of what is meant by the Tradition of the Church. We also have a reasonably clear understanding of what, who and where the one Church of Christ was and is. We need now to see how the Church discerned and discerns the revelation of God from within the Tradition.

The two processes—the process in the past and in the present—have some superficial differences. The councils of the time of the Eastern Roman Empire, which was conquered by the Turks in 1453, were a major element in such discernment. Like every phenomenon they developed. These councils had characteristics peculiar to their times. These passed with the passing of the Roman Empire. We shall see what it was about them which was central to the nature of a council and which was, and would be, held in common with other councils and what was inessential to their character as general councils. As it happens it is generally accepted by churches other than the Roman Catholic Church that the last ecumenical council was the Seventh in 787. That was the last, almost universally recognized, council.

Some Protestants only recognize the first four councils. It is worth noting at this point that when referring to a council the word, "ecumenical" does not refer to discussions intending to lead to church union as in "Ecumenical Movement." It means a council that represented the whole of the *oikumene*, the whole of the civilised world, i.e. the Eastern Roman Empire. There have been attempts in recent writing to distinguish between ecumenical councils and general councils. "Ecumenical" is used to describe those councils which were, a priori, convened according to the custom and practice of the time so as to possess the authority of a council of the whole Church. "General" is used to describe those ecumenical councils whose deliberations were subsequently received by the whole Church and, for that reason, deemed to form part of the corpus of the Apostolic Faith. This distinction has no real value. As we shall see, "ecumenical" and "general" came to be used to describe councils which would, in the definitions just set out, have been called general i.e. whose definitions have been received by the whole Church and were deemed, for that reason, to be part of the Apostolic Faith.

It will be recalled that the Tradition is one: the Scriptures and the life of Christ in his Church, as we have discussed it. The period when the conciliar discernment of revelation and the formulation of dogma within the Tradition was most frequent and formally necessary was the period from about 45 AD to the eighth century — that is between the Council of Jerusalem and the Seventh General Council, more particularly from 325, the date of the First General Council. This was the period in which the Apostolic Faith was defined in the form we have described. This Faith is enshrined in the Creeds. The irreversible fundamentals of the Faith were set out in this period. It would be correct to say that no authentic dogmatic definition which broke new ground has been made since the end of the Seventh Council (787) and the term, "broke new ground," does not truly represent the case even in respect of that council. The definitions of that council did not break new ground as such but made definitions that followed logically from earlier definitions. They made explicit what was implied earlier. Indeed all conciliar definitions are nothing more than the definition of what is already believed. Dogmatic definitions are definitions of what has been the essence of the Apostolic Faith from the beginning. The Apostolic Faith, as defined, was held from the beginning. It must have been, otherwise the Apostolic life would not have been lived from the beginning and it has been lived from the beginning.

Definitions, in reaction to innovative errors, state what has been the faith from the beginning and have a conservative effect. They seek to conserve the dogmatic basis of a life that is already being lived in the Church. Councils know that there is an immediate connection between dogmatic definitions and life lived out by the believer. That is why doctrine is important. Councils acting authentically do not, therefore, add to what has been believed. To do so would be to seek to change, in a radical way, the way of discipleship and Christian living. Councils define and preserve what is already believed. We will examine the concepts of the development of dogma and the development of doctrine, two different things, below. We can say, however, that definitions do not develop dogma or doctrine. They tell us what the faith of the Church was from the first. Definitions are made when a doctrine already believed is threatened by heresy.

We have examined the characteristics of dogmatic definitions in chapter one. A development of the description of those characteristics will be useful. Three characteristics of dogmatic definitions emerge from a study of the way they have been defined. Firstly, a dogmatic definition is not innovative but definitive. It defines what is already believed. It does not define something new. It is not innovative. It does not seek to state a new dogma to be believed but points to what was always believed but has not yet been defined; the point stressed above. Thus the Chalcedonian definition of the person of Christ was the final stage of a process in which, point after point, the person of Christ was defined. It brought into one integrated definition what was already believed from the beginning, what was demanded by the logic of salvation. This had been defined bit by bit, reactively, as the Apostolic Faith was questioned. The definition of Chalcedon brought these into one complete definition of our Lord's person against the heresies of Appolinarius, Eutyches and Nestorius.[1] Certain matters were left undefined at that

---

[1] Nestorius (died c. 451), Patriarch of Constantinople, taught that there are two separate persons in the Lord Jesus as opposed to the orthodox teaching that the Incarnate Christ is one single person, who is both God and man. Apollinarius, Bishop of Laodicea (c. 310–c. 390) taught a) the unity of the Godhead and the

council because they had not been questioned. The principal one concerned whether our Lord has two wills or one will. This matter was defined later in the Sixth Ecumenical Council (680-681) by drawing out the implications concerning it in the Faith that had been held from the beginning. The characteristic of dogma, which we have discussed in this section, will cause us to raise questions when we consider the Roman Catholic dogma of papal infallibility and other dogmas.

Secondly, and following from the discussion above, dogmatic definitions are reactive not proactive. The assumption is that the Faith is known, clear and lived. There is only a need to define it if it is questioned. For example, when Arius[2] said that there was when Christ

---

manhood in Lord Jesus; b) the full deity of the Lord Jesus; c) that there was no moral development in the Lord Jesus. All this was all right in itself but he then went on to say that in the Lord Jesus there was no human spirit, the human spirit having been replaced by the Logos. He therefore taught an incomplete and imperfect manhood in the Lord Jesus. It was, incidentally, in respect of this heresy that St Gregory of Nazianzus wrote in Letter 101 to Cledonius: "What has not been assumed is not healed." He was referring to nothing else and certainly not to the ordination of women. Despite that his words are constantly used as the only reference in the Fathers which supports such ordinations. Eutyches, archimandrite of a monastery in Constantinople (c. 378–454), confused the two natures, divine and human, in the Lord Jesus saying that the manhood of the Lord Jesus is not consubstantial with ours; thus he taught that the Lord Jesus is not both fully God and fully man.

[2] Arius was a priest of Alexandria (c. 250–c. 336). The essence of his heresy was that the Lord Jesus is not of one substance with the Father but created. The Lord would, therefore, not be divine.

was not (he did not say *a time* when Christ was not) he said, in effect, that Christ is not God but a creature. Arius' teaching had several implications. The Son is a creature and thus inferior to God. If He is not God He cannot forgive. His saving work is of no effect. Only God, who is without sin, can forgive. It follows also that God is not a Blessed Trinity. In one form or another the teaching of Arius was widely accepted, even by the Bishop of Rome. Only a tiny group, supporting the teaching of Saint Athanasius of Alexandria, opposed Arius. When, at last, a Council was called at Nicaea in 325 AD the decision was made that the Son was God, being of one substance (*homoousios*) with the Father. *Homoousios*, a Greek word meaning "of the same substance," is not a New Testament word.[3] The Fathers of the Council could, however, find no other word that matched the need. No other word adequately set out the relationship of the Son to the Father. The issues raised at Nicaea were not completely settled until the Council of Chalcedon in 451 and the definition of that

---

[3] The word means "of the same substance" (*homo*, the same; *ousia*, substance). This is not to say that God has substance and the Orthodox usually translate the word as "essence" or "one with". The word is designed to protect the truth that the Lord Jesus is God as the Father is God and the Holy Spirit is God, "but there are not three Gods but one God". It is a truly dogmatic word seeking to define what must not be denied rather than what must be asserted. Different translations of the word *ousia*, especially its translation into Latin as *substantia*, was a rich source of conflict and confusion between the East and the West—one side accusing the other of believing in three gods and vice versa the one side accusing the other of denying the Trinity.

council is in the appendices. The logic of salvation led to the rejection of Arianism.

Any definition that is not reactive to heresy may be deemed a sort of dogmatic luxury and there is no place for such in the Church. This is expressed well in a letter, already quoted, from Newman to Bishop Ullathorne over the question of the definition of the dogma of papal infallibility. Newman wrote: "What have we done to be treated as the faithful never were treated before? When has the definition of doctrine *de Fide* been a luxury of devotion, and not a stern painful necessity?" A wholly Orthodox sentiment from the pen of a great Roman Catholic theologian.

The dogmatic definition by the Bishop of Rome in 1950 that belief in the Assumption of the Blessed Virgin is necessary to salvation is a further case in point. The Orthodox keep the Feast of the Dormition of the Blessed Virgin (the nearest equivalent Orthodox belief to the Roman doctrine) as a solemnity, preceded by fourteen days of fasting and it is believed to be historically true *but* as Fr John Meyendorff points out, "no theological necessity seems to justify its inclusion among facts which realised the salvation of mankind."[4]

The Orthodox believe that it is true but do not include it in the body of the Apostolic Faith because belief in it is not deemed to be necessary to salvation. This leads to the third characteristic of dogmatic definitions. It is indeed the fundamental criterion for making such definitions: "Is the definition necessary for salvation?"

---

[4] Meyendorff, *Living Tradition*, p. 19.

"Does the logic of salvation lead us to this definition?" Negatively stated it is "Does a failure to believe this put a person's salvation at risk?" Dogma must only be defined when the dogma is necessary to salvation or when a failure to define creates the possibility of error over a doctrine necessary for salvation. We can see that principle applied in the Orthodox refusal to define the Dormition of the Blessed Virgin as a dogma of the Faith although the Orthodox believe that the doctrine is true in fact.[5]

The definition of the person of Christ made at Nicaea was clearly necessary for salvation. If the terms of that definition were not true then man's salvation would be impossible. If the Lord Jesus is not truly God He cannot forgive and heal; if He is not truly man He cannot redeem and heal human nature and bring it into union with God the Father. The failure to define that dogma as an article of the Apostolic Faith would place

---

[5] It has been suggested by Fr Michael Harper, Dean of the British Antiochian Orthodox Deanery, in his book, *True Glory*, that not all Orthodox believe in the Dormition as though belief in this doctrine is an optional extra to Orthodox belief. Bishop Kallistos Ware in his book, *The Orthodox Church*, p. 264, suggests that a few Orthodox rejected the doctrine in reaction to the Roman Catholic definition of the Assumption of the Blessed Virgin. Bishop Kallistos also observes that this is not representative of the Orthodox Church as a whole. Fr Harper's observation, which is without this qualification, is hard to justify. It seems to infer that it is consistent with being Orthodox not to believe in the Dormition of the Blessed Virgin. It is not. What does an Orthodox who does not believe in the Dormition of the Blessed Virgin do for the first fortnight of August when the rest of the Church is fasting?

people's salvation at risk. Once the matter was raised it was so important that it had to be defined. The Roman Church, speaking through the Bishop of Rome, deems that the dogma of the Assumption of the Blessed Virgin is necessary to salvation and thus makes belief in it a condition of salvation.

The Orthodox, as we have seen, do not agree with him in this nor can the dogma reasonably be drawn from the dogmatic definitions of the first seven councils of the Church as necessary to salvation. In other words if the Blessed Virgin had not been assumed into Heaven our salvation would not be affected in the way in which it would be affected if the Lord Jesus Christ had not risen from the dead, for example. The same can be said of the dogma of the Immaculate Conception of the Blessed Virgin defined in 1854 and the dogma of Papal Infallibility defined in 1870. It can be further argued that the dogma of the Immaculate Conception seriously damages the saving work of Christ and that the dogma of Papal Infallibility produces an heretical structure in the Roman Church.[6] The second definition, papal infallibility, also lacks several necessary characteristics of a dogmatic definition as we shall see when we examine it in detail below.

The question that must always be asked is, "Which path leads us to salvation?" No other question leads to an authentic definition of dogma. This is the final criterion. We should examine definitions, dogmatic or oth-

---

[6] The problems caused by the dogma of the Immaculate Conception are examined in Appendix 4.

erwise, which a church wishes to lay upon its members in a binding way with great care. If we find that they are not consistent with the characteristics we have set out above then we are wise to be very, very cautious indeed. They are likely to be inauthentic.

We shall examine the dogma of papal infallibility more fully below. It is important, when considering it, to be clear of the correct meaning of the dogma rather than popular misconceptions about it. We shall attempt to do that below. A preliminary examination of some aspects of its form will, however, be useful at this point. We shall be able to see that it lacks the characteristics we should expect to see in a dogmatic definition. This dogma is one of the ways, indeed the principal way, in which the Roman Church believes the Apostolic Faith as revealed by God can be discerned from the Tradition. We can, however, observe that the definition arose not in response to innovative heresy but rather to the political reality of nineteenth-century Italy in which Pope Pius IX found himself losing control of the Papal States. It is well known that less than ten years before the definition of papal infallibility at the First Vatican Council (1869-1870) a Roman Catholic catechism, Keenan's Catechism, published with full episcopal approval, an imprimatur, called the doctrine a Protestant heresy.[7] It

---

[7] This catechism is widely referred to in many documents critical of the dogma of papal infallibility but the present writer has never seen a copy or been able to verify its existence except that it has been widely quoted. It should not be taken to do more than indicate that claims that the doctrine was widely believed in the Roman Church before its definition are open to question.

would be fair to say, however, that there is not widespread evidence of general opposition to the doctrine elsewhere in the Roman Church in the nineteenth century. What opposition there was, and it was not insignificant, is dealt with in the record of the Council by Dom Christopher Butler.[8] It was perhaps strongest among German Roman Catholics led by Dr Dollinger. He, with others, subsequently left the Roman Church for the Old Catholics.

The doctrine had been widely argued by senior Roman Catholics from the sixteenth century onwards. Cardinal Bellarmine was a strong advocate of it and he was followed by a succession of advocates of the doctrine over the years. There was, however, substantial opposition to the definition of the dogma within the First Vatican Council. The opposition was on two grounds. Firstly, that it was wrong in itself, i.e. that the Bishop of Rome does not have the powers set out in the definition. Secondly, that it was inopportune to define it at that time. The position of the out and out opponents is understandable. It is possible to argue, as we shall below, that the dogma is not a true part of the body of the Apostolic Faith but a heresy. The position of the inopportunists is incomprehensible. If the doctrine is necessary to salvation then there is no question of the definition being opportune or inopportune. It must be defined if true. It must not be defined if it is not true. To believe the doctrine true but to believe that it is inopportune to define it at the time is an untenable posi-

---

[8] Butler, *op.cit.*

tion – nor does it look as though it was a real position of many of those who held it. The inopportunists were, in many cases it seems, truly opponents of the doctrine and sought to prevent its definition by arguing, bizarrely as we have seen, that the definition was inopportune. The background to the decision and the workings of the Council are well set out in Dom Cuthbert Butler's book, *The Vatican Council 1869–1870*, to which we have just referred.

The substance of the definition raises problems itself. (The definition itself can be found on page 103 below.) We shall examine those fully below. It is appropriate, however, to observe that the following characteristics of the definition are not consistent with the characteristics we should expect in dogmatic definitions:

a) The definition does not have that negative and apophatic quality that we find in earlier dogmatic definitions. That is, it does not set boundaries of belief that must not be crossed. It defines in a proactive and positive way, quite differently from earlier definitions.

b) It creates a series of definitional minefields that confuse rather than clarify and which would not be present in a negative and apophatic definition.

c) The definition fails to do what it purports to do, that is, give clear and infallible guidance on faith and morals. Nobody can say for certain which definitions are infallible and which are not.

d) The definition is not implied in the Apostolic Faith and is unknown from the earliest times. It is not, therefore, the definition of a belief held from the beginning. There are no early claims for it and there are no examples of the Bishop of Rome claiming to exercise this gift in the life of the early Church although there were plenty of occasions when it would have been appropriate.

e) The definition concerns jurisdiction rather than the fundamentals of the faith i.e. it is concerned with the power of the Bishop of Rome to define dogma rather than some aspect of the doctrine of God or of salvation. It raises to the level of dogma necessary to salvation what is truly a matter of jurisdiction writ large rather than a fundamental theological matter. Hitherto dogmatic definitions have concerned fundamental theology, e.g. the nature of the Blessed Trinity, the Person of Christ and the saving work of Christ. This definition is of a quite different quality. It does not touch the essentials of the Apostolic Faith. From this spring the many difficulties associated with it. It is, in fact, the only dogmatic definition that has this character. It defines how dogma is to be infallibly defined in a way which potentially omits all the safeguards and principles that surround such definitions that have been built up over the centuries.

Mgr Ronnie Knox attempted to answer the serious objection that we do not know which decisions of the Bishop of Rome are infallible in the terms of the definition and which are not. He said that we do not have to know which decrees are infallible to know that decrees are infallible any more than we have to know how many swans there are on the Dee at Chester in order to know that they all belong to the Queen. That is just silly. Not all papal decrees are thought to be infallible. If infallible decrees were announced as such or if all decrees of the Bishop of Rome were deemed infallible then there would be no problem in this respect. The trouble is that decrees are not announced as being infallible or otherwise. This leaves a large area of uncertainty. It is, precisely, knowing which decrees are infallible which would give the supposed gift of the Bishop of Rome any value. Logically, all those who decide which definitions are infallible must share the infallible gifts of the Bishop of Rome. They must infallibly decide which definition is infallible if, until their decision is known, there is no other indication as to infallibility or otherwise of a definition of the Bishop of Rome. The question of heretical popes is also a problem. It is not clear how the fact that some Bishops of Rome have been condemned as heretics sits with the definition of papal infallibility. Who is to judge the Bishop of Rome's definitions as heretical or otherwise if they are irreformable of themselves and not from the consent of the people — especially when there is no certainty as to which definitions are infallible and which are not? We shall deal with the whole question more fully below. We can see, however, some of the problems beginning to emerge.

Another example of a proactive definition is the decision of several provinces of the Anglican Communion to ordain women to the priesthood. This had many of the characteristics of the definition of papal infallibility. For this reason it is defective in the same way. The decisions were essentially proactive rather than reactive. They were not negative and apophatic. They were not reacting to an innovative heresy. Nobody can explain why the ordination of women is necessary to anyone's salvation. It lacks patristic and biblical support. The only way a patristic writer can be called in support of the decision is by the quotation, out of context, of a saying of St Gregory Nazianzus.[9] It has not been demonstrated that the decision is implied in the Apostolic Faith so that it is consistent with the body of the Faith of the Church held from the beginning. The reverse seems to be the case.[10] Indeed the debate of the Church of

---

[9] St Gregory Nazianzus, *Letter 101*. In this letter to the priest Cledonius St Gregory was arguing against the heresy of Apollinarius (see footnote 1, above). He made the obvious point that what had not been assumed i.e. the spirit of man, could not be healed. The silliness of applying this to the ordination of women by saying that female human nature would not be redeemed if our Lord had not assumed it is demonstrated in Appendix 2.

[10] See Appendix 2.

England Synod was marred by serious misquotations of Anglican doctrinal formulae at crucial points in the course of the debate.[11] The dynamic of the decision was sociological and political, not concerned with people's salvation. Its effect has been, quite literally, diabolical. It has split Christians apart rather than thrown them together.[12] It has caused, as the definition of papal infallibility caused, a very great deal of confusion with the bending and distortion of theological and doctrinal concepts, e.g. reception, so that we are never really sure

---

[11] The most significant and inexcusable misquotation in the debate came when Dr Carey, seeking to persuade the Synod that it had the authority to change the nature of Holy Orders, misquoted Article 20 of the Articles of religion of the Church of England. The article says "The Church hath....authority in controversies of faith," a self evident truth. All commentators on the articles say that in this case the "Church" means the Universal Church. Dr Carey quoted the article as "The Church *of England* hath... authority in controversies of faith." (Page 22 of the Verbatim Report.) This statement is, in itself, ludicrous and would have been rejected by the Anglican reformers. It does not make sense to say what Dr Carey said and still claim that the Church of England is part of the One, Holy, Catholic and Apostolic Church. Either Dr Carey deliberately misquoted the article to persuade the Synod it had a power it plainly does not and cannot have, which is inexcusable; or he misled the Synod by negligence, again inexcusable.

[12] The word, "symbol" comes from two Greek words *sym* (together) and *ballo* (throw); so a *symbolon* is something in which two or more things are brought together, a sign by which one knows or infers something which is not present materially.*Diabolos* is slander, backbiting that which separates and throws apart--thus diabolical, of the devil.

of the meaning of the terms in the discussion. It is to reception that we must now turn.

Reception

Reception of a doctrine by the People of God is a central element in discerning the authentic Tradition of the Church. Until a definition has been received by the people of God it is not the Faith of the Church. It is easy to misunderstand the concept of reception. Many do.[13] We must, therefore, clarify what is meant by "reception" and define as closely as possible who does the receiving. The people of God receive the definition — or not. There have been councils whose definitions have not been received and which, for that reason, have not been deemed to be ecumenical. There exists, at some point in the process, therefore, the possibility of the doctrine not being received. That, however, is a more complicated idea than it seems as we shall see. The final step in the definition of a dogma is its reception by the whole people of God *in some way*. The whole people of God must, *in some way*, accept it as necessary to salvation.

The reception of a doctrine is simply defined. It is the assent of the Faithful to that doctrine so that they accept that it is as necessary to salvation, an authentic discernment of the Apostolic Faith. Until the Faithful

---

[13] Bishop Richard Holloway is one such. For him reception is the process by which everyone eventually accepts a decision. It is not, for him and many Anglican bishops, a process that can reject a decision. See Chapter 10 of *Dancing on the Edge* by Bishop Richard Holloway.

have assented to a doctrine, in some way, it is not a dogma of the Church. The nature and form of that assent, the process of reception is a little complicated and needs clarification but the essence of it is clear. A doctrine is defined by an ecumenical council or sometimes by a provincial or local synod. If it is a provincial council the definition, in time, comes before an ecumenical council. The ecumenical council then comes to a decision and that decision is then put to the Faithful for reception. What that involves we shall examine in due course.

The definition of a local council that was received by the whole Church would be a doctrine of the Faith. It may be that, after the fact of making a definition, reception of a council's definitions by the whole Church constitutes that council as ecumenical. This is uncertain since all the universally accepted ecumenical councils were summoned by emperors and took to themselves, in the way described above, the decision of local synods—some councils called in this way were, however, subsequently deemed not to be general councils.[14] Certainly early in the Church's life local synods acquired great authority from time to time.[15] We also have the

---

[14] Volume 14 of the *NFPNF* Series of patristic writings gives a full account with commentaries of the first seven Councils, those universally recognized as ecumenical, as well as details of smaller councils whose decrees were adopted by general councils.

[15] For example, the councils of Orange (the second, 529) and Carthage (the sixteenth, 418) defined the saving work of Christ and these definitions were the basis of the dogmas of our Lord's saving work.

problem that all generally accepted ecumenical councils occurred during the period of the Eastern Roman Empire. Some characteristics of councils developed in that time have not, clearly, survived the fall of that Empire in 1453. Equally clearly, the possibility of an ecumenical council still exists. The characteristics of such a council must therefore be independent of its Byzantine origins. We do not, for example, need an Emperor of Rome before a council can be called. Probably a decision of the patriarchs of the Church would be enough—it is not clear.

We only know that a council is an ecumenical council after the event. Reception after the event authenticates the council's definitions and thus the council itself. We shall see below that there is even a view that subsequent reception by the Faithful indicates that an infallible papal decree was, from the moment of its declaration, infallible. We shall see where that leads us. What is clear is that until the definition of papal infallibility the reception by the Faithful, in some way, was universally understood to be the effective authentication of a definition. That is still the belief of Christians not in communion with the Bishop of Rome, even if they ignore the implications of that belief from time to time.

We need now to examine some definitional minefields which bedevil the understanding of reception and then attempt a definition that stands up to history.

We have spoken of reception by the Faithful, that is, by believers. The Faithful are, says the Second Vatican Council in the Decree, *Lumen Gentium*, infallible:

The whole body of the faithful cannot err in matters of belief. This characteristic is shown in the supernatural appreciation of the faith on the part of the whole faithful, when "from the bishops to the last of the faithful" they manifest a universal consent in faith and morals. By this appreciation of the faith, aroused and sustained by the Spirit of Truth, the People of God, guided by the sacred teaching of authority receives the faith once for all delivered to the saints. The People unfailingly adheres to this faith, penetrates it more deeply with a right judgement, and applies it more fully in daily life.

It has even been suggested that the whole Church constitutes a council forever in session.[16]

There are problems in the definition of *Lumen Gentium*. When we say "reception by the Faithful" do we mean the whole Church? Do we mean that each member of the Faithful has a say in this process of reception. This idea itself raises a host of problems. In any case, as we shall see in due course, the infallible decrees of the Bishop of Rome, in the necessary conditions, were defined in 1870 as "irreformable of themselves and not from the consent of the Church." It does not matter if the People of God are infallible because the Bishop of Rome is. The problems mount. Are the words of *Lumen Gentium* effectively nothing more than rhetoric? They sound good and if not tested seem acceptable. The

---

[16] Florovsky, *op.cit.*, p. 96.

problem is giving effect to this statement. The whole people of God may be infallible but we have, first, to decide what constitutes being a member of the people of God and, second, how this infallibility takes effect. What function does this attribute of the people of God have? Infallbility that is not or cannot be practically applied really cannot be said to exist in any real way.

The problem, for Roman Catholics, comes with the dogma of papal infallibility. For everyone else the problem comes, as we have seen, from the sheer impossibility of giving meaning to the words of *Lumen Gentium*. If there is no effective way to test the beliefs of or to consult this infallible group what is the point of saying that they are infallible. If the whole Faithful, down to the last peasant, do not consent to a dogmatic statement is it received or not? How are we to know if they consent unless we ask everyone. The reception of a doctrine by the whole People of God is a sign of its truth. The whole People of God is preserved from error: "the whole body of the faithful cannot err in matters of belief." How are we to know if the whole Body of the Faithful has received the doctrine? Does each of them have to asked? And which is this Body? What are its boundaries? By the time we have asked everyone the constituency will have changed by normal processes, birth, death and conversions, and we would have to start again. The problem emerges yet again. The vicious circles in seeking answers to these questions defy enumeration.

The decree, *Lumen Gentium*, is based on the proposition that the one Church of Christ "subsists in the

Catholic Church which is governed by the successor of Peter and the bishops in communion with him" that is, Roman Catholics. We can see the near impossibility of giving meaning to the proposition that a doctrine is a doctrine of the Universal Church when it has been received by all the Faithful if "the Faithful" are defined as only those in communion with the Bishop of Rome. In any case, in the Roman Church, there is a source of infallible decisions, irreformable of themselves and not derived from the consent of the Church. We are left with the ludicrous case that we shall not know if the Faithful have received a doctrine until we have asked them. How else can we find out? Is their consent, however, even wanted or necessary? We are also left with the odd conclusion that if a small number do not receive it then it is not a doctrine of the Church—or perhaps, and more troubling, they were not among the Faithful to start with. Cardinal Manning, perhaps unconsciously, raised this problem at the First Vatican Council. He assumes that papal infallibility is the Faith of the Church before the Council decides that it is—and so wishes to exclude the opponents of the definition as heretics.[17] Then there is the problem of how all this sits with papal infallibility.

---

[17] Manning's remark was "...heretics come the Council to be heard and condemned, not to take part in formulating doctrine." Butler p. 146. Two points arise from this; a) why have a council at all if you have decided that your opponents are heretics and, as it must follow, that you know the truth and b) depending upon what he means by "formulating", councils gather to define existing

We have not, in all this—perhaps because we dare not—considered the problem of some number of the Faithful changing their mind.

We find ourselves with all sorts of unanswerable questions. For example, if an individual or a group dissents from a doctrine that the Pope has decreed as necessary to salvation, are they, for that reason, no longer to be numbered among the Faithful? If that is the case does membership of the Church depend upon agreeing with the Pope? That is the problem Manning raises at the First Vatican Council. Perhaps, however, the doctrine was not infallibly declared originally. It was not perhaps, in fact, a doctrine of the Church in the first place. Can we come to that conclusion? After all it was not accepted by *all* the Faithful before its definition. There were dissidents. We shall see below an intriguing but not very convincing attempt to get round this impasse to which we have referred briefly above. This is the proposition that subsequent reception by the Faithful certifies a definition as infallible when it was made. It would not have been infallible initially if it had not subsequently been received by the Faithful. To be unkind but practical, the case of Poland sets some serious problems for the doctrine that the Faithful are preserved from error. In that country the Roman Church has one of the highest mass attendance rates. That country also, as a whole, has the highest abortion rate in Europe. The use of artificial means of contraception in

---

doctrine in the face of error. "Formulating" sounds the same as "originating"; perhaps it is not.

Roman Catholic countries, e.g. Italy, presents a similar problem.

The definition of *Lumen Gentium* that the whole body of the Faithful is infallible looks at once impractical and tautological. In the end it tells us nothing. We have seen, also, that the definition is impractical. That it is tautological is also fairly self–evident. If a person is faithful he infallibly believes the truth. He would not be faithful otherwise. If he ceases to believe the truth he ceases to be faithful and if he ceases to be faithful he ceases to believe the truth and so ceases to be infallible. This makes the definition meaningless. The overwhelming problem with attributing infallibility to a person or group is giving a predictive and certifying quality to the attribution so that we know, simply because someone or some group has spoken that what they have said is infallibly true. It is what people want but it is not to be had. All this, however, gets us not one inch nearer to answering the question, "What is the truth?" All we can say—and it is worth saying—is that a person who is faithful holds the truth. Of course he does.

Even if we take the criterion of *Lumen Gentium* back before the days that the Church was world-wide and the practical problems were smaller, we still have other sorts of problem. If we apply the criterion to that much more easily locatable entity, e.g. the Church in the early fourth century when it was a largely Mediterranean phenomenon, we still find difficulties. We have referred to them. A council of the Church consented to a mild form of Arianism—a heresy. The Bishop of Rome and most of the bishops in communion with him consented to the decrees of the council. Were those who consented to it among the Faithful? Or had they, by consenting, excluded themselves from the number of the Faithful? Upon what basis and who decided that they were wrong and not right? Where, as we have wondered before, was the Catholic Church then? It is only historical reflection that enables us to see the truth that the Fathers of the Council of Nicaea decreed. That is that, by inference, the one Church of Christ was in a boat fleeing up the Nile—namely St Athanasius of Alexandria and his followers.

The practice of the process of reception and its nature come under serious question in face of the following circumstances, one actual and one hypothetical. They are important circumstances. If a church conducts itself in such a way that the reception of a doctrine is either seriously misunderstood or ignored then the whole process is at risk. Further to that the church loses sight of the truth.

The first circumstance concerns the bishops of the Church of England. They issued a report on the ordination of women to the priesthood in 1988. In that they said that until the ordination of women to the priesthood had been received by the Universal Church[18] the decision could not be deemed to be the mind of Christ for His Church. This was a classic statement of the orthodox and traditional understanding of reception and

---

[18] Paragraph 177 of the Church of England Bishops' Report on the Ordination of Women to the Priesthood (London, 1988).

consistent with the Church's practice. Four years later they led the Church of England along a path they did not deem to be the mind of Christ for His Church. While the decision was not accepted by the whole of the Church of England, the whole Anglican Communion and indeed the Universal Church they should not have done so. They should not have done so while any significant objection persisted. Significant objections from over a third of the Church of England, more than half the provinces of the Anglican Communion, the Roman Church and the Orthodox Church still persist. Do the bishops of the Church of England fall under their own condemnation? It is hard to avoid the conclusion that they do.

The claim that the doctrine has developed will be examined below. It is an unconvincing claim. It may be that the bishops of the Church of England really meant what they said in their report of 1988. If they did why did they proceed as they did in 1992? Do they argue that the doctrine and practice of reception developed so much in four years as to permit the ordination of women? When will they concede that the decision has not been accepted? When will they accept that because it has not been accepted in the way they stipulated it cannot be deemed to be the mind of Christ for His Church? When, as they must if they are honest, they concede that the decision has not been accepted how will they unscramble the muddle?

The second circumstance is hypothetical. The Roman Church and most other churches have disciplinary procedures for those who deny fundamental doctrines of the Faith. The whole concept of heresy means that there are criteria that can be applied to a doctrinal statement to indicate whether or not it is orthodox. Let us suppose that a significant number of people disagree with these criteria and the doctrinal statements that flow from them—say in the Roman Church. Do these doctrinal statements cease to be doctrines of the Church. After all not all the Faithful consent to them and the whole body of the Faithful are preserved from error. How do we deal with that situation? We cannot seriously contemplate consulting all the Faithful. As we have seen we would never get an answer—ever! Or do we follow Manning's line at Vatican I and exclude them from consultation thus deciding what the truth is before the fact of reception; but who is to make that decision?

We can see that reception is not such a simple matter. Just what, practically, constitutes reception is harder to define than it seems. The very concept raises questions that make a simple solution impossible. The first obvious practical question is, "How are the Faithful to be consulted?" The second is, "Who are the Faithful?" That is a problem even if we suppose, which we do not, that the whole group of Faithful is coterminous with the Roman Church. We shall now attempt some answers to these questions.

When we come to examine the nature of councils we shall discover that unity in doctrine and eucharistic communion are the characteristics of councils which survive the passing of the Eastern Roman Empire. Originally the Faithful were consulted in the person of their bishop. The bishops were elected by the people.[19] In St Cyprian's words, "The bishop is in the Church and the Church is in the bishop." In St Cyprian's teaching each bishop was the successor of Peter. Further each local church was "The Church" in much the same way as Orthodox believe that the whole Church subsists in each faithful Orthodox. The local Church, therefore, subsisted in each bishop. Thus when bishops gathered for episcopal consecrations and for the settlement of other matters they brought with them the mind of the People of God in their diocese. As these local and provincial councils developed the locus of authority shifted to the province but the bishop still carried with him the mind of his people.

The development was intensely practical and realistic so that the ideal of consensus between the bishops on matters of doctrine was mitigated in certain cases. Canon 6 of the Council of Nicaea knew that stubborn minorities might resist the will of an overwhelming majority. The council ruled that

> if…two or three bishops shall, from natural love of contradiction, oppose the common suffrage of the rest, it being reasonable and in accordance with ecclesiastical law, then let the choice of the majority prevail.[20]

From the point of view of our concern with reception this development had the following effect. It

---

[19] Hippolytus, *Apostolic Tradition*, 1.2. Bishops are to be elected "by all the people."

[20] Canon 6 of the Council of Nicaea. Vol.14 of *NFPNF*, p. 15.

moved decision making from a consensus of bishops in the truth to a more legalistic practice. As the number of bishops increased and the significance of doctrinal definitions became more important for the Empire at large the process and results of councils became more formal in their practice, governed by the principles of Roman Law. The Emperor or his representative was usually present and sometimes presided. Larger councils developed which did not include all the bishops and very rarely included many western bishops. The patriarchate of Rome was usually represented by papal delegates who were deemed to speak for the whole of Western Christendom.

Despite these developments the fundamental power of reception remained with the people of God. As the system developed the certainty that the bishop would bring with him the mind of his people waned. The mind of the people of God, however, worked in other ways. Other channels of expressing reception or non-reception grew up. Councils that defined dogma against the mind of the Faithful were rejected. Councils such as Sardica - 343, Rimini - 359, Ephesus - 449 and Constantinople – 754, all had the a priori pedigree of an ecumenical council but were either rejected completely or in part or not accepted as such. The Faithful may not be consulted formally nor may bishops bring with them the mind of their people but the Faithful make themselves heard in some way. Charismatic power overcomes legalism. The suggestion by one Roman Catholic writer that reception lies largely with those who are competent is odd and unacceptable.[21] Are the Faithful not competent and if not who are the judges of competence — the university examiners in research degrees? That would be salvation by scholarship again.

At several points in setting out the bare bones of the idea of reception we used the qualification "in some way." We are going to leave it at that. The definition of a doctrine must be received *in some way*. We are aware that this still leaves a degree uncertainty in the matter. The reception must be real i.e. neither a foregone conclusion once a council has come to a decision nor a theoretical process the result of which is settled before it begins; nor must the opposition be defined out as Manning tried to do at Vatican I. There must, therefore, be a real possibility of rejection. It is quite wrong to suppose that reception means wearing down the opposition until it gives in from exhaustion or dies. The definition must not be acted upon until it is received. To do so creates confusion. Pre-empting the process in this way creates the possibility of doctrinal disorder. If the doctrine has a real effect upon the life of the Church relating to the salvation of souls then reception must be real. Ignoring dissidents or seeking to push them to the margin of the life of a church is usually a sign of lack of openness and reality in the process of reception. Even the effect of Canon six of the Council of Nicaea — ignoring the stubborn two or three — would have meant that, for a time, Saint Athanasius of Alexandria would have been ignored. He, the reader will recall, was in the

---

[21] McBrien, *Catholicism,* Study Edition (London, 1984).

right and in a tiny minority. The process of reception may be lengthy and the response of the Faithful to innovations may take time to develop as we shall see over the response to Iconoclasm but it emerges eventually.

We need to consider if doctrine and dogma can develop and how such purported developments are to be judged. If development of some sort is possible, can we test the reception of the development and so the authenticity of the development? We shall examine that question in Chapter Seven. Now, however, we must return to the basic question and possible answers to it.

The Basic Question and some Attempts to Answer It

In view of the difficulties we have seen surrounding the question of reception we need to examine in detail the fundamental question underlying this study: "How do we know that such and such a doctrine is orthodox?"

This question has been put in other forms. It occurs in the Commonitorium of St Vincent of Lerins (434) who posed the question in these terms: "How can I secure a fixed, and as it were, general and guiding principle for distinguishing the true Catholic Faith from the degraded falsehoods of heresy?"[22] Fr Georges Florovsky posed the question in these terms: "What are the ultimate criteria of Christian truth?"[23]

---

[22] Vincent of Lerins. *Commonitorium*, 2.1. See Bettenson, *Documents of the Christian Church* (London, 1959), p. 118.

[23] Florovsky, *op.cit.*, p. 97.

We need to make some preliminary observations. The first concerns the way in which we hold dogmatic definitions, the way in which we believe in them. Because we are dealing with a doctrinal belief in which a person always acts with freely willed faith, the idea of certainty about a doctrinal proposition may not be entirely appropriate. St Vincent of Lerins and Florovsky are not suggesting that we can arrive at an absolutely demonstrable certainty in respect of the truth of a doctrine. If we are looking for that we are looking for fool's gold. Certainty takes us out of the arena of freely willed faith. We cannot prove a dogmatic definition as we might prove a theorem in mathematics or a proposition in science or even as a lawyer might prove a case from evidence. If knock down arguments could be brought to bear we would have no choices in respect of doctrine. We would have to accept the argument unless we were incapable of following it. In that case the use of the words "believe" and "faith" would no longer be appropriate. If we had to decide whether the resulting condition would be intellectual certainty rather than spiritual enlightenment the decision is not a difficult one. The final condition would not be one of salvation but of intellectual certitude. It would bring us to intellectual knowledge rather than repentance. The two conditions may be connected but not necessarily so.

The absence of proofs does not reduce the certainty with which the doctrine is held or one's certainty of its truth. We cannot demonstrate, by a simple logical argument, that the Son is begotten of the Father before all time. We cannot show that He is very God and very

Man in the same way that we can demonstrate that the square on the hypotenuse of a right angled triangle equals the sum of the squares on the other two sides. That does not mean that the doctrine is less true or less firmly held. We can demonstrate why the doctrine of the person of Christ must be as it is if He is to save us. We have called that the logic of salvation. We can say that men and women have come to salvation on the basis of that belief. We can show that it is a coherent part of an integrated set of doctrines. Martyrs were so sure that it was true that they died for it. On the other hand while it is inconceivable that anyone would threaten another with death for maintaining Pythagoras' Theorem, if they did, perhaps only the most fanatical mathematician would think that it was a truth worth dying for. Belief is powerful and its effects are more powerful than knowledge of fairly easily provable facts but what we cannot have, in respect of belief, is certainty, absolute proof.

Florovsky points out that we get into some vicious circles if we insist on formal guarantees.[24] We have seen the nature of some of those vicious circles when we looked at the definition of the Church and we shall see more when we examine papal infallibility. So eager can we become for complete certainty and for guarantees that we can easily, as we have seen, lock ourselves into conceptual and theological nightmares in which certainty depends upon an undefined and probably indefinable set of concepts. We must treat the doctrine of

[24] Florovsky, *op.cit.*, pp. 51 and 97.

papal infallibility with respect and the defences of it seriously. It is believed by serious men and women and defended by the most able intellects. It is, however, difficult to take seriously the simplest apologetic for the doctrine, that is the question, "Surely God would not leave us without an infallible guide in matters of salvation?" The answer to that is to say that he has done so. He has done so for good reasons connected with our free will. There are additional problems that can lead us up the garden path. Just as there are philosophical infinite regresses i.e. lines of reasoning that never finish, so too there are several theological infinite regresses.[25] They never finish and lead nowhere.

It has been necessary, as we have gone along, to deal with various answers to the basic question in order to see that they are dead ends or lead to vicious circles. We have had to knock them off, so to speak, as they came into the argument because they are often plausible and tempting. We will now examine some of the more substantial answers to the basic question before suggesting a set of criteria for deciding if a doctrine is orthodox before it comes before a council for judgement. It is unlikely that a doctrine that fails to match these criteria will be orthodox.

The question was answered, with what success we shall see, very early in the life of the Church in the

----

[25] An example of this sort of thinking is the question, "Who created God?" If the answer is, "X created God," then the question can become, "Who created X," and so on. The answer to the original question is, of course, that God is by definition the uncreated One.

Commonitorium of St Vincent of Lerins in 434. He posed
the question we have set out above. Florovsky, in a paper in the first volume of his collected works, is unhappy with the answer St Vincent gives, the Vincentian
Canon. Later in a paper in the same volume he is more
approving. Florovsky does St Vincent something of an
injustice in his first criticism but his criticism has value,
however, because it successfully dismisses all simplistic
presentations of the Vincentian Canon and adds further
necessary criteria.[26]

St Vincent's answer was a developed answer. The
simple form in which it is often quoted, i.e. "that which
has been believed everywhere, always and by everyone" — and which Fr Florovsky criticises — does not
convey its strength. "We ought," says St Vincent, "to
fortify our faith in a twofold manner; first by the
authority of God's word and secondly by the Tradition
of the Catholic Church." This is a venerable answer, defining Tradition, with the rest of the Fathers, as the
whole life of the Church and including in that life a profound, orthodox, principle of Biblical interpretation.
The teaching and the practice which grows from this
teaching is given life in the life of the Church. The Orthodox understanding of Tradition was never simply of
a body of teaching. That is a later Roman distortion.

St Vincent then deals with those who depend solely
upon a simple application of the Bible to answer his
question. These can be called the *sola scriptura* school.
His answer is that because of the very depth of scrip-

---

[26] Florovsky, *op.cit.*, p. 51.

ture all men do not place identical interpretation on it. He then lists the heretics who have failed to interpret Scripture in an orthodox way, that is according to the interpretive principle that is the Tradition of the Church, i.e. applying the logic of salvation. He then gives us his rule, the Vincentian Canon, the heart of which we have just quoted: "now in the Catholic Church itself we take the greatest care to hold that which has been believed everywhere, always and by everyone."[27]

That is a very easy definition to take apart precisely because it sets up empirical and practical criteria that cannot be tested. To do that is fatal. If I wish to find out if a doctrine is believed by everyone I must ask everyone and so on. We met this problem with the definition from *Lumen Gentium*. That cannot be done and so the criterion is useless. It leads us into a further vicious circle that we have already examined. Does a member of the Faithful who does not consent cease to be a member of the Faithful or is the doctrine no longer orthodox because he does not consent? The vicious circles begin again.

St Vincent does not leave it here, of course, and neither can we. This is how he continues:

> That is truly and properly "Catholic", as is shown by the very force and meaning of the word, that comprehends everything *almost* universally. (Our emphasis) We shall hold to this rule if we follow universality (ie. ecumenicity),

---

[27] Bettenson, *op.cit.*, pp. 118ff.

antiquity and consent. We shall follow universality if we acknowledge that one Faith to be true which the whole Church throughout the world confesses; antiquity, if we in no wise depart (note the negative, apophatic nature of the words) from those interpretations which it is clear that our ancestors proclaimed; consent, if in antiquity itself we keep following the definitions and opinions of all, *or certainly nearly all* (again our emphasis), bishops and doctors alike.

What then shall a Catholic Christian do, if a small part of the Church has cut itself off from the communion of the universal Faith? The answer is sure. He will prefer the healthiness of the whole body to the morbid and corrupt limb.

But what if some novel contagion tries to affect the whole Church, and not merely a tiny part of it? Then he will take care to cleave to antiquity, which cannot now be led astray by any deceit of novelty. (This is brilliantly simple point; antiquity does not change but remains as catholic and orthodox as it was in the past.)

What if in antiquity itself two or three men, or it may be a city, or even a whole province be detected in error? Then he will take the greatest care to prefer the decrees of the ancient General

Councils, if there are such, to the irresponsible ignorance of a few men.

But what if some error arises regarding which nothing of this sort is to be found? Then he must do his best to compare the opinions of the Fathers and enquire their meaning, provided always that, though they belonged to divers times and places, yet they continued in the faith and communion of the one Catholic Church; and let them be teachers approved and out-standing. And whatsoever he shall find to have been held, approved and taught, not by one or two only but by all equally and with one con-sent, openly, frequently and persistently, let him take this as to be held by him without the slightest hesitation.[28]

We can see that St Vincent's rule and his commentary on it are more subtle and valuable than at first seemed the case. The passages we have emphasised by italics point to real flexibility and practicality. It relies upon universality rather than "everyone." It relies on antiquity rather than 'always'; ubiquity rather than "everywhere." This removes the weight of Fr Florovsky's criticism that we cannot tell if a belief has been held everywhere until we ask. Florovsky, however, uses this criticism to develop a valuable criterion of truth that is not brought out well in the rule of St Vincent. We shall examine that in a moment.

---

[28] Bettenson, *op.cit.*, p. 119ff.

In its simplest form the rule would, as we have seen, have failed in the Arian controversy. Then almost nobody, almost nowhere and, for those reasons, not always, held the Catholic Faith. When, however, we apply the rule in its fullest form, we can see that we have a very valuable if slightly incomplete, and because of its incompleteness, flawed rule which goes a long way to answering the question St Vincent posed. What clearly emerges from his developed statement is that the slice of history studied in antiquity needs to be a broad one. The reception of doctrines takes time. Some of the decrees of the Seventh Ecumenical Council (787) were designed to counter the teaching against the veneration of the holy icons. This teaching had begun nearly 60 years before and it was over 60 years before the opposition to the decrees died down. In all, from the first onset on Iconoclasm, as the heresy was called, until its final disappearance some 120 years passed.[29] The slice of history needs to be a broad one so that a whole process can be examined.

Fr Florovsky criticizes the Vincentian Canon in the third chapter of the first volume of his collected works but is more approving in the fifth chapter. He success-

---

[29] The Iconoclast Controversy began c. 725 when the Emperor Leo III, under Muslim influence, banned icons. A synod in 753, called by Constantine V at Hieria, endorsed the ban. Later the persecution died down and in 787 the Seventh Ecumenical Council declared Iconoclasm a heresy. Not to be able to portray the Lord on an icon is to deny his full humanity. Later emperors tried to revive iconoclasm and it was not finally defeated until 843 following the death of the Emperor Theophilus in 842.

fully disposes of it only by dealing with it in its simplest form. We have seen that this is not adequate. In fairness to St Vincent this was not his complete answer to the question he poses. In that regard Florvovsky's criticism loses force. His critique however sets out clearly the weakness of all practical and empirical tests of catholicity such as are implied in Lumen Gentium: "the whole body of the faithful are preserved from error." Such practical tests are valueless because they are impossible to apply.

Florovsky also provides us with an invaluable criterion of Catholicism which, taken together with the Vincentian Canon and other accepted criteria, provides us with a very powerful set of criteria for deciding what are the ultimate truths of the Christian faith. These criteria are more effective than the dogma of papal infallibility. We shall show that this dogma has some serious deficiencies as a tool for answering St Vincent's question, "How can I secure a fixed, and as it were, general and guiding principle for distinguishing the true Catholic Faith from the degrading falsehoods of heresy?" These deficiencies stem from the a priori nature of papal infallibility and the effective absence of the consent of the Church from its exercise. It purports to guarantee the certainty of an answer. In fact it does not because it cannot. It cannot because the consent of the people of God, in some form, is dispensed with. As we shall see below there is a subtle but unconvincing attempt to give reception a place in papal definitions deemed infallible. We have already briefly referred to this above.

Now to Florovsky's critique. We have edited slightly for the sake of brevity. It is an effective disposal of the Vincentian Canon in its abbreviated form and sets out with great clarity the weakness of all empirical and practical tests.

> The ... formula of St Vincent ... is very inexact when he describes the catholic nature of the Church in the words , what has been believed everywhere, always and by all — (*quod ubique, quod semper, quod ab omnibus creditum est*). First of all it is not clear if this is an empirical criterion or not. If this be so, then the "Vincentian Canon" proves to be inapplicable and quite false. For about what *all* is he speaking? Is it a demand for a general, universal questioning of all the Faithful, and even of those who only deem themselves such? At any rate, all the weak and poor of faith, all those who doubt and waver, all those who rebel, ought to be excluded. But the Vincentian Canon gives us no criterion, whereby to distinguish and select. Many disputes arise about faith, still more about dogma. How then are we to understand *all*?... There is actually no need for universal questioning. Very often the measure of truth is the witness of the minority. It may happen that the Catholic Church may find itself but "a little flock"... It may happen that the heretics will spread *everywhere* and that the Church is relegated to the background of history... In history

this was more than once the case and may be so again. The word *all* is to be understood as referring to those that are orthodox. In that case the criterion loses its significance. To what do *always* and *everywhere* relate? Is it the experience of faith or the definitions of faith that they refer to? If the latter case the Canon becomes a dangerously minimising formula. For not one of the dogmatic definitions satisfies the demand of *always* and *everywhere*.....

It appears that the Vincentian Canon is a postulate of historical simplification, of harmful primitivism. This means that we are not to seek for outward, formal criteria of catholicity; we are not to dissect catholicity in empirical universality. Charismatic tradition is truly universal; in its fullness it embraces every kind of *always* and *everywhere* and unites *all*. But empirically it may not be accepted by all; at any rate we are not to prove the truth of Christianity by means of universal consent.[30]

We make no apology for that long quotation. It very clearly sets out the weaknesses of most tests of catholicity which are based on an oversimplified version of the Vincentian Canon. It shows the impossibility of having a body which, before the process, we can be sure will give us an authentic and authoritative answer to the questions that St Vincent and Fr Florovsky pose

---

[30] Florovsky, *op.cit.*, p. 41.

about the criteria for finding catholic truth. Finally he begins to introduce his own profound criterion for answering the questions the Vincentian Canon sets out to answer.

We must take the Vincentian Canon in its fullest form being aware of the weakness of its simplified form. We must understand the Canon within the limitations that Fr Florovsky places upon it. We must then apply it together with the comments of the nature of Catholicity and the functions of councils that Fr Florovsky goes on to set out and which we shall shortly examine. If we do that we may then have as secure a basis as we can hope to find for making authoritative judgements on the truth or falsity of a doctrine. The Vincentian Canon and Fr Florovsky supply the each other's needs. We shall propose certain criteria, in Chapter Six, based on these, for testing doctrinal propositions.

Florovsky's standard of Catholicity is easily summed up. He observes that the word, "catholic" comes from the two words, *kath' holou* (according to wholeness), and not from the two words, *kata pantos* (according to everything). The universality of catholicism is not demographic or quantitative or geographical. It is seen in the quality of catholic wholeness in a person and in a community. It is seen in sanctity and union with Christ. This wholeness can be found and is possible everywhere and in all circumstances. It is everywhere to be striven for and all people can strive for it and receive the gift. It is, however, not actually seen everywhere, in all and at all times. Universality flows from catholicity for catholicity is a universal truth and reality. It is universally knowable, universally to be experienced. The universality, as we have defined it, is a sign of catholicity. Catholicity comes first. It is not to be discerned on the basis of certain questionable, practical criteria.

We cannot tell that a doctrine is Catholic because almost everyone holds it. History has shown that this, by itself, can be a misleading guide. Catholicity is the authenticating reality. It is "according to wholeness" — an inner wholeness and integrity which itself leads to and is a sign of communion with God — sanctity. We cannot, therefore, test the reality of catholicity by an empirical and practical test because we cannot test sanctity and wholeness in a practical and measurable way. There are no empirical and practical tests of salvation. We cannot ask if such and such a test of acceptance has been passed because there are no tests. If, however, the doctrine purporting to lead to catholicity was not, in fact, received as catholic by the Church we could conclude that the dogma was not authentically catholic. If a doctrine is not discerned as leading to wholeness, salvation and holiness by the whole Church then it is difficult to believe that it is catholic and orthodox. The process is negative in substance as we would expect. We cannot draw such conclusions from tests of external phenomena, a succession of bishops in the church teaching the doctrine and so on. We would be morally certain in concluding that a doctrine cannot be catholic and orthodox if it does not lead to wholeness and sanctity. The experience of the whole people of God has told us that.

We cannot test the catholicity of a dogma by examining certain external phenomena of the church that holds the dogma as we have just observed. Its order, the nature of its communion will not reveal its catholicity. The absence of certain integrated characteristics from a community — as from a person — would, however, indicate the absence of saving, Catholic dogma. Catholicity, as we have seen, defines the essence of the Church. It is concerned with its very being. An examination of the external dimensions of the Church reveals very little about its inner nature. If we were satisfied that a Church meets certain external criteria that would not, of itself, ensure that what it defines as Catholic dogma is, on these grounds alone, i.e. its conformity to certain criteria about its characteristics — the phenomena we can observe — an authentic doctrine of the Faith. It is not a succession of bishops or recitation of the Creed of Nicaea and Constantinople, which ensures the catholicity of a church although their absence would indicate that the church is not catholic. The process of examining external phenomena no more reveals the truth of the Church than a scientific examination of the Eucharistic elements would reveal the truth about them. The truth of both is revealed to faith and known in faith.

Florovsky makes the point comprehensively:

> Yet the Church itself is not catholic because of
> its outward extent, or, at any rate, not only be-
> cause of that. The Church is catholic, not only
> because it is an all embracing entity, not only
> because it unites all its members, all local

Churches, but because it is catholic all through, in its very smallest part, in every act and event of its life. The *nature* of the Church is catholic; the very web of the Church's body is catholic. The Church is catholic because it is the Body of Christ; it is union in Christ, oneness in the Holy Ghost—and this unity is the highest wholeness and fullness. The gauge of catholic union is that "the multitude of them that believed be of one heart and of one soul."[31].

The absence of certain criteria e.g. adherence to the Creeds of the Church, a succession of bishops from Apostolic times, the sacraments of the Church and an orthodox doctrine of Biblical authority, would, on the other hand, give serious cause to question the doctrines of that church.

The Catholic Church is where Jesus Christ is: "Where there is the bishop, let there be the whole multitude; just as where Jesus Christ is there too is the Catholic Church."[32] Thus says St Ignatius, developing the words of the Lord Jesus in Matthew 18.19–20:

Again I say to you that if two of you agree on earth about anything that they may ask, it shall be done for them by my Father who is in heaven. For where two or three have gathered together in my name there am I in their midst.

---

[31] Florovsky, *op.cit.*, p. 41.

[32] Ignatius of Antioch, *Letter to the Smyrnaeans*, 8.2. Cf. Meyendorff, *op.cit.page.*, p. 47.

The presence of Christ, of the wholeness of Christ, is a self–authenticating reality. "Where every kind of sin is healed... and men are called to repentance and brought on by the Holy Spirit to holiness of life—there is the Catholic Church," says St Cyril of Jerusalem.[33] Catholicity is self-evident. It is reasonable to add that an essential precondition for that life, for that presence of the Lord, is that the Apostolic Doctrine tested, lived and taught by the people of God, is held as the rule of faith. Behind the lived reality of Catholic life there is, and must be, the dogma which both constitutes and is a sign of the lived reality of the Catholic and Apostolic Faith. We seek always, in resolving doctrinal disputes, to assert in an apophatic way those doctrines that bring us to Apostolic life. That is what the Faith of Apostles held by the One, Holy, Catholic and Apostolic Church is. It is salutary to observe, in response to modern heresies that dismiss the teaching of the Fathers, that both Ignatius and Irenaeus are said to have known Polycarp. He

---

[33] St Cyril of Jerusalem (315–386), *Catechetical Lectures*, 18.23. He extends his point in this way: "It (the Church) is called Catholic then because it extends over all the world, from one end of the earth to the other; and because it teaches universally and completely one and all the doctrines which ought to come to man's knowledge, concerning things both visible and invisible, heavenly and earthly; and because it brings into subjection to godliness the whole race of mankind, governors and governed, learned and unlearned; and because it universally treats and heals the whole class of sins, which are committed by soul and body, and possesses in itself every form of virtue which is named, both in words and deeds and in every kind of spiritual gifts."

was taught by St John the Divine. With these Fathers we are but three generations from the Lord Himself.

To return to the proposition that the presence of Christ, the wholeness of Christ, is a self-authenticating reality; there are obvious signs of this. One of the signs of this self authentication, in addition to those we have quoted from the Fathers immediately above—St Ignatius and St Cyril of Jerusalem—is the desire to adhere to the true Christ. The sign of this is opposition to the false ecumenism described by Archimandrite Constantine in the passage quoted above. Oneness, holiness, catholicity and apostolicity are definitions of the community within which the one Christ dwells. He is one, holy, catholic and apostolic. The Church, which is his Body, must also be.

Councils

The Church (to which, at this point, we give a broad definition) has acted or has purported to act through two major channels, by two major means. We must now examine these. They are the Councils of the Church and the Infallibility of the Bishop of Rome. We have referred to both of these already. Now is the time to examine them more fully.

Councils have a history of development.[34] We can distinguish three phases in this development. They are

---

[34] Meyendorff, *op.cit.*, chapter 3, "What is an ecumenical council?" gives a concise and authoritative account of the development of councils. See also Florovsky,*op.cit.*, chapter 6, "The

broadly the pre-Byzantine, the Byzantine and the post–Byzantine phases. Like all periodisation in history these phases are slightly misleading. It was not that tidy. It never is. There were no neat cut-off points. Councils first emerged as ad hoc meetings of bishops in a particular area for the settlement of problems and the election and consecration of new bishops. They had no certain place in church government or in the definition of doctrine. In time they responded to particular doctrinal innovations. We can see this even in the Council of Jerusalem in Acts 15 where a decision is required over several matters that have arisen in the experience of the mission of the Church. The decisions are listed.

The significance and importance of councils developed in the second century in Asia as they met to combat Montanism.[35] Over time and in reaction to heresy the councils, and so the Church, built up a corpus of the Apostolic Doctrine i.e. what had been believed from the beginning. This happened reactively, that is the Church reacted to the emergence of doctrinal error and the distortion of what had been believed from the beginning. The councils defined the doctrine of the Apostolic

---

Authority of Ancient Councils." Both give a full account of the nature of the early councils.

[35] Montanism was an heretical movement of the second century. Its leader, Montanus taught that the Holy Spirit would be poured out on his sect and that the Heavenly Jerusalem would soon descend to earth. It taught and enforced a very strict ascetic discipline. Tertullian joined the sect in Roman Africa in about 206. It was condemned by various Eastern synods and by Pope Zephyrinus of Rome (d. c.217).

Church, codifying and restating the Apostolic doctrine in dogmatic form. The council, as an instrument of decision making and for the expression of the unity of the Church in the unity of Faith, grew in significance in the life of the African Church. Councils asserted the Apostolic tradition which was the Church's life and the one faith upon which the unity of Catholic Christians was founded. Life within the Apostolic Church was not founded, as it later comes to be in some places, upon an institutional and jurisdictional principle. Unity grew from unity in Christ rather than from membership of an institution. Membership of an institution followed from communion with all those living the Apostolic life and believing the Apostolic Faith. We find, in the early councils, the features which, in time, are seen to constitute the essence of a council i.e. unity in the Apostolic Faith and eucharistic communion.

With the conversion of Constantine in 312 the life of the Church became an imperial concern. The universality of the Church, which had always been one of its marks, became more obvious. It was the Church of the Empire and of the Emperor. The effect of a dispute in the Church was felt throughout the Empire. The settlement of disputes became, therefore, the concern of the Emperor. The Emperor called the councils as an instrument of his will and government to resolve disputes which damaged the unity of the Empire and the Church. We shall see that this form of council disappeared, obviously, with the fall of the Empire in 1453.

As the Emperor used the means of a council, called by him, to settle disputes the councils began to change in their nature. They became more remote from the local churches and more formal, reflecting the practice of Roman Law. Even with this very significant development there was never any canonical doctrine of conciliar power or even a developed theory. There is no canonical set of rules for calling councils which, of themselves, would ensure that the council is ecumenical nor has there ever been. Nobody codified the principles upon which a council came to decisions or the nature of its power. The one persisting reality was and is unity in doctrine and eucharistic communion. Where this broke down as, for example, in the union councils of the fifteenth century there are no dogmatic definitions.[36] These councils, called to restore unity between Eastern and Western Christendom, were not called in response to a heretical innovation. They were called to heal a di-

---

[36] These were councils—or more properly one council that moved around between Ferrara, Rome and Plorence in the years 1438–45, held between the Church of Rome and the Orthodox Church. The Church of Constantinople was under great pressure from the Turks--the Empire fell in 1453—and sought union with Rome, as much as anything, to obtain Western military help. Some degree of agreement was reached on the contentious issues of the primacy of Rome, the doctrine of Purgatory, the use of unleavened bread at the Eucharist and the Filioque clause. Under great pressure from the Byzantine Emperor a decree of union was signed. St Mark of Ephesus was the only bishop who refused to sign. In this he represented more truly the mind of the people and monks of the Orthodox Church. The decree of union was rejected by the Orthodox synods. This council was plainly not ecumenical lacking, as it did, the essentials of unity in faith and eucharistic communion. The whole idea of a union council is without theological foundation. See Meyendorff, *op.cit.*, p. 57.

vision that had many doctrinal, political and cultural causes. The absence of dogmatic definitions from these councils is not therefore surprising. They lacked the essential characteristics of a council, unity in the Faith and eucharistic communion. They failed in their purpose.

If we are concerned to understand the nature of the decisions of ecumenical councils we are faced, obviously, with the problem of what constitutes an ecumenical council. We have seen some of those problems already. The fact that we cannot be sure, before the event, if a particular council is in fact ecumenical is a major problem in the search for clear definitions of what constitutes, a priori, an ecumenical council. Such a search is doomed to failure. There are no characteristics we can look for which will tell us, before the reception of the definitions of a council, that a council is, in fact, an ecumenical council.[37]

There is a Reformation definition of a council that is similar to that of Cedrenus, the eleventh-century Byzantine historian. The definition of Cedrenus is quoted below. Article 21 of the Articles of Religion of the Church of England suggests that councils must be called by princes and that their decrees must not be inconsistent with Scripture where a doctrine necessary to salvation is defined. That looks like a good start. There have, however, been councils called by a prince, namely the Eastern Roman Emperor, at which the representatives of many particular churches have been present. These councils have made decrees which the members

---

[37] Meyendorff, *op.cit.*, p. 58.

believed were consistent with Scripture but which have been deemed on reflection not to have been ecumenical because their definitions have not been received by the Faithful. The Robber Council of Ephesus in 449, to which we have referred above, was just such a one – the details are below. There have been councils not called by a prince that have been fairly small and yet which have authentically defined dogma. Who authenticated them, who made the decisions? The Faithful upon reflection received the definitions and this authenticated the council.

Cedrenus defined an ecumenical council in this way; he said that councils "were named ecumenical because bishops of the whole Roman Empire were invited by imperial orders and in each of them, and especially in these six councils, there was a discussion of the faith and a vote, that is, dogmatic formulae were promulgated." That, as we can see, defines the council after the event and does not give us an *a priori* definition even if, at first sight, it seems to do so.[38]

We cannot, therefore, be sure, before the fact of the meeting of the council and the reception of its definitions, that the council is ecumenical — "ecumenical" and "general", as we noticed above, effectively mean the same thing. We cannot be sure because its definitions may be rejected by the Faithful. This has happened more than once. We have seen above that a council was called by the Emperor Theodosius II, at Ephesus in 449. It sought to reverse the condemnation of Eutyches at a

---

[38] Cedrenus, *History*, 1.3, Bonn Edition (1838), p. 39.

synod at Constantinople the year before. The legates of Pope Leo were insulted and ignored. The decisions of the council, which came to be known as "The Robber's Council", were soon reversed. They were reversed because although the bishops present consented to them they were not received by the absent bishops, St Leo, the Bishop of Rome or the laity and monks of Constantinople and the Empire.

The principal problem in this field is that we have very little to work on in terms of accepted definitions. There are very few definitions upon which there is general agreement and which can form the basis for proceeding. This is true even in the case of papal infallibility, as we shall see. Despite the fact that the definition was exhaustively discussed and has been the subject of a great deal of examination, uniformly accepted definitions of its terms are still hard to come by.

No council was known, therefore, to be ecumenical in advance. A person could not wait for the decision of an ecumenical council knowing, before it spoke, that what it decided would be the certain settlement of a dispute. It was not known, before the council spoke and its definitions received, that it would define true dogma unerringly. The doctrine had, in some way, to be received by the Faithful, as we have seen. Several councils which were formally called by emperors to settle a dispute were subsequently deemed not to have ecumenical authority.[39]. Some councils which were local synods made decrees which were subsequently received universally and incorporated into the canons of a council, itself subsequently deemed to be an ecumenical council. We have explored this matter above in the section on reception.

The authority of a council was, therefore, charismatic not legalistic. The subsequent reception of the decrees of a council authenticated the decrees of the council and made it ecumenical. Reception by whom? By the Faithful. There was and is no formal theory of reception although the development of such a theory is urgently necessary for churches which assume the authority to bring in innovations which lack the consent of the Universal Church. It would preserve them from serious error.

Reception was deemed to have occurred because the doctrine put to the Church was seen, universally, to be consistent with the Apostolic life of the Church and to have unfolded or disclosed a doctrine which was implicit in the Apostolic Faith from the beginning. The definition fitted, so to speak, into the whole life and belief of the Church. It was recognised as true. The Apostolic Life founded on the Apostolic Faith was there, being experienced. It was this experienced faith against which the doctrine was tested. Change was therefore assumed to be incorrect and had to be shown to be cor-

---

[39] The two councils referred to in the next footnote are the most obvious examples. See also Florovsky, *op.cit.*, chapter VI, "The Authority of Ancient Councils."

rect. Dogmas did not and do not change or add beliefs to the Apostolic Faith. They revealed what was already believed. If the doctrine did not match the criteria it was — sometimes after a long delay — deemed not to be consistent with the Apostolic Faith and rejected. The process of reception was lengthy. The answers did not suddenly emerge. It takes time, in certain cases, to see that a certain doctrine leads or does not lead to Catholicity and, therefore, whether it is Catholic or not, whether it is truly part of the Apostolic Faith or not. That is to be expected. Argument cannot always conclusively demonstrate that a doctrine is in error. The doctrine has to be lived and experienced, tested in the following of Christ. We have seen above that it is not always easy to show that a false doctrine leads to deviations from the Christian way. The effect may have to be experienced and reflected on before the truth is seen.

Heretical conciliar definitions about the person of the Lord and the Holy Icons were both initially accepted and held sway.[40] It was only, over time, as the doctrines and their meaning settled into the experience of the Faithful, that the false doctrines were rejected. The councils were then deemed, after the event, not to be ecumenical councils. The process could be confused further by the activities of civil authorities, usually the Emperor, whose motives were political and designed to satisfy the religious sentiments of an influential group of his subjects. There were cases when the Emperor at-

---

[40] For example, the Council of Ephesus (449) and the Synod of Hieria (753).

tempted, successfully for a time, to force a heresy on the Church not so much because he believed it to be orthodox as to restore civil order.

It has been said that the whole Church is council that never adjourns.[41] This raises yet again the question to which we have proposed an answer—where is the Church? It reveals that councils are best understood as authoritative slices of the life and Tradition of the Church, giving the whole Church's understanding of true doctrine through the Council Fathers at a point in time. The Council speaks for the Church and the reception of the doctrine certifies that.

It happens that no councils after the fall of the Constantinople in 1453 have received universal recognition. The Seventh Council in 787 was the last universally recognised ecumenical council. We can also suggest that such a council may never meet again or at least not before the reunion of East and West. This is not because there is no Emperor in Constantinople—a peripheral consideration—but because the fundamental preconditions of unity in the Apostolic Faith and eucharistic communion no longer exist. The two churches which might be considered to have a claim to be the successor of the Apostolic Church, i.e. the Orthodox Church and the Roman Church have fundamental dogmatic differences. For that reason there is no eucharistic communion.

Before any of the very serious doctrinal questions prevalent in the churches today can be authoritatively

---

[41] Hans Kung, "Council" in Rahner, *op.cit.*

answered, doctrines defined and errors condemned, a preliminary process of unification must take place. This can only take place on the basis of the Apostolic Faith already defined. This does not, however, mean that we cannot come to firm conclusions about the whether or not certain innovations in doctrine and order are authentic or inauthentic developments of the Apostolic Faith. We do not have to wait for a general council to come to a very high degree of certainty about such matters, at least negatively. A synod or group of synods may propose an innovation. This innovation can be tested intellectually and practically. Its rejection or acceptance can take place. While we may not be sure that a partial acceptance — even by a fairly large part of the Church — constitutes sufficient reception to constitute the innovation as part of the Apostolic Faith, it is clear that rejection by a significant part of the Church means that the innovation has not been received and is not, therefore, an authentic expression of the Apostolic Faith.

The response that this effectively blocks developments in doctrine and dogma is easily answered. It does not, in fact, prevent development of doctrine — and dogmas, as we shall see below, cannot develop. It is precisely because error in doctrine is so damaging that the safeguards against innovative error in doctrine and order — and order is an expression of doctrine — are so weighty. The theological flippancy that can be detected in the justification for some damaging innovations is remarkable.

Infallibility

An alternative to councils has been introduced by the Roman Church. Very simply, it is the way of defining that the Bishop of Rome in his role (assumed role to everyone but Roman Catholics) as Supreme Pontiff and Vicar of Christ constitutes a one man council. This description would, it is likely, be vigorously contested by members of the Roman Church. We believe, however, that it is the simplest and most accurate way of describing the nature of papal infallibility. It fits the doctrine into the historical development of the exercise of authority in resolving doctrinal disputes. It can be seen as the next, albeit false and mistaken, stage of conciliar development.

For many the imprecision and uncertainty of the conciliar process we have been describing was too cumbersome. By 1869 the conditions for calling a truly ecumenical council barely existed. The problems of the conciliar process, with definitional difficulties at every turn and no a priori certainties when it comes to the resolution of doctrinal differences, let alone the practical problems, led to an almost ecstatic welcome, in some quarters, to the dogma of papal infallibility. Papal infallibility appeared to cut through all the confusion and uncertainty. It seemed to be the solution to all the problems and it was very simple. The Bishop of Rome, under certain carefully defined circumstances, decides what is the faith of the Church. His definitions are irreformable of themselves and not from the consent of the Church. As Pius IX is said to have observed, "*Io son tradizione*" ("I am the tradition"). The dogma was decreed by Pope Pius IX in 1870—as the Times reported—amidst flashes of lightening and claps of thunder over the Eternal City. As an alternative to the conciliar process for resolving doctrinal disputes it seemed much more effective and efficient. Nor did it take much working out that the conditions for the calling and working of a council along the lines of the Byzantine or pre-Byzantine councils no longer existed. Agreement in doctrine and eucharistic communion no longer existed between the Orthodox Church and the Roman Church. The papal definition seemed a much more satisfactory way forward than councils.

The definition had the support of a significant majority of Council fathers. Butler seems to indicate that there was a substantial minority opposed during the discussion of the definition but in the end only two or three resisted consenting to the doctrine. Every bishop did so in the end.[42] This is the definition promulgated by Pius IX:

> It is divinely revealed dogma that the Roman Pontiff, when he speaks ex cathedra that is when acting in the office of shepherd and teacher of all Christians, he defines, by virtue of his supreme apostolic authority, a doctrine concerning the faith and morals to be held by the Universal Church, possesses through the divine assistance promised him in the person of Blessed Peter, the infallibility with which the Divine Redeemer willed His Church to be en-

---

[42] Butler, *op.cit.,* chapters 24 and 25.

dowed in defining the doctrine concerning faith and morals; and that such definitions are irreformable of themselves, not because of the consent of the Church (*ex sese non autem ex consensu ecclesiae irreformabiles esse*).

Before examining this definition in more detail we need to observe that its terms, whatever they mean, are only accepted by the Roman Church. Other churches do not suppose that the Bishop of Rome has an office of shepherd and teacher of all Christians. Other churches do not believe that he possesses supreme apostolic authority. They do not believe that he is the recipient of promises made to the Apostle Peter or even that the promises were made to St Peter rather than to the whole Apostolic College. It seems to the Orthodox, for example, that the claims of the Bishop of Rome, even before the definition of his infallibility, are unhistorical and unbiblical and a denial of the principles of episcopal authority and union expressed by St Cyprian. They do not accept the premises from which the Roman Church proceeds. These premises are not accepted outside the Roman Church, or even universally accepted within it! Nor, of course, is the definition itself accepted elsewhere outside the Roman Church or in any effective way by many inside the Roman Church. Anyone reading Roman apologetic for this definition comes across arguments that seek to minimalize the definition into meaninglessness. The dogma, for some members of the Roman Church is fairly empty of meaning. They do the work of those who are critics of the definition for them.

Taking the definition on its own terms it clearly goes further than saying that when the Bishop of Rome makes a definition he is giving voice to the infallible mind of the Church. That is, that he embodies in his office the whole Church and is a sort of one-man council. If he was, in fact, acting as a one man council then his definitions would have to be received by the Faithful to be expressions of the Apostolic Faith. The consent of the Faithful is, however, not necessary to the making of an infallible dogmatic definition — "irreformable of themselves and not from the consent of the Church." This distinguishes his definitions from conciliar definitions. In fact great care was taken to ensure that all the council fathers eventually received the decree itself although the acceptance by every bishop was not complete for some little while after the definition.[43]

What soon becomes clear is that while we seem to be escaping from uncertainty and definitional confusion we have, in fact, entered on an even more confused path. What seems straightforward is, in fact, very hard to tie down. What purports to be clear is, in fact, very confused. The simple and straightforward meaning of the words is not what is meant even if Pope Pius IX meant them in that sense. Certainly some Roman Catholics at the time of the definition expressed relief that at last the confusion was over. They looked forward to the arrival of infallible definitions on every subject. The convert W. G. Ward said that he looked forward to an infallible definition every day with his

---

[43] Butler, *op.cit.*, chapters 24 and 25.

copy of the Times! It seems that the straightforward and obvious meaning of the words is the meaning accepted by many Roman Catholics. They are, however, mistaken. The words do not mean what they seem to mean. That is the only conclusion that one can come to if one reads through the vast literature on the subject. In this definition we have something other than the words tell us. We have something other than the proposition that the Bishop of Rome, when speaking under the conditions set out, speaks with irreformable authority and without the need of the consent of the Church. The definition excludes, apparently, even approval before a new dogma is defined. The Bishop of Rome is not understood to be defining what everyone already and has always believed although that is, sometimes, said to be the meaning of infallibility. There would hardly be any point in him telling us what we already know. The real power of the gift of infallibility, if it existed, would be in the resolution of matters about which there is uncertainty.

The Bishop of Rome is not infallibly telling us what has been believed from beginning. That position is, apart from being pointless and tautological, historically untenable. Things did not happen in that way. Bishops of Rome have erred dogmatically. Bishop Honorius of Rome (d.638), for example, held that our Lord has only one will. He intervened in a dispute between Patriarch Sergius of Constantinople and Patriarch Sophronius of Jerusalem saying that our Lord has one will and ordered the patriarchs to be silent on the subject. His action certainly looked as if it was intended to be the final word on the subject. His actions fitted into the conditions of infallible definitions. A dispute existed and he settled it — or at least thought he did. His successors and the Council of Constantinople in 681 condemned him as a heretic. His decision was not received. In any case papal infallibility was not believed from the beginning nor can it be demonstrated that such a belief is implied in the Apostolic Faith. It is not the case, either, that the dogma of the Immaculate Conception of the Blessed Virgin defined in 1854 is a definition of the faith of the Church held from the beginning.

The Bishop of Rome when making an infallible definition is not always defining the existing faith of the Church in the way that councils did (e.g. the Immaculate Conception and Infallibility). He is, in some cases, making new doctrine and dogma and does not require the consent of the Church before or after he does so.

We have a further complication. We have seen that the Bishop of Rome has fallen into heresy in the past. It could happen again — indeed the Orthodox Church believes that he is in heresy now.[44] If, while in heresy, he defines a dogma, saying he is speaking under the conditions set out, does he retain the gift of infallibility? Clearly not for heretics are not members of the Church; and if clearly not who decides that he is or not, at the time that he makes the definition, in heresy and so deprived of his gift of infallibility? The whole body of the

---

[44] Papal heresy; the four dogmas referred to in Appendix 4 are the four points on which the Orthodox regard the Bishop of Rome to be in heresy.

Faithful are preserved from error but their consent to a papal definition is not required for the decree to be infallible How can the Pope be judged by the Faithful if his decrees are irreformable of themselves and not from the consent of the Church?

The very act of pointing out that he was not fulfilling the conditions of the dogma in a case where he asserts that he is would, in effect, be judging the Pope. The Church would be saying, "You think that you are speaking under the required conditions. We judge that you are not and so your decree is not binding." He would say, "I am and it is." Who can settle this question which effectively judges the Pope's infallibility—a gift which is defined as not being capable of being judged? That in turn raises another question. Is the Bishop of Rome infallible in judging himself to be infallible in any particular definition or in the original definition of 1861 itself? If he is not then the gift has no value. The Bishop of Rome and the Roman Church could find themselves in this position. These are real possibilities.

We are told that all this will never happen because the Pope is only infallible when declaring the doctrine of the Church and so on. But this simply raises the question in another form. Who is to judge what is the doctrine of the Church before it is declared, before the fact of definition so to speak; after all it is precisely this judgement that the gift of infallibility is supposed to deliver? Can anyone judge—according to the definition, other than the Pope, what is the doctrine waiting to be infallibly defined in the conditions set out when we remember that the definitions will be irreformable of themselves and not from the consent of the Church? A decision has to be made by someone—the Pope or the whole people of God—as to whether what he is defining is the doctrine of the Church. Infallibility rules out the possibility of anyone, but the Pope, making that decision and yet the very fact that the gift is defined in the way it is defined points, paradoxically, to the fact that this judgement may theoretically lie with a body other than the Pope. The Pope is infallible when defining the faith of the Church it is said. That begs the questions, "What is the faith of the Church that he is defining? Who is to answer that question?"

In the conditions set out there is nobody other than the Roman Pontiff able to judge the Roman Pontiff as far as the Roman Pontiff is concerned. He alone can judge what is the faith of the Church.

Many explanations of the dogma seem to say, in the long run and when boiled down, no more than that when the Pope declares the faith of the Church he is infallible. Then, of course, in those conditions, so is everyone infallible. The statement is meaningless because it is tautological. To say that I am infallible when I declare the faith of the Church means nothing of itself. It is like saying that when I am healthy I am healthy. I am obviously without error when I declare the faith of the Church. This is not the issue. Infallibility concerns a decision that brings a new dogma into the Church such as the dogma of the infallibility of the Pope, a decision in which it is asserted as a dogma of the Church that the Bishop of Rome is preserved from error when defining dogma in certain conditions. The issue is not the consistency of one's beliefs with the Apostolic Faith but the supposed capacity to define, infallibly, new elements in that Faith. It would only mean anything to say that I am infallible if I could decide infallibly what the faith of the Church is. That is what the Bishop of Rome purports to be able to do. What cannot reasonably be assured is that the Bishop of Rome is infallible in defining a dogma which has not been discerned by the whole Church, that is when he is acting as a one man council. Neither can it be assured that we shall ever know which definitions are made under the correct conditions to ensure their infallibility.

With one or two rare exceptions definitions are not, before, at, or after their definition, defined as being an exercise of the gift of infallibility. The exceptions are the definition of Infallibility itself, though that is tricky — defining the definition of the dogma of Infallibility as infallible, the dogma of the Assumption of the Blessed Virgin and the canonisation of saints. These are the only certain infallible definitions. There have, however, even been canonizations of saints that have been reversed! They were, one supposes, not infallibly canonised in the first place. Apart from these there is no sure list of infallible definitions. Surely, however, such a list is essential in giving real effect to papal infallibility. A gift whose exercise is uncertain or unknown cannot be infallible except at a theoretical level. It can have no practical effect. The gift of infallibility exists, if it does exist, essentially in its exercise. If the discernment of the infallibility of the Bishop of Rome's definitions depends upon a process, scholarly or otherwise — accepting this, rejecting that—then that process itself must be also be infallible. The person or group that decides which definitions are infallible must be infallible. Indeed infallibility must reach down to the translators, the explainers, and the faithful who must obey. They must understand the definition infallibly correctly. One Roman Catholic theologian maintains that there is no list of dogmas to which all Roman Catholic theologians agree! Yet the same theologian goes on to say that rejection of a dogma places one outside the Catholic Church and makes one a technical heretic. (Technical heresy is a very odd concept indeed. One is either saved or not. One cannot be technically saved.) One can, it seems, be cast out of the Church for rejecting an article from a list about which there is no agreement and the contents of which are either uncertain or unknown.[45]

We can see that what seemed a simple solution to a degree of uncertainty in a process, a theological untidiness, leads to worse confusion. It is salutary to recognise, in all this, that this dogma is deemed to be necessary to salvation. What would a person be asked to assent to in order to be saved? There is a fatal uncertainty at a crucial point.

Further to all this we must consider what place the reception of the dogma plays in its definition as infallible. It appears, in fact, to have no place at all. But that view is not universally held. One view seeks to find a place for reception by the people of God in the process of definition. The reader must decide if this ingenious

---

[45] McBrien, *op.cit.*, p. 71.

answer, which seeks to bring reception into the exercise of infallibility, is convincing. The answer is set out by Fr Edward Yarnold in an article in the *Way*. He refers to the teaching of Fr Yves Congar. The sections in italics and brackets are our comment. It seems the simplest way to point out the problems which this passage raises:

> Although subsequent reception is not the constituent factor in an infallible definition, infallibility cannot be attributed to a definition which has failed to gain the subsequent approval of the Church. *(That seems contradictory.)* In other words reception is a guarantee that the definition, when it was made *(Remember that it is not announced as infallible when it is made and thus depends upon some subsequent discernment of infallibility.)*, fulfilled the conditions of infallibility. Vatican II clarifies this point. Congar, however, envisages the possibility that a valid definition *(How will we know that it is valid?)* might not achieve subsequent recognition *(But the whole people of God is infallible—do we have two infallibles in disagreement?)*[46] Just as reception does not

---

[46] An attempt to overcome this problem was made by Joseph Descuffi, Archbishop of Smyrna in the Second Vatican Council. He is concerned to remove misunderstandings that might arise from the juxtaposition of the two phrases 1) *of themselves* and 2) *not from the consent of the Church*. He firstly refers to the prior co–operation of the Church in the decision. This was referred to by Bishop Grasser, the relator (explainer) at Vatican 1. Secondly, while suggesting, that the infallibility of the Pope and the Church have

constitute the juridical validity of the definition, non – reception would not signify necessarily that decision was invalid or false, but rather that the decision has no "vital force and does not contribute to edification." (*However, it is still an infallible definition; presumably a useless and meaningless infallible definition. The whole point of them seems lost if such a thing is possible.*) Arguing both historically and theologically, he suggests that what reception adds is not juridical validity, but greater "power" (would "authority" be a better term?), because the Faithful recognise in a decision "the good of the Church which

---

different origins, he says that they must be joined in one infallibility. The Pope's gift is defined as a special divine help – not divine inspiration or revelation, although the preamble to the definition itself refers to divine revelation. The fatal step the Archbishop makes, however, is to suggest that the Pope, as head, and the Church, as body, form one reality thus making a clash of infallibilities, so to speak, impossible. Such a definition of the relationship of the Pope to the Church is wholly unacceptable for it is the Lord Jesus, and him alone, who is the head of the Church and who, with the Church forms the whole Body. (See Augustine, "For if he is the head we are the members: the whole man is he and we.... for Christ is not simply in the head and not in the body, but Christ is entire in the head and the body" in Evangelium Joannis tract, XXI, 8. and p.44.f. Council Speeches of Vatican II.Ed.Congar, Kung and O'Hanlon. London. 1964. See also the New Testament references.) The Archbishop does not succeed in overcoming the problem and reveals the profound difficulty in giving meaning to this dogma. In seeking to solve one problem he raises other, more serious, problems.

they too have a vocation and the grace to build up."[47]

Fr Yarnold continues with reference to the theories of Peter Chirico but these simply have the effect of dissipating further the concept of infallibility as a papal gift to arrive at a position which is not Roman Catholic, however valiantly it is maintained that it is. However we construe Fr Yarnold's words it seems hard to conclude other than that the exercise of the infallible gift of the Bishop of Rome is discerned by the people of God or by the theologians. This must in itself be an infallible discernment as we have argued above. There is no occasion, however—or very, very few—in which the Bishop of Rome says, "Now I am going to say something infallible and that is an end of the matter."

When Pope Paul VI issued the decree *Humanae Vitae* on the morality of artificial means of contraception it had all the looks of an infallible definition. He had waited for the decision of a committee, had consulted the bishops of the Roman Church and finally had spoken. He did not say that he was speaking infallibly and his teaching has been widely challenged and watered down both in practice and by teaching. Yet he merely repeated well-known Roman Catholic teaching. If ever a matter required the exercise of an infallible gift of discernment it was this. Roman Catholics are, however, no wiser now than they were before.

Further to all this, even if the Bishop of Rome defined a dogma as infallible and promulgated it as such

---

[47] Yarnold, *The Way* (January, 1980), p. 64.

the gift of infallibility would have to stretch to the translators and interpreters of the dogma and so on as we have suggested above. The whole process from the declaration of a dogma to its apprehension by every last Roman Catholic must be covered by the gift of infallibility. If it is not the process collapses and is worthless. That either leads us into the greatest vicious circle of all or to the start again in which the whole Church is preserved from error, but we have been here before. We can conclude that what seemed simple and straightforward is in fact of no value at all in coming to an answer to the question raised in different forms by St Vincent of Lerins and Fr Georges Florovsky. We cannot find the definitional grail of knowing before a decision is made, by pope or council, that the answer will be true and correct, without error, because the definitional grail does not exist. It is not to be had.

We cannot know, from the nature of the definor, a council or the Bishop of Rome, before the fact of the definition, that the definition will infallibly be the Apostolic Faith. The definition of papal infallibility seemed to suggest that we can. We have seen, however, that this either breaks into pieces when we try to use it or it melts in our hands. The dogma of papal infallibility has been called "the papal fact factory" by the distinguished Anglican, Austin Farrer. That is unfair. That is what a number of people want it to be and wanting it, suppose that it is, but it is not. Nowhere, except in statements that lack any seriousness, do we find the dogma defined in this very simple way and yet it is this simple answer that people want and expect. It does not exist. It is not to be had.

The Criteria of Christian Truth

Preliminary Observations

The foregoing leads us again to the question which in one form or another lies at the heart of this study. We will use the words of Fr Georges Florovsky to express it: "What are the ultimate criteria of Christian truth?" Before answering that question as fully as we can we need to observe the following points about the nature of the question as framed by Florovsky.

First of all, it is significant that Florovsky asks "what are the *ultimate* criteria?" We believe that it is in the Last Day when the secrets of all hearts shall be disclosed and we shall know as we are known that the truth of all things will be revealed. The basic question and the answers to it relate to the consummation of all things. They are—that difficult word—eschatological. This is not to avoid difficult questions but to observe that the Truth is a Person, the Lord Jesus Christ, and that discovering Him brings us face to face with the End of all things for He is our Judge and our Saviour. Christ is the End and purpose of all things; see eschatology in the glossary. Encountering the Truth in our

Lord Jesus Christ is, after all, the fundamental purpose of this study.

The Truth is discerned in penitent prayer as we come before the Lord Jesus. It is not discerned in theological debate or in books. They have their place but the Place of Meeting with Christ is a different and more significant place. The experience is more profound. We take off our shoes and fall on our faces in the dust. The Truth of the Church's Doctrine and Faith is the Lord Jesus Christ. However adequate or inadequate the criteria we set out they are nothing more than the tests we apply to doctrines and practices with doctrinal implications. Doctrines are maps. All we can see is if the map is misleading or not. Doctrines cannot themselves bring us where we want to be; i.e. in union with the Blessed Trinity although false doctrines can prevent us coming to the Truth. There is more to the wonder of our salvation than true doctrine but untrue doctrine excludes the possibility, in the long run, of meeting the Truth. Doctrines are like musical scores. We can examine them for false notes and bad harmony and so on. They make good music possible, but music still has to be well played to be good.

The word, "ultimate" warns us against unrealistic expectations and slick answers. It warns us against supposing that the experience of conversion and repentance that precede, again and again, our union in grace with God are simply tied up in the words of a doctrine. The doctrine is necessary but it is not enough of itself. We must live Catholic dogma out in its fullness to come to God as we must play the music as well as we can to give life to the composer's vision.

Secondly, we must remember Florovsky's observation that "catholic" comes from *kath' holon* (according to wholeness), not *kata panton* (according to all things). This again brings us before the End, before our Saviour and our Judge. Our wholeness lies in the tears of repentance not in the sharpness of debate. It is shown in holiness not in intelligence. We become whole when we are touched by the cleansing fire of the Saviour. Catholic Doctrine is tested by its power to bring us to that encounter with the Saviour. It is according to wholeness. Wholeness is possible because the Eternal God enters the Created Order in the Son. It is fulfilled when the Son takes the Created Order to present it to the Father as everything is restored to its head.[1] It is witnessed in a person living catholically, according to wholeness, presenting us with the reality of the Lord Jesus now — in other words, in a saint.

Thirdly, the Truth, who is the Lord Jesus, has to be discerned, lived with and lived out by people making free, faith-filled choices within the limitations of existence, and we can get it wrong again and again. That simply means that we do not know everything. The whole Church is, in the long run, preserved from error but in the short term errors occur. Life is lived for real

---

[1] *Anakephalaoisis.* This doctrine found in the Epistle to the Ephesians and in the Fathers, particularly in Irenaeus, teaches that the fullness of Christ's saving work is to be seen in the restoration of the whole created. See the glossary.

and when lived for real by real people things can go wrong.

The history of the Church is filled with times when people thought they had discerned the Truth according to accepted principles and then found out that they were wrong. It seems likely that many honest people accepted Arianism without realising the implications of the heresy. They were terribly mistaken and in time the Church rejected the heresy. The honest people were, however honestly, in error. This is the great importance of the time of reception and discernment. It gives the Church time to see whether the decision settles into its life and experience in a way that leads to wholeness, integration, a growth in love and a growth in holiness. The grail of an *a priori* guarantee of truth is not to be found. If it was available it would mislead because it would lack the beneficial and essential effect of reception by the whole people of God. The very Christological nature of the Church, that it is an inseparable union of the human and the divine, Christ and us in Christ, creates the possibility of error by sinful men and women.

Five Criteria

These preliminary observations were necessary to set what follows in context. So what then are the ultimate criteria of Christian Truth? We suggest the following five criteria presented as questions:

1) Is the doctrine consistent with the Biblical revelation? Asking the question in this way secures the

essentially reactive and negative (apophatic) nature of decision making. It liberates the process of decision making so that it is a truly free process. Consistency with Biblical revelation, at its simplest, means that a doctrine should not openly contradict Biblical revelation or what can properly be shown to follow from Biblical revelation. It is more secure when applied to doctrinal matters but can be applied to ethical questions.

The use of this criterion is only possible if we give to the Bible the authority that we have set out above. This means that we take a whole view of Biblical teaching rather than sustaining something we rather fancy to teach by the use of Biblical quotations. For example there is a verse in Ecclesiastes (4:12) which says that a threefold cord is not quickly broken. It would be very hard to count the number of times that this verse has been quoted to sustain the proposition that there are three sources of authority: Scripture, Tradition and Reason. That proposition is mistaken and not sustainable as we have shown above. It does not become sustainable because a piece of wisdom literature is misapplied to support it. It is a gross misuse of the Biblical text. Nor is it proper to dismiss apostolic teaching because it is not consistent with the thinking of today, i.e. Christian reason/common sense.

It is assumed, upon what grounds it is not clear, that St Paul was a misogynist. For that reason it is thought that his teaching on certain matters can be discounted. Do a misogynist's words have no value? If they do not why do a feminist's words have value? We do not know if St Paul was a misogynist. The matter is irrelevant. Even if he was his teaching cannot to be dismissed because we are not accustomed to it or because it is not consistent with some twenty-first-century ideas and beliefs. St Paul's writings in the New Testament are inspired Scripture discerned as such by the Church. It must be treated as such and due regard given to its authority.

It is, of course, the case that within a large corpus of Scripture there may be found elements that contradict each other. There may be elements that, for some reason or another, do not have obvious application. Before, however, deciding to accept as a doctrine a proposition that is inconsistent with a broad element of Biblical teaching one should be very, very careful and then reject it. For example there is consistent teaching on sexual ethics throughout the Old and New Testament indicating that heterosexual physical sexual relationships within marriage are the only sexual relationships consistent with the Christian understanding of human sexuality and its function and meaning. A proposition that conduct contrary to this teaching is acceptable among Christians (or anyone!) because it is conscientiously believed to be acceptable by persons involved and is for that reason not sinful, is seriously misguided.[2]

2) Is the doctrine consistent with the Vincentian Canon, the complete version of which is to be found in

---

[2] See *Issues in Human Sexuality*; p. 15, note 5 for the text of this passage.

Bettenson's *Documents of the Christian Church*?[3] As we have seen when we examined this Canon it is not the complete answer and it has some weaknesses. It also has great strengths and if we are aware of the nature of the weaknesses and the strengths then we can use it. It is a very powerful criterion for discerning the Truth.

Firstly, it requires a very critical examination of novelty. Novelty has, historically, been a sign of doctrinal error. We can see this in the early history of the Church. It can be seen more recently in Protestant churches. Here liturgy, which is expressive of doctrine, has ceased to have any form and is conditioned by what is pleasing to the religious sentiments of the worshippers. This is a problem that is summed up in the short aphorism, *lex orandi, lex credendi* — the law of praying is the law of believing. Novelty and appeal to the emotions of the "worshippers" are now principal characteristics of much Protestant liturgy,[4] self indulgence replacing doctrinal orthodoxy.

---

[3] Bettenson, *op.cit.*, pp. 118.ff.

[4] One of the surest signs that a church has lost its firm hold on the Apostolic Faith is disorder in liturgy. Dr Carey's encouragement of the Nine O'Clock Service in Sheffield, which was more like a popular music show and finished in sexual scandal, and his suggestion that the Church should experiment in worship using the skills of poets and musicians in designing exciting worship are signs of a profound misunderstanding of the nature of worship and its function. It turns worship into a human work rather than the work of the Holy Spirit in the Body of Christ. It further reveals that the center of attention, the flow of concern, so to speak, is to the worshipper rather than God. When the worship becomes people-centered rather than God-centered it becomes

We shall examine the question of whether and in what way we might consider it possible for dogma and doctrine to develop in the next chapter but we can say with certainty that novelty has always been a sign of heresy. Novelty, of itself, needs close examination. This is obvious. The fundamental dogmas would naturally be settled in the early years of the Church's life. Even in the later councils we find that the issues being dealt with are matters which are essentially implicit in the earlier definitions. For example the Orthodox definition following the Iconoclast controversy, which occupied some of the time of the Seventh Ecumenical Council, was concerned, basically, to make the very simple observation that if the Lord Jesus was really man then his likeness could properly be painted on an icon. It was defending the real manhood of the Lord Jesus, which had been defined earlier. It drew out the implication of that as it applied to the question of painting an icon of the Lord.

Secondly, the Vincentian Canon subjects a new doctrine to comparison with that which is believed everywhere else or at least over a wide area. This is not by any means a conclusive test. As we have seen the Catholic Church can, at times, be a tiny minority and if a doctrine deemed on all other grounds to be Catholic was held by a tiny minority it would not, for that reason alone, fall under the condemnation of the Vincen-

---

diabolical. It divides the Church. The recent adoption by the Church of England of eight(!) alternative eucharistic prayers—"to suit everyone's tastes"—really means that worship is being conformed to the taste and pleasure of the worshipper.

tian Canon. It must, however, be said, that the "everywhere" of the Canon should be regarded with great seriousness in the present day i.e. a novel doctrine held by a small group in the Church would be presumed to be in error. Today the "everywhere" also encompasses the 'everyone' as we have just seen. The Vincentian Canon is not watertight but it is a significant set of criteria of truth when taken together with the other criteria.

3) Is the doctrine consistent with the dogmas of the Universal Church? One of the features of the Apostolic Faith of the Universal Church is that it has a strongly integrated quality. One dogma fits into another. The belief about the person of the Lord Jesus fits in with the dogma of the Trinity. The dogma of the being of the Holy Spirit is integrated with the teaching on the person of the Lord. If a doctrine can be shown to be inconsistent with a dogmatic definition, such that we have to change the dogma to accommodate the doctrine, then we may assume that it is an error. We should have to be persuaded that the doctrine is truly of a piece with the whole dogmatic corpus before we accepted it.

It is assumed that the opponents to the ordination of women to the priesthood are motivated by misogyny. That is not the case in general. The reason for the opposition is dogmatic. The Tradition of the Church, restated by Dr Carey in an interview in March, 1991,[5] is that the ordained ministry of the Church is symbolic and representative of the Lord Jesus. Any other basis

---

[5] *Reader's Digest* (March, 1991).

for the ordained ministry — skill, charisma and so on — creates a ministry of skill and works rather than of grace.

If the Lord Jesus is symbolized and represented by a woman such that He is believed to have assumed unsexed and ungendered human nature then the Lord Jesus ceases to be a real human. Real humans are either men or women and He is — there is no real argument about this — a man. Human nature, as such, is not something that can be assumed except by becoming a man or a woman. Human nature is simply a set of definitions that distinguish human beings from other species. It does not, as such, include reference to sexual differentiation.

The objection to the ordination of women to the priesthood is that it is inconsistent with the dogma of the person of the Lord who became a man to save us. His real gendered humanity, because that is the only humanity there is, is essential for our salvation; which leads to the next question, below (d). If He lacked gender He would not be really human.

One final test in this class of criterion is this: is the doctrine consistent with our experience of reality understood in faith. There is no ultimate conflict between science and religious belief. Too many good scientists are believers for that to be likely. The Created Order speaks to us as eloquently of the truth of God's providential love as any other channel of revelation. It is tricky sometimes and we need to take a deep and broad view but in the end a belief that is radically inconsistent with our experience, in faith, of reality certainly needs at least to be questioned.

4) Is the doctrine necessary to our salvation? The dynamic behind all dogmatic definitions is our salvation. We have called this dynamic the logic of salvation. For this reason Fr John Meyendorff can observe that although Orthodox believe in the Assumption of the Blessed Virgin, calling it the Dormition of the Blessed Virgin, it is not part of the dogmatic corpus of the Universal Church. Why? Because "no theological necessity seems to justify its inclusion among the facts that realised the salvation of mankind."[6]

Doctrines are never luxuries designed to honour the Blessed Virgin, the apparent basis of the damaging doctrine of the Immaculate Conception of the Blessed Virgin, for example. As we shall see below,[7] this dogma, if true, actually makes salvation impossible. It is the duty of those discussing and coming to conclusions on doctrines to demonstrate that they are necessary to salvation. This judgement must be made not because a presumed infallible pontiff has said so but because it can be demonstrated with reference to revelation and theological reasoning, the logic of salvation. If it cannot be demonstrated then it should not be defined as dogma necessary to salvation. Some doctrines, if defined as dogmas, would make salvation impossible. The dogma of the Immaculate Conception of the Blessed

---

[6] Meyendorff, *op.cit.*, p. 19.

[7] Appendix 4.b.

Virgin is such a one; that Christ is androgynous is another.

5) Related to the former question and following from it we must ask, does the doctrine lead to catholic wholeness and the integration of the person and the Church? This is a very important criterion that grounds the other criteria that might, otherwise, float off into an unverifiable theological stratosphere. More simply the question might be put as, "Does the doctrine make saints?" The relationship of doctrine and dogmatic definitions to the experience of the Christian life is similar to the relationship between a printed page of music and a performance, that is the statement, the music, must be realized. It may be brilliantly and authentically realised or poorly and inauthentically realized. Trite, discordant and unmusical music on the page cannot lead to a brilliant performance. A brilliant performance authenticates the music on the page as good music. Sanctity and wholeness in persons and in the Church authenticate the doctrine and in cases of doubt sorts Truth from error.

If a doctrine passes all these tests then we are safe to assume that it is orthodox Catholic doctrine—subject to what might best be called settlement, that is the working out of the final criterion above, the experience of the Faithful. Martyrdom and sanctity have a very powerful effect in authenticating a doctrine. We have, however, to observe that there are exceptions to this, e.g. the Jehovah's Witnesses in Auschwitz whose conduct was noted by everyone to be exemplary (but perhaps not holy). They hold an heretical doctrine of the person of our Lord Jesus Christ.[8]

Finally we must deal with the question of the development of doctrine and dogma since it can be argued that innovations in doctrine are authentic developments. The question of whether dogma and doctrine can develop is the subject of the final chapter.

---

[8] Jehovah's Witnesses believe in an Arian understanding of the person of the Lord Jesus.

CHAPTER SEVEN

The Development of Doctrine and Dogma

We need to see in what way we can sensibly speak of developing doctrine and developing dogma — for they are two separate concepts — and, if we can sensibly speak of this kind of development, how the development occurs. The question of whether the development is authentic is simpler. We just apply the criteria we have discussed in the last chapter.

What is the difference between doctrine and dogma? A dogma is a formally defined doctrine that has the following characteristics. First of all, those dogmas, universally held, have been defined as dogmas by councils accepted as ecumenical and received by the Faithful. The Roman Church also accepts as dogmas those doctrines so defined by the exercise of papal infallibility.

It is, secondly, a doctrine of the Universal Church forming part of the Apostolic Faith. It is a statement that a doctrine has been held from the beginning as an essential part of the Apostolic faith.

Thirdly, it is a doctrine, belief in which is necessary to our salvation. This needs some slight expansion. The truth is that a person may well come in complete penitence to our Lord and receive forgiveness and come, by living in grace, to union with our Lord without ever having a clear grasp of any dogma. That is obvious. If we probed that person's beliefs we should find, at every crucial point, that his or her belief was orthodox. If a person said that he did not believe in the divinity of the Lord Jesus it is very difficult to see how he could come to salvation through the saving work of Christ. It is precisely because Jesus is both man and God that His life, death and Resurrection are for us men and our salvation.

Dogmas define the fundamentals of the faith of Christians, the basic building blocks, that which has been believed from the beginning. Rejection of a dogma is rejection of the Apostolic Faith and is self-exclusion from the Church.

Dogmas are expressed and defined in the way we have dealt with above. They define what must not be denied. For this reason alone it is very difficult to give any value to the idea of the development of a dogma since development implies change and dogmas are so framed as to make change destructive. The very apophatic and negative nature of a dogma defies the idea of development.

Our Lord Jesus is the second member of the Blessed Trinity, the Logos of one substance with the Father and He is also the man Jesus who walked the earth two thousand years ago in Palestine. We may debate the way in which our Lord is both God and man but we must not deny it.[1] How are we to develop this dogma? It has a very simple function i.e. to stop us denying that the Lord is both fully God and fully man. Its very simplicity makes the idea of development inappropriate. Development means change. If we are to change it, what are we to change? We can reduce the definition in some way so that we do not have the two, hitherto central, poles of the definition. We can make it permissible to deny some aspect of the Godhead or some aspect of the humanity. That, however, is not to develop the dogma but to destroy it. The dogma then no longer brings people to their salvation. It cannot. The Lord is God and man with all the implications of those two words, "God" and "Man". We may legitimately discuss the nature of his divinity and his manhood. We may legitimately discuss the various doctrines and theories which have been held during the history of the Church.[2] We cannot, however, deny the irreducible minimum of the dogma without destroying the dogma and rendering it useless. The dogma ceases to be for our salvation if we remove its force. Dogmas are not luxuries but the irreducible minimum necessary for salvation.

Alternatively we could make the dogma more specific in some way. We could limit the boundaries; build the dogma up, so to speak, define it more closely and more fully, make the holes in the net narrower. We

---

[1] The definition of the council of Chalcedon is in Appendix 1.

[2] See Macquarrie, *Jesus Christ in Modern Thought* (London, 1997) and Pelikan, *Jesus Through the Centuries* (London, 1985).

could require people to believe that the Incarnation involved particular precise characteristics about the nature of the Godhead in Christ not hitherto defined. We could do the same with the nature of the manhood of Christ. We could limit doctrinal speculation quite radically and quite easily. The effect would be to remove the life from the dogma. It would be to root it in a particular age and culture. It would destroy the legitimate freedom of theological debate. The processes by which dogmas are continually represented to the world as doctrinal flowers, so to speak, growing from a dogmatic stem would cease.

We can see the danger of this process most dramatically in the various doctrines and theories of the atonement, the saving work of Christ, over the centuries. The dogma of the saving work of Christ is that the Lord's life, death, resurrection and ascension are for our salvation. Every addition and refinement of that dogma is designed to preserve that truth in its fullness. Throughout history, different ages and cultures have sought to explain how the Lord's saving work was and is effective in itself. There have been many doctrines and theories, the majority of which have reflected the culture, particularly the political culture, of the time in which they were born. We have referred to this in an earlier chapter of this study. As long as the theories are not inconsistent with the dogmatic definitions then they are acceptable. Indeed they have great evangelistic value. There has been a tendency among some churches and groups, however, to isolate the theory of penal substitution as the only authentic doctrine of the atonement. In this our Lord is said to take to Himself the punishment due to us for our sins. This doctrine presents various problems that are beyond the scope of this study. By insisting upon it as the *only* acceptable doctrine of the atonement the churches and groups which hold this view have, by elevating it into a sort of dogma limited the capacity to bring home the power of the atonement to those who cannot accept this particular theory. They have done so by tightening and limiting the terms of the dogma. This is an example of dogmatic development i.e. adding elements that are unnecessary in order to preserve the Apostolic Faith. The effect is damaging.

It is true that the language of any statement, and so of a doctrinal definition, is conditioned by time and culture. The expression of truths and the meaning of words may change. It may be necessary to define a dogma more exactly in contemporary language. Such linguistic changes are, of course, acceptable if they are not inconsistent with the substance of the dogmatic definition. It was necessary, for example, to find words in Latin and English—and every other language—in order to express the truth of consubstantiality. The original word is Greek (*homoousios*), but this re-expression is not development. Indeed it is the reverse of development. It brings the contemporary reader back to the original truth not to a dogma changed by development. Such a process does not change the truth or develop the dogma.

If we supposed dogmatic definitions to be positive statements putting before us what we must believe rather than what we must not deny then the process of development might just make sense. That supposition is incorrect but for the sake of thinking it through let us accept it for the moment. The nature of dogma would be in constant flux as age succeeded age and linguistic and philosophical changes piled in on each other, each new phase requiring a new definition in contemporary terms. We would have new dogmas for each age and each place, new changes in the conciliar definitions. The faith would no longer be certain and universal. We can see that abandoning the negative and apophatic nature of dogma is the only way in which we can sensibly speak of development. We can also see that this is a disaster.

It seems therefore that the concept of developing dogma is meaningless. Can doctrine develop? We take doctrine to be teaching based on dogmas. We might as well refer to doctrines and theories for they have many of the same characteristics. Doctrines/theories are the result of exploring and applying the effect of a dogma. We have seen that the dogma of the atonement has been applied, brought to life to some degree, explained, in various ways at various times. Doctrine is sound doctrine when it is not inconsistent with dogma. Doctrines may be sound and true, not inconsistent with a dogma, but they do not set out the fundamental irreducible elements of the Faith so that they are, as such, not necessary for salvation. Doctrines may express facts believed to be true but not believed to be necessary to salvation. We have seen, for example, that the doctrine of the Dormition of the Virgin is believed but not defined as necessary to salvation by Orthodox Christians.

New circumstances, new politics, new science even may cause a doctrine to change and develop. We can test the authenticity of the development by the canon of the dogma. We ask the simple question, "Is it consistent or inconsistent with the dogma?"

Here is a theologian who is seeking to set out the nature of our Lord or the nature of the Blessed Trinity. The doctrine is set out and developed and people are invited to accept the new expressions. This development must, however, be tested first against the dogmas. The doctrine may have an inner consistency but lack consistency with the rest of the body of the Apostolic Faith. It may be reasonable to modern thought but inconsistent with the dogma.

One of the dangers of assuming that dogmas are positive statements is that when we do so we cannot cope with the paradoxes within the dogma. It is very difficult to read the Athanasian Creed[3] and not come to the conclusion that a mighty effort is being made to hold together propositions that simply cannot be held together in a rational way. Either God is one or God is three. Both beliefs cannot be true, but they are. The mysteries of the Faith transcend human reason. The wonder of the Blessed Trinity is too great for us to put into tidy concepts. All we can say is what must not be

---

[3] This creed was not the product of St Athanasius but is Western in origin as the presence of the Filioque clause in it makes plain.

denied. We know that the Lord Jesus is both God and man. That belief is necessary for his saving work to be effective. Equally we know that He referred to the Father. So, and this is *not* meant to be a complete statement of Trinitarian theology, we must first accept that the Lord Jesus is God and that there is also a differentiation between the Son, the Lord Jesus, and the Father in the Godhead. The Church's experience and the Biblical teaching on the Holy Spirit, and other reasons, caused the Church to define a third differentiation within the Godhead, the Holy Spirit. We have used the inadequate word, "differentiation," to avoid explaining the meanings and differences between *hypostasis, persona, prosopon, substantia* and *ousia*. Life is complicated enough sometimes. We can manage, for the moment, without setting off on another journey to explain those terms that were the currency of Trinitarian debate and differences in the early life of the Church. The paradoxes of the Athanasian Creed are intolerable unless it is understood to be apophatic and negative in form expressing what must not be denied.

The idea that dogma can be developed does not stand up to examination but we can see that it is reasonable to speak, in certain circumstances, of the development of doctrine.

We have not made more than a passing reference to Newman's teaching on the development of doctrine. In referring to development he is referring partly to the re-expression of dogma in contemporary doctrinal terms and partly to the definition of dogma in response to heresy, defining what has been believed from the beginning. He does not teach that dogmas can change and develop. He does not, however, deal with the apophatic and negative nature of dogmas which logically, in addition to the historical and doctrinal grounds, makes nonsense of the concept of developing dogma. Proceeding, as he does, from the premise that doctrines are positive rather than apophatic in form he deals with the question in a quite different way from its treatment here. Nothing he teaches could be used to justify the concept of changing and developing dogmatic definitions.

Afterword

The purpose of this study has been very simple: to provide guidance in understanding the way in which disputes over doctrine might best be resolved. To do that at least half adequately it has been necessary from time to use terms with which the reader may be unfamiliar. We have tried to keep these to the minimum and where they seemed necessary, to provide a glossary and appendices.

It would be a grave mistake to suppose that this is all a sort of intellectual game played by people with a taste for it. That is not correct. No sane man or woman wants to be involved in this sort of controversy. Energy and time are better spent in prayer and growing in love, but problems come and they are serious. They are serious because they create an environment of belief and conduct, a religious milieu, which draws people away from the best. The best is union with our Blessed Lord, and nothing but the best is good enough for the People of God. The Lord Jesus died to bring us to that best and to settle for less than the best is to set his loving sacrifice at nought. A development that causes this cannot be ignored. It is profoundly unloving to do so. Our mothers and fathers in the Faith, upon whose prayers with those of the Blessed Virgin and the Saints, we depend, did not seek controversy but when it came they faced it, and many of them died for the Truth. In veneration and love for them and out of love for all men we have a duty to oppose errors that lead people from salvation.

This study has been written with a strong awareness of the seriousness of the issues and from the experience of doctrinal error at work in a church drawing people from the following of Christ. Serious concern sometimes brings anger in its wake. If anger has led the author to unfairness he apologises. Perhaps, however, anger at some of what has happened is not out of place. Irresponsibility in matters of the faith of the Church is a proper cause for anger.

The persian soldier, quoted by Herodotus, is reported to have said, "the most bitter of all griefs, to see clearly and to be able to do nothing." By the mercy of God something can be done. This study is a small contribution, inadequate and poor, to what must be done to restore the fearful collapse in the churches affected by a misconceived liberalism and secularism, a collapse which is clear for anyone to see.

APPENDIX 1

The Definition of Chalcedon

Therefore, following the holy Fathers, we all with one accord teach men to acknowledge one and the same Son, our Lord Jesus Christ, at once complete in the Godhead and complete in manhood, truly God and truly man, consisting of a reasonable soul and body; of one substance (*homoousios*) with the Father as regards his Godhead, and at the same time of one substance with us as regards his manhood; like us in all respects, apart from sin; as regards his Godhead, begotten of the Father before all ages, but as regards his manhood begotten, for us men and for our salvation, of Mary the Virgin, the God Bearer (*Theotokos*); one and the same Christ, Son, Lord, Only begotten, recognised in two natures, without confusion, without change, without division, without separation; the distinction of the natures being in no way annulled by the union, but rather the characteristics of each nature being preserved and coming together to form one person and subsistence (hypostasis), not as parted or separated into two persons, but one and the same Son and Only Begotten God the Word, Lord Jesus Christ; even as the prophets from the earliest times spoke of him, and our Lord Jesus Christ Himself taught us, and the creed of the Fathers has handed down to us.

APPENDIX 2

Sexuality and Symbolism

This is an attempt to show the relationship between belief, symbol and action by showing that there is a fundamental causal connection between the ordination of women to the priesthood and the growing acceptance of the rightness of homosexual, genital acts. It is an attempt to show that they come from the same doctrinal basis and the same way of understanding the world.

Nobody who knows the present writer will suppose for a minute that he wishes to say more than that we cannot say that homosexual genital acts are consistent with the Judaeo–Christian ethical tradition.

The Lesbian and Gay Christian Movement soon realised that the vote to ordain women proceeded from the same theoretical basis as their own. They saw that the arguments which support the ordination of active homosexuals, the acceptance of the rightness of homosexual genital acts and the ordination of women to the priesthood spring from the same conceptual basis. Is there a correlation between these two phenomena? It is clear that, in general, the same people hold the one belief as hold the other. Even where someone like Dr Carey seems to deny the rightness of homosexual genital acts the denial is not consistent. His refusal to subscribe to the terms of the Synod decision on the subject when put to him, his support for "Issues in

Human Sexuality", which permits homosexual relationships, and his acknowledgement that the teaching which says that homosexual acts are sins might change all show that he is equivocal on the subject. (When asked in Los Angeles if the condemnation of homosexual genital acts might change he said that it might.) The Episcopal Church of America provides ample evidence of a strong correlation between these two beliefs. The acceptance of the ordination of women and the acceptance of the moral and social equality of heterosexual and homosexual unions as having the status of marriage have gone together there.

The four Anglican primates who subscribed to an advertisement advocating the ordination of active homosexuals were also the principal advocates of the ordination of women. The bishops of the Church of England, with very few exceptions, declined to subscribe to a statement issued by Reform, an Anglican evangelical society. This statement repeated, in substance, the terms of a Synod resolution asserting the immorality of homosexual genital relationships. The same bishops issued the report, *Issues in Human Sexuality*, which we have referred to above. The Anglican Bishop of Newcastle said that "homosexuality within a loving stable relationship is no sin." The Anglican Archbishop of York formally judged this statement to be consistent with the doctrine, worship and practice of the Church of England. The Anglican Bishops of Oxford, Bath and Wells, Portsmouth and Worcester have made broadly similar statements. The former Anglican Bishop of Southwark was a vigorous advocate of the ordination of sexually active homosexuals. Since only those who support the ordination of women are appointed as bishops by the archbishops and the responsible bodies, the Church of England House of Bishops, almost to a man, supports of the ordination of women. There is, therefore, a correlation among many Anglican bishops.

The correlation can also be seen in the academic life of the churches in England and elsewhere. Dr Adrian Thatcher, Director of the Centre for Christian Theology and Education in Plymouth is a thoroughgoing advocate of both views. The substance of one of his books, *Liberating Sex*, is the basis for a course on the subject for the Church Colleges' Certificate. The new doctrine of inclusivity that is becoming a distinguishing mark of Western liberal Protestant thought demonstrates the same correlation. Dr David Holgate, the director of a theological training scheme, locates the distinctive identity of Anglicanism in its inclusivity, which includes homosexuality.

We need, however, to do more than show that there is a correlation. There is a venerable fallacy which proceeds from correlations to presume that there is necessarily a cause i.e. because event B follows event A it is caused by event A. It is know as the fallacy of *post hoc ergo propter hoc* (after this, so caused by this). We must not fall into that error.

We must try to demonstrate why and how the two beliefs which we are examining are connected. To do so we will examine four areas that demonstrate the connection at the level of causation. These areas of study are (a) symbols and dogma, (b) hermeneutics, (c) social theology and (d) the effects of gnosticism.

(a) Symbols

We need to distinguish between conventional symbols such as flags which we understand because there is a convention that tells us what they symbolise and received or intrinsic symbols. These are symbols like the nature of the ordained ministry that is given to us by the Lord and the Apostles or a symbol like an open hand that conveys lack of hostility. While it is not always clear where the boundary between these symbols lies nor is this classification exhaustive we take it that the symbols we encounter in the Church are received or intrinsic symbols.

Dr Carey, in an interview with the Reader's Digest, suggested that to say that a woman could not represent Christ at the altar was a heresy. The issue of the ordination of women is, as he recognised then, (a) one of representing and of representation and (b) of heresy. Sacramental representation is symbolic representation. It can only be a heresy to say that a woman cannot represent Christ at the altar if to do so implies a statement in Christology, a statement about the nature of Christ. If this is not the case then the statement that a woman cannot represent Christ at the altar cannot be heretical. It is clear from those who have written in support of Dr Carey, particularly Dr Torrance, the Presbyterian theologian, that a statement in Christology is implied. The matter concerns therefore the nature of the Lord Jesus Christ.

The argument that lies behind Dr Carey's remarks goes something like this; our Lord assumed human nature and He must therefore have assumed the whole of human nature. If He had not done so what He had not assumed would be unhealed. This argument is usually supported by the teaching of St Gregory Nazianzus in Letter 101 to Cledonius. St Gregory is writing against the views of who taught that our Lord Jesus did not have a human spirit. St Gregory argues that this is not correct because if it was the human spirit would be unredeemed: "what is unassumed is unhealed." If the Lord assumed whole human nature then, the argument runs, He must be able to be symbolised by a woman because He must have assumed female human nature if He assumed human nature completely. To deny that He assumed female human nature is, it is said, to deny healing, i.e. salvation to women and perhaps to all men because the Lord will not have become completely human. It is on the grounds of Christology—the full humanity of the Lord—and of its effects on the saving work of Christ that Dr Carey condemned as heretics those who do not share his views. His argument is based on three fallacies and therefore cannot stand.

The first fallacy is to suppose that human nature is something more than a definition of characteristics that distinguish *homo sapiens* from other creatures. It is, in fact, just that i.e. a set of characteristics; nothing more. Since sexual differentiation is not exclusive to *homo sapiens* it does not form part of the definition of human

271

nature. It is not one of the distinctive characteristics of human nature. Our Lord did not, however, assume human nature. He became human. That is a quite different thing, as we shall see now.

The second fallacy is to suppose that it is possible to be fully human but not to be either a man or a woman. Human nature, the characteristic of being human, only subsists in men or women. To be human is to be either a man or a woman. To assume human nature that is sexually undifferentiated is to assume an idea, a classification. It is not to become human. To say that our Lord assumed human nature and to say nothing more is to say that He is not really a man. If He is neither a man nor a woman He is not human and to say that Christ is not human is heretical. It is, in fact, heretical, by implication, to say that He assumed human nature; that does not say enough and does not adequately define the Incarnation. Detailed analyses of the meaning of *vir* and *aner* and the rest are irrelevant. The answer does not lie in the meanings of the word, "man" but in the reality of being human. The logic of salvation demands a real human Incarnation. Anything else, all the other arguments, are the reverse of the logic of salvation and heretical. To say that the Lord assumed humanity or human nature and to say nothing more is a serious theological error. It leaves Him unincarnate.

The third fallacy in Dr Carey's argument concerns the nature of the saving work of Christ. It is the teaching of the New Testament and the Fathers that the saving work of Christ restores the whole created order to the Father. According to Dr Carey's argument our Lord, in order to restore all things to the Father, would have to have assumed bovine nature, canine nature, equine nature and so on for any unassumed nature would be unhealed and all natures are healed. All that is, of course, nonsense. Our Lord entered the created order, creaturely existence, as a man and restored all creation to the Father.

If the Lord Jesus Christ was and is a material being (i.e. "is" in the sense that it was true that He was a material being when He walked the earth in Palestine and that He is now not less than He was then but the same, glorified) that had assumed both male and female human nature He must have been androgynous—a view that has been advocated by the Reverend David Power, the former adviser in Evangelism of the Anglican diocese of Portsmouth—otherwise the Lord Jesus would only have appeared to have become human; (that heresy is called docetism).

This heresy was vigorously opposed in the New Testament, e.g. 1 and 2 John, and the early Church. A Christ represented and symbolized—Dr Carey says that is what a priest does—by a woman is a docetic Christ, one who assumes human nature and does not become a real human. The next step, as we shall see, leads to the acceptance of homosexual genital acts.

The fundamental symbol of our faith, the Lord Jesus, and here we use the word, "symbol" in the strongest way, lacks sexual differentiation. The Symbol of the Father, the only-begotten Son of the Father, the second member of the Blessed Trinity, The Word Incarnate, the Perfect Man, the Author and Finisher of our faith, the one to whom we must be conformed, who restores all things to the Father and who is ideal, perfected humanity is sexually ambivalent when symbolised by a woman. The Lord does not share in the sexual differentiation of other humans. Human sexuality is unassumed. Unassumed human sexuality is unhealed with truly terrible effects. Indeed because He is not human but has simply assumed human nature He has assumed nothing and nothing is healed.

The sexual expression of love can, therefore, in accordance with the symbolism of a docetic and asexual Christ, take place within any sexual pairing, homosexual or heterosexual. Since human sexuality is believed to be unassumed it is unhealed. The result is that human sexuality is trivialised and distorted with disastrous results. What is clear is that sexual intercourse is no longer believed to require sexual differentiation. In addition to this, with the acceptance that procreation is no longer the function of sexual differentiation and sexual intercourse, a direct result of human sexuality being unhealed because unassumed, the loss of the significance of sexual differentiation is made almost complete. It would be trying and beyond the scope of this brief study to point out the serious negative effects that the desanctification of human sexuality, following from the unhealing of human sexuality — what is not assumed is not healed — has caused. The desanctification of human sexuality and all the evil that flows from it follows, however, as night follows day, from the acceptance by a church of an asexual, docetic Christ symbolised by a woman.

It is important to say that we do not suppose, for an instant, that women priests in general or any woman priest, in particular, is part of some plot to undermine sexual morals. It is just that the implications of ordaining women have not been fully worked out.

There is one final consideration in the area of symbolism and dogmatic theology. This point has been made by an Orthodox theologian but we are unable to trace the reference. The point is this; the Blessed Virgin conceived by the Holy Spirit. Women conceive by that which is male. While we are not suggesting, for a moment, that the Godhead is male or has gender — the idea is nonsense — the Virginal Conception of the Lord, by the Holy Spirit, brings into the conception of the Lord very strong male symbolism. Incarnation is not possible unless the Lord is born of a woman and this presents us with a further example of male symbolism.

If this male symbolism is rejected, as it is by those who accept the ordination of women, there is a further cause for concern. The conception of the Lord, in this case, is either symbolic of asexuality or of conception by a female. The former is docetic and cannot bring salvation and the latter is a homosexual union. We have seen an increase of such homosexual unions and births in which the man is simply an inseminator or the woman an incubator. The effects of this on children in the long term is unknown. The symbolism of representing the Lord Jesus by a woman asserts, in the most powerful way, the moral equality of homosexual unions and heterosexual marriage. The defective symbolism of the advocates of one view strengthens the advocacy of the other view.

(b) Hermeneutics

There is a connection between the two beliefs we have been discussing in the field of hermeneutics—the principles upon which the Bible is interpreted. A senior Anglican minister has observed that the hermeneutic which allowed the ordination of women has also made possible the acceptance of homosexual genital activity. In both cases we have Biblical injunctions indicating that neither is correct. How is it possible to interpret the Bible in such a way as to negate those injunctions?

The argument which leads to this possibility is fairly simple. It is believed, by those who deduce from texts teaching that is explicitly denied in them, that the texts of the Bible are temporally and culturally conditioned. They only apply to the particular conditions in which they were written. The texts are understood to have value only as reflections of the mores and moral and social understanding on the people of God at a particular time—either of the people of Israel or of the early Church. Since the times have changed, and the mores and morals with them, the texts no longer have binding authority. They may provide interesting historical sources of religious sociology but are principally valuable as giving insights into ancient thought. They are simply examples of intellectual archaeology.

Scripture can be re-interpreted according to the mores and moral and social understanding of our time.

The reader may recall Dr Santer's theory of Christian reason/common sense. In this view Scripture takes second place to Christian reason/common sense. Biblical authority is despatched at a stroke. It is a remarkable and totally misguided achievement. On liberal principles of Biblical interpretation, such as we have described, the Bible has no more authority than the Anglican Articles of Religion or the latest Swedish government report on sexual equality.

As we have seen the Bible speaks to us on matters relating to our salvation. The nature of the Church and its ministry and what act is and is not a sin are matters concerning our salvation. This is particularly so when we recall Dr Carey's attribution of Christological significance to the nature of the ministry — the priest represents Christ — expressed in his *Readers' Digest* interview. This orthodox view of Biblical authority is not accepted by those who teach the kind of liberalism we have been discussing. Since sexual equality including the ordination of women and the moral equality of homosexual relationships with heterosexual relationships are part of contemporary morals, of Christian reason/common sense, as defined by Dr Santer, they are accepted by some churches despite Biblical revelation to the contrary. The Biblical teaching to the contrary is believed to be out of date and irrelevant.

(c) Social Theology

A number of miscellaneous issues come under this heading. Firstly, we have the exaltation of justice over grace, particularly justice as a fundamental human right. Archbishop Desmond Tutu supported the ordination of women solely on grounds of justice and the present Anglican Bishop of Rochester is prepared to risk the unity of his church because of a fundamental to justice. Archbishop Tutu also supported the ordination of sexually active homosexuals on the same grounds.

Many advocates of the ordination of women see the issue as a matter of human rights. While it is clear that we have a duty to do justice to others it is hard to argue, in a community of grace—the Church—and before a God who is gracious, that anything can be claimed as a right. It also does not seem correct, under these circumstances, to suggest that justice as judged by twentieth century principles of social justice—the values of Western social democracy are not eternal—should override the authority of the Bible and the Fathers, at least for Christians.

To claim something as of right in a community of grace and before a God of grace is a contradiction in terms or it means that we have a church and a god before whom grace has given place to rights. Rights and grace cannot exist together. One necessarily excludes the other. If I have a right to something it cannot be given to me as of grace precisely because I have a right to it. I can demand it if I have a right to it. That is what "having a right" means. If I can only receive something as a gift, of grace, without having a right to it then it is nonsense to try to assert at the same time that I do have a right to it. The two things are mutually exclusive and cannot exist together in any relationship. I cannot be in a relationship of love and grace and at the same time, within that relationship, demand things as of right. Above all love cannot be demanded as of right. Nobody has a right to love. Every Christian has the duty to love. It is from the exercise of this duty and in its exercise that justice finds a place. I must exercise justice as part of the duty of love. I cannot, within a loving and gracious relationship, demand justice.

It is, further, simply incoherent to speak of fundamental human rights, especially in the Church. It is a sort of gibberish that sounds good but means nothing. If rights are fundamental they must attach to each human just because he or she is human, and so these rights must be capable of being asserted before God; but before God we have no rights. God is essentially a God of love and everything we receive from Him is of grace. We can demand nothing as of right. There are, therefore, no fundamental human rights—only a fundamental human duty of love. Ordination is spoken of as a matter of justice and of right. That is a sort of gibberish that means nothing. Ordination is a matter of God's gracious choice.

Secondly, the argument put forward by Dr Carey that the great abilities of women are lost to the ministry if they are not ordained exalts talents and ability—works—over grace. A person, on these terms, is a good priest because of his or her gifts and skills rather than because of a loving gift of the whole self to God, an act of grace. The priest is essentially useless at the level of gifts and skills, an empty person in whose emptiness God's grace works.

Dr Carey's argument from gifts and skills is essentially the same argument as that put forward by the former Anglican Bishop of Southwark to justify the ordination of active homosexuals. He argued that active homosexuals ought to be ordained, regardless of their actions, because they had many gifts, skills and talents to offer the Church. Again the ordained ministry is seen as a matter of abilities and talents rather than of grace. A woman who is not a symbol of the Lord can be ordained because she is talented and able to do the work. The same is true of an active homosexual.

We have, in this way of thinking, a meritocratic priesthood, which is a symbol of a meritocratic way of salvation. That is a great comfort for the good, able, gifted and talented but very bad news for us sinners. It destroys the way of grace shown us by the Lord Jesus Christ. It is also an example of the effect of gnosticism, salvation by knowledge; of which more below. We see, again and again, in the thought of those who support the ordination of women, and in Dr Carey in particular, an abandonment of the grace of God in favour of human works, e.g. in worship, in the ministry of the Church and in church government.

Thirdly, we find that acts are judged to be right or wrong by the degree of satisfaction that is afforded to those involved in them rather than by an accepted set of moral principles. It is deemed wrong to withhold satisfaction from the person who wants something and right to afford satisfaction. One hears the argument that it would be wrong to deprive such and such a person of happiness — a bishop marrying the divorced wife of one of his priests, a woman who wants to be ordained or someone who wants a homosexual relationship. It should be made clear, at this point, that the writer has nothing but admiration for celibate homosexuals and loving sympathy for many active homosexuals. All we cannot properly do is say that there is nothing wrong about it. The exaltation of personal satisfaction as a significant moral criterion is a further link between the acceptance of women priests and the acceptance as right of homosexual genital acts.

Fourthly, militant feminism, which is the engine of much of the motive for ordaining women has been observed to have the effect of robbing men of their male role. The confusion of sexuality that follows from the spread of militant feminism is matched by an increase in moves to justify homosexual activity. The two phenomena seem to spring from the same understanding of the insignificance of sexual differentiation. This is not the place for a critique of militant feminism or militant masculinity but it is worth noticing that both lead to moral chaos.

(d) Gnosticism

The belief that the material has no ultimate moral significance and is debased is a characteristic of the gnosticism which is so prevalent in western liberal Protestantism. This leads—as a conference held in Chelmsford Anglican Cathedral was titled—to a "Blurring of the Boundaries." (Note also that salvation by knowledge is a characteristic of gnosticism and we see this at work when Dr Carey speaks of the gifts of women priests or Dr Williamson, former Anglican Bishop of Southwark, shows himself ready to ordain active homosexuals if they are able men and women.) This blurring of the sexual boundaries and the trivialization and debasement of the material together with salvation by knowledge constitutes a further intellectual ground, i.e. gnosticism, held in common by the advocates of the ordination of women and those who accept the rightness of homosexual genital activity.

The priest as symbol

Plainly the argument of this appendix stands or falls upon the proposition, as stated by Dr Carey in his Readers' Digest interview, that the priest is a representative, symbol, icon and type of the Lord Jesus. It has been argued extensively elsewhere[1] that there is a continuous understanding of this from the New Testament to the present day. This understanding can be found in the East and the West, in Orthodox, Roman and Reformed thought. It cannot seriously be argued that a priest represents the Lord – Dr Carey's words – in any way that is not symbolic. He cannot represent the Lord Jesus morally or in terms of holiness. To suggest that would be blasphemous. Article 26 of the Anglican Arti-

---

[1] Chapter 6 by Bishop Kallistos Ware, in *Man, Woman, Priesthood,* ed. by Peter Moore and the present writer's John Keble lecture published in *Costings* (September, 1996) by Cost of Conscience.

cles of Religion, which we have already referred above and which teaches an almost universally held view, would not make sense except upon the basis of symbolic representation. Those who reject the representative symbolism of the ministry do not follow through the logic of their position and dispose of the ordained ministry altogether. That follows from the rejection of ministerial symbolism. Once the symbolic nature of the ministry is rejected the Church becomes a different sort of body, not the organic Body of Christ with differentiated parts and each part valued as each other, growing up into the fullness of Christ. It becomes a works and ability centred organisation ripe for management. Its structure is no longer an utterance of the Gospel but an utterance of the message of justification by works and it is no longer the Church.

APPENDIX 3

"Outside the Church there is no Salvation"

St Cyprian's words are extra ecclesiam nulla salus, "outside the Church there is no salvation." This has been taken to mean, by some, that there is no salvation outside the Roman Church. This is an untenable argument since for a considerable time St Cyprian was in dispute with Bishop Stephen of Rome and out of communion with him. For some time ecclesiastical relations between Rome and Africa were severed.

In a synod in 256 St Cyprian differed radically from Bishop Stephen over baptism by heretics which he held to be invalid. He believed that the original Church founded by Peter was in Rome but he never attributed any primacy to Rome nor would he accept Roman interference in the affairs of his diocese. We need to look back to an older doctrine of the Church in which each local church constituted the Catholic Church, even where two or three are gathered together. "There is Jesus Christ and where Jesus Christ is there is the Church," as St Ignatius puts it. To be outside the Church is to be separated from Christ. As Florovsky puts it, "Outside the Church there is no salvation because salvation is the Church. For salvation is the revelation of the way for everyone who believes in Christ's name. This revelation is to be found only in the Church."[1] St Cyprian's statement is a much more immediate and less theoretical proposition than it has been taken to be. The bishops are united in their common origin and in fraternal love and concord. Adherence to the Church is adherence to one's bishop. That is the basis of Church unity.

---

[1] *Bible, Church and Tradition: An Eastern Orthodox View,* p. 37.

Appendix 4

The Dogmatic Additions made by the Roman Church to the Apostolic Faith

There are four primary additions to the Apostolic Faith that have been made by the Roman Catholic Church: the addition of the *Filioque* clause to the Creed, the doctrine of the Immaculate Conception, the doctrine of papal infallibility, and the doctrine of the Assumption of the Blessed Virgin. Because I have already dealt with the latter two issues in some detail, I shall focus on the *Filioque* and the Immaculate Conception.

I. The *Filioque* Clause

(a) Introduction

What follows is not, and could not be, more than a brief account, and inadequate because brief, of this Western addition to the Creed of Nicaea and Constantinople and a brief assessment of its significance. An adequate account of the *Filioque* clause would take another book. For those who wish to understand the history and substance of the dispute between the Holy Orthodox Church and the Roman Church—and subsequently all western churches—on this matter, more fully, the following books are recommended: Volume 2 of Jaroslav Pelikan's *The Christian Tradition*, Meyendorff's *Byzantine Theology*, Lossky's *Mystical Theology of the Eastern Church* (the chapter on the Trinity) and *In the Image and Likeness of God*, Papadakis' *Crisis in Byzantium*, and Piault's *What is the Trinity?* This last is by a Roman Catholic who is particularly unsympathetic to the Orthodox position. We have included the book by Piault because he presents, in accessible language, a typical Western understanding of the Blessed Trinity. We shall refer to his understanding below.

(b) A brief history of the Filioque controversy

In the late sixth century there was alarm in Europe, especially in Spain, at the effect of the Arian heresy and other heresies that had the effect of denying the full divinity of the Son. The reaction to this led to the decision of the Synod of Toledo in 589 to emphasize the consubstantiality of the Father and the Son. It was decided that this could be achieved by saying that the Holy Spirit proceeded from the Father "and the Son"—*Filioque* means "and the Son"—rather than from the Father alone. This insertion into the Creed spread through Europe largely under the influence of Charlemagne (742–814) although the Bishop of Rome resisted including it for some time. By the eleventh century, however, it was included in the Creed in the Western

Church and became, until the definition of the Immaculate Conception of the Blessed Virgin, the only canonical and dogmatic dispute between the Holy Orthodox Church and the Roman Church. It was the formal cause of the breach between the Holy Orthodox Church and the Roman Church, which was almost complete by about the middle of the twelfth century.

It is important to note that at every stage in the development of the dispute genuine doctrinal differences mixed with political motives—on both sides. It is further important to notice that there is a real difference of dogma between the Holy Orthodox Church and the Roman Church on this matter and that the difference has significance consequences. It has been dismissed as a non-dispute but that is a mistake. There are real doctrinal issues involved with real practical effects. It is not correct to say that East and West say the same thing in essence. They do not.

It is true to say that in respect of the work of the Holy Spirit in time, what is called the economic procession of the Holy Spirit or the temporal mission of the Holy Spirit, the dispute is less acute and some degree of agreement between the Orthodox Church and the Western Church may be possible. (See below for a fuller treatment of the economic and the theological Trinity.) When, however, we come to consider the eternal procession of the Holy Spirit, that is the place of the Holy Spirit in the inner life of the Blessed Trinity—what is called the theological Trinity, there is no basis for agreement.

A further cause of dispute between the Orthodox Church and the Western Church concerns the canonicity of the decision to add a clause to the Creed agreed at Nicaea and Constantinople without the authority of the whole Church. The Orthodox Church does not accept that the Bishop of Rome had the power to change the Creed in this way. This unauthorised change, in itself, made the Filioque unacceptable to the Orthodox in addition to the disagreement as to substance. Full accounts of the history of the dispute are available in Pelikan, Papadakis, Meyendorff and many church histories.

(c) The substance of the dispute

This is not an easy matter to discuss. It involves the paradoxes of theology at their most acute. The only way to get through it is to be very clear about the nature of the discussion and the definitions. After every sentence describing the Trinity say to yourself, "I do not have to understand everything about this sentence nor do I have to assert it. I must just not say anything inconsistent with it."

The introduction of the Filioque clause and the dispute that flowed from it started as an attempt to stress the consubstantiality of the Son—that is that the Son and the Father are of one substance. This was a response to a trend to subordinate the Son to the Father in the sense of diminishing the divinity and consubstantiality of the Son, i.e. of making the Son not wholly divine and one with the Father.

The effect of the response to this development was, however, to emphasise the consubstantiality of the Son and the Father at the expense of the Spirit. The Spirit is seen no longer to be in the same rank of consubstantiality as the Father and Son although speaking of ranks of consubstantiality is a very inadequate way of speaking and thinking.

The debate was and is bedevilled by two principal problems: 1) A failure to distinguish between the economic Trinity and the theological Trinity, which we referred to above, and 2) a difference between the Western, philosophically based, Augustinian, understanding of the Trinity and the Eastern, theologically based, basically Cappadocian, understanding of the Trinity. This goes together with a tendency in the Western churches to begin the exploration of the meaning of the Blessed Trinity with the unity of God and then proceed to the persons/*hypostases*. The Orthodox begin with the reality and experience of the *hypostases* and then move from them to the unity of God.

The Trinity can be described and understood at two levels. The first, the theological Trinity, concerns the life of the *hypostases* within the Trinity, within the Godhead. Each *hypostasis* is God. The fullness of God subsists in each *hypostasis* equally, each *hypostasis* being fully God. For this reason we can, paradoxically, say that each *hypostasis* is God but there are not three Gods but one God. That would be nonsensical if we were making a positive statement but we are not. We are describing what we must not deny about a reality our minds cannot grasp. We need constantly to remind ourselves that these are statements that we must not deny rather statements that we must assert—apophatic definitions.

There are three *hypostases* in each of which subsists the fullness of God but only one God. There is not a primary Divine essence, a Divine reality proir to the *hypostases*, in which the three *hypostases* share, a reality or original Divine essence prior to the *hypostases*. There is not a primary essence of God that precedes *hypostases*, a kind of basic Divine essence in which *hypostases* participate or share or from which each *hypostasis* is made.

The whole being of God is Trinitarian and subsists in the three *hypostases* and in each *hypostasis* fully. The Father is God, the Son is God and the Holy Spirit is God but there are not three Gods but one God. The difference between the *hypostases* is that the Father is unbegotten, the Son begotten and the Holy Spirit proceeding. This is the differentiation of the *hypostases*. The Father is the only source of the Godhead who begets the Son and from whom the Spirit proceeds. This is the inner nature of the Godhead.

The three *hypostases* are said to have a community in relationship, reciprocity of life, each living in the other; this is called *perichoresis* or circumincession. (See, e.g. John 14:10 and 1 Cor. 2:10) The Three Divine *hypostases* are said mutually to indwell in each other. The Divine nature is entire in each person though the *hypostases* are distinct from each other. There must, therefore, be a mutual indwelling of *hypostases* in each other.

Never is the value and strength of apophatic definitions more clear than when defining the Blessed

Trinity. They express what we must not deny about a reality that the human mind cannot grasp or express positively. The very nature of the Trinity means that it is impossible to produce analogies from human experience or from human anthropology or psychology. The Trinity is not like the spirit, mind and soul of a man or any other set of three attributes or functions of a man or part of human psychology. These things are attributes of a person. The Father and the Son and the Holy Spirit are not attributes of God. Augustine, while not going that far and strongly protecting his orthodoxy (see *de Trinitate* 5.9. and 8.1) sometimes comes near to a sort of modalism or Sabellianism. He sees analogies to the Trinity in the mind, its knowledge of itself and its love of itself; or the mind as remembering, knowing and loving God; or the mind's knowledge of itself—the memory, understanding and love of itself. These look very like functions or attributes of the mind and The Father and The Son and the Holy Spirit are not functions or attributes of God.

All we can properly say is what must not be denied if the Blessed Trinity is to be understood in a way consistent with the Biblical revelation, the experience of the Church and the logic of our salvation. Analogies are dangerous because they seek to be positive explanations of what cannot be explained. They fall at this point. Despite using analogies Augustine understood their weakness.

The second level at which the Trinity can be understood, the economic Trinity, is that which is experienced, that which works in the world. The dispute about the way this is spoken about is much less severe. Much of the confusion in the conflict over the *Filioque* arises over the failure to distinguish between these two Trinitarian realities i.e. using the language concerning the theological Trinity as though it is referring to the economic Trinity. Biblical and patristic references to the economic Trinity are used as though they referred to the theological Trinity in an attempt to provide Biblical and patristic support for the Filioque clause. This inevitably leads to further confusion in a confusing subject. The tendency to make positive statements about the Trinity and to find analogies for The Trinity are further causes of difficulty as we have seen. We must be rigid in distinguishing between the economic and theological Trinity, rigid in understanding the definitions to be negative and apophatic and rigid in avoiding misleading analogies.

Because the understanding of the economic Trinity grows more from the experience of the *hypostases* of the Trinity while the understanding of the theological Trinity is developed more from the logic of salvation there is a tendency to give a primary role to the economic Trinity. It takes time and experience to see that the understanding of the theological Trinity provides the theological and conceptual environment, so to speak, within which we can understand and locate our experience of the economic Trinity. It is the same Blessed Trinity and the same Persons in each case. In one case we are looking at fundamental relationships within the Being of God; in the second we are reflecting on our experience of them and upon God's self revelation.

If we say that within the Godhead the Spirit proceeds from the Father and the Son (*Filioque*), something we might say to stress the equality ("consubstantiality" is a better word) of the Father and the Son — that they are *homoousios* (see glossary) i.e. of one substance, we finish up with serious problems, as we shall see.

The first effect of the *Filioque* clause is that we lose sight of the consubstantiality of the Spirit which has also been defined as being of one substance (*homoousios*) with the Father and the Son. The Spirit becomes subordinated to the Father and the Son as an inferior consequential part of the Trinity. Much of the development of "charismatic" Christianity is a distortion of the life of the Spirit. The Liturgy is the work of the Holy Spirit in the Church and speaking in tongues while serving the Liturgy looks more like a diabolical intervention than the work of the Spirit. The Charismatic Movement is a reaction to the faulty teaching on the Holy Spirit in the West as is the tendency to ignore or to formalise the work of the Spirit.

Second, if the Spirit is believed to proceed from the Father and the Son then the Father and the Son become one principle of origin within the Godhead, together forming an a prior divine essence. "Distinct in virtue of their properties, these hypostases are none the less identical, consubstantial, *since there is in God but one essence which all have in common.*"[1] Thus says Piault. He probably does not mean that the *hyspostases* share an essence or that they are the same — consubstantial does

---

[1] Piault, *op.cit.*, p. 112.

not mean identical—but he could be understood that way. As we have stressed there is no prior divine essence in which each *hypostasis* participates. The fullness of God subsists in each *hypostasis*. Piault's language is ambivalent and it is ambivalent because it is not apophatic. It is also problematic when he refers to the differentiation of the *hypostases* as distinct in virtue of their properties. The Father is eternally the Father, the Son eternally the Son and the Spirit eternally the Spirit. "Distinction by virtue of their properties" could be a misleading way of speaking of the differentiation. The *hypostases* are distinct because of their origin within the Godhead; the Father unbegotten, the Son begotten of the Father and the Holy Spirit proceeding from the Father, not by virtue of their properties.

Third, if the Holy Spirit proceeds from the Father and the Son the origin of the Godhead then ceases to be the Father, a hypostasis, and becomes a diffused and impersonal essence shared by the Father and the Son. The monarchy of the Father, which is the differentiation of the Father, is destroyed and the personal nature of God radically diminished. God tends to become a depersonalised essence in which the *hypostases* participate. Further the balance of the *hypostases* within the Blessed Trinity is destroyed with the subordination of the Spirit. This has effects upon the nature of the Church, which is an icon of the Blessed Trinity. We shall explore those below.

Fourth, the western understanding of the Trinity is fundamentally Augustinian. Augustine spoke, among other things, of the Spirit as the mutual love of the Father and the Son. (We have discussed his analogies of the Trinity briefly above) This way of speaking of the Blessed Trinity and the balance or relationship of the *hypostases* causes problems. It is hard to understand how the fruit of a relationship of love can be a *hypostasis* consubstantial (*homoousios*) with the other *hypostases* of the Trinity or that we can say that the fruit of a relationship of love can be said to intercede with the Father as in Romans 8:14–17, 26. A loving relationship exists between two persons. It cannot be understood to do more than describe something that exists between them. It is not a separate, differentiated reality. St Paul teaches that the Holy Spirit is a distinct *hypostasis*, as does all orthodox Trinitarian theology.

It seems that, in some sense, Augustine almost speaks of the *hypostases* as relationships within the Godhead. Again this is an inadequate way of speaking of the Blessed Trinity. It leads to a form of modalism, that is that God is sometimes in the mode of the Father, sometimes the Son or sometimes the Holy Spirit, that he appears in different modes of operation. The *hypostases* are confused. They are understood as temporary phenomena within the Godhead or roles played by the one impersonal divine essence. That is Sabellianism and was condemned in the third century. The *hypostases* are eternal.

However we find something like Sabelliansism in Piault: "But in God faith discerns three 'subjects'. Why? Because the divine essence, although one, possesses characteristics which enable it to exist in three different ways." This statement by Piault subordinates the *hypos-*

tases to the essence of God and seems to be on the very edge of, if not actually, Sabellianism.

God does not exist in three different ways. The three *hypostases*, the Father, The Son and the Holy Spirit, in each of whom the fullness of God subsists and each of whom are consubstantial, *eternally constitute together and constitute each* the reality of the Godhead. Each is eternal and their being precedes existence.

We cannot say that the *hypostases* share the Godhead or the essence of God, or that there is only one *hypostasis* appearing in different modes, appearing to be three different *hypostases* or that there are three Gods. That is heresy because it suggests that the *hypostases* are not each eternal and so the fullness of God does not subsist in each.

The effect of the *Filioque* clause is to unbalance the internal reality of the Blessed Trinity as we have observed above. All understandings of theological dogmas affect the way that the Church and individual Christians lead their lives so we can expect to see the Filioque have effects in the way of life and form of church life and structure of Christians who believe that the Spirit proceeds from the Father and the Son. It is a difficult and lengthy process to trace the line of causation between dogmatic propositions and their effects; we have seen this. For that reason we will simply suggest some effects which might flow from the *Filioque* without attempting to show the line of causation in any fullness. That is the task of a study on the *Filioque* itself.

The centralized nature of the Roman Church in which the Church finds its centre of authority in one man, the Bishop of Rome, indicates—despite assertion to the contrary—a diminution in significance of the People of God. The fullness of the Roman Church effectively subsists in the Bishop of Rome. That cannot be said of any other Roman Catholic. If the Church is an icon of the Blessed Trinity, and the belief of the Orthodox Church is that it is, then the Church of Rome is an ikon of an unbalanced Trinity in which the Holy Spirit proceeds from the Father and the Son with distinctions between the teaching Church and the listening Church. That is to be expected. The charismatic spirit-filled people of God are subordinate as the Spirit is subordinate.

The true catholicity—the true wholeness—of Orthodoxy in which the Church subsists in each faithful Orthodox is the result of being an icon of an Apostolic understanding of the Blessed Trinity. In the Apostolic dogma of the Trinity the inner personal reality of God is not diffused by losing sight of the *monarchia* of the Father—the Father as the personal origin of the Person of the Son and Spirit by begetting in one case and by procession in the other—by the procession of the Spirit from the Father and the Son. As the fullness of God exists in each *hypostasis* so the fullness of the Church exists in each faithful Orthodox. One cannot say that the fullness of the Roman Church exists in each faithful Roman Catholic because being an icon of a distorted Trinity it has an heretical and distorted structure.

The unbalanced understanding of the Holy Spirit among Pentecostal Charismatics, a denial of the true life of the Holy Spirit in the Church, which has some diabolic characteristics from time to time, is another effect of subordinating the Holy Spirit. The absence of the true doctrine of the Spirit and the true experience of the Spirit in the Western churches in general leads to a distorted and false experience of something, which is often mistakenly taken to be the Holy Spirit, but is not.

The general absence of fully developed understanding of divinization (see the glossary) as the aim of the Christian life and growing dependence upon emotion- producing, people-centred forms of worship and prayer are further examples of the effect of the inclusion of the Filioque in the Creed. When the fullness of God is believed to subsist in the Spirit—a truth easily lost sight of when the Filioque is believed—then the Holy Spirit can work in each Christian to bring each to fullness with the Father so fulfilling the work of the Son.

As we said at the start of this section a full understanding of the Filioque clause can be made in the recommended books. This has been nothing more than a brief sketch to indicate the nature and content of the subject.

II. The Immaculate Conception of the Blessed Virgin

In 1854 the Bishop of Rome defined the dogma of the Immaculate Conception in the Bull, *Ineffabilis Deus*. (This dogma is not to be confused, as it is even by some Roman Catholics, with the dogma of our Lord's Virginal Conception and Birth of the Holy Spirit and the Blessed Virgin.) He defined:

That from the first moment of her conception the Blessed Virgin Mary was, by a singular grace and privilege of Almighty God, and in view of the merits of Jesus Christ, Saviour of mankind, kept free from all stain of original sin.

The belief had an uncertain history and although many Eastern Fathers had extolled the actual sinlessness of the Blessed Virgin and a feast of her conception had been kept, the doctrine of the Immaculate Conception, as such, had not been believed. It was opposed by Bernard of Clairvaux, Albert, Thomas Aquinas, Bonaventure. Many others opposed the doctrine on the same grounds, in essence, that it is rejected by the Orthodox Church. The grounds of its rejection are simply set out:

First of all, only the Lord Jesus Christ is immune from the effects of original sin and in Him alone was the image of man renewed by the Father. It is the saving work of the Lord Jesus that brought this about in the rest of creation and for all other people. To believe that this happened to the Blessed Virgin before the saving work of Christ, before even his Incarnation, is to diminish his saving work or to render it unnecessary. This is the point made by Bishop Mayfield, the Anglican Bishop of Manchester when he spoke for the motion that "Jesus Christ is not necessary to eternal life" in a Durham University Union Debate. If God can bring the Blessed Virgin to redeemed perfection without the saving work of Christ then the Liberal Protestants are correct; the saving work of Christ is not necessary. We are back in the graceless world of the Liberal Protestants.

Secondly, and more seriously, if our Blessed Lord did not assume fallen humanity in the womb of the Virgin, but humanity already redeemed by God's act in the Immaculate Conception, then how is our fallen humanity redeemed? "What is not assumed is not healed," says St Gregory Nazianzus. If our Lord Jesus did not take on our fallen humanity but the already redeemed humanity of the Blessed Virgin, redeemed other than by the saving work of Christ, how are we saved by his Incarnation and saving work?

Thirdly, if God can renew fallen humanity other than by the Incarnation and saving work of Christ why is the Lord Incarnate and why did He suffer?

Finally, this dogma, far from honouring the Blessed Virgin for her sinlessness turns that sinlessness into an unavoidable circumstance resulting from an act of God in the Immaculate Conception. It was her real sinlessness and her real consent to the calling of God by which she conceived the Lord Jesus of the Holy Spirit, which is the source of our wonder and our veneration of her. What seems to honor her — this dogma — diminishes her and makes the saving work of Christ of no effect and pointless. For these reasons the Orthodox reject the dogma and honour the Blessed Virgin the more by doing so.

APPENDIX 5

Heresy

Some clarification of the concept of heresy may be useful. The word, "heresy," originates from the Greek word meaning "to make a choice." A heresy can be defined as a doctrinal opinion that is inconsistent with a dogmatic definition of the Apostolic Faith. Thus to say that Jesus was only a very good man would be a heresy as would any statement about Jesus which denied that He was both fully God and fully man.

The effect of a heresy is understood to be the opposite of a dogmatic definition. A dogmatic definition preserves the essential doctrinal basis of salvation by means of an apophatic or negative statement that indicates what must not be denied. A heresy denies, or changes in such a way as effectively to deny, doctrines necessary to salvation. It is essential to understand dogmatic definitions as apophatic in order to understand the true nature and effect of heresy and the circumstances under which a doctrine might be defined as heretical.

In view of the tendency of some western churches to recoil from the idea of describing an opinion as heretical or, alternatively, of reaching for the heretical gun rather quickly it is necessary to explore the question a little more. In his "Some Thoughts on Heresy,"[1] the distinguished Anglican theologian, Dr John MacQuarrie examines the nature of heresy and finds himself uncomfortable with it. He explains his discomfort by setting out five propositions the first of which reveals as clearly as anything does the grounds of his discomfort. It is that "all theological formulations are approximate." That must be true since our minds cannot grasp the wonder of God and every positive theological statement must be a poor approximation of the truth. The mistake, however, is to confuse dogmatic definitions with positive theological statements. They are quite different in nature and effect. A dogmatic definition says, in effect, "You may discuss the matter in any way you like as long as you do not deny the terms of the dogma or say something inconsistent with the dogma."

MacQuarrie goes, next, on to observe that genuine heresy is extremely rare. This is again true and it is essential to distinguish heresy from any other sort of opinion such as one which questions some aspect of the Church's life not connected with a dogmatic truth. A heresy is such because it creates a situation that bears on the way of salvation—and nothing else.

MacQuarrie next observes that theological freedom carries an element of risk that must be tolerated. It is, however, the Orthodox understanding of the nature of dogmatic definitions, i.e. as apophatic, which creates

---

[1] J. MacQuarrie, "Some Thoughts on Heresy," originally a letter sent to the American House of Bishops about Bishop Pike. It then became chapter four of *Thinking About God* (London, 1975).

the necessary conditions for the correct exercise of theological freedom. An exercise of theological freedom which sought to promote a doctrine that would lead people from the way of salvation is an incorrect use of such freedom. Indeed it is hard to see how persistence in the promotion of a proposition which can be shown to lead people from the way of salvation can be regarded as a theological act at all. That does not mean that theologians should not explore to the limit of their devotion and intellects the nature and work of God in all its aspects. They can do that in the freest way possible secure in the knowledge that whatever their conclusions are they can be tested against the wisdom of the Church as expressed in dogmatic definitions. There is nothing oppressive about this. Oppression is more likely to be found in the attempts of those who adopt a doctrinal innovation that is deemed heretical to silence the orthodox believer. That is what is to be found in the history of the Church. There is a line of martyrs for the Apostolic Faith who were victims of the civil authority or of ecclesiastical authorities. Dogmatic definitions, properly understood, give the theological explorer freedom and preserve him from the one thing he does not want to do, that is, mislead the Faithful.

MacQuarrie next discusses some practical objections to the use of the concept of heresy and finally suggests that heresy or suspected heresy is best combated by a clear statement of the Church's position. Such a statement might fall into the problem he raised in his first proposition, i.e. that theological formulations are approximate, and essentially approximate. Better is a careful exposition of the reasons for the dogmatic definition , the way in which the formulation concerned may be inconsistent with it and the reason why such an inconsistency, if believed and lived out, will lead someone from the way of salvation. There may come a time when a person so persists in a proposition that can be shown to be heretical that he can properly be called a heretic. If and when such a time comes the person concerned automatically excludes himself from the Church. It is the responsibility of those whose duty it is to guard the Apostolic Faith to make public what that person has done. Because other matters enter the process — the dignity of the hierarchs, the need to maintain unity, the desire to limit confusion and distress among church people — the greatest clarity of motive is necessary in the process of dealing with a theological proposition which is deemed to be heretical. The process must be shot through with the zeal of love not the desire for order or conformity for conformity's sake. But it would be foolish not to recognise that heresy is still dangerous. The heresies of the early Church re-emerge again and again. It is, because it refers to the situation in North America and Western Europe, a valuable examination of the causes of the collapse of churches and a reminder that the dangers met by the early Fathers of the Church persist.

None of it would matter if we were simply discussing matters of intellectual speculation. To seek to limit that except for serious reasons is not only offensive in itself but radically inconsistent with the spirit of the age. Freedom of thought has brought down intolerable tyrannies and nobody can suppose that the process was not good; but doctrines and practices that lead men and women from the way of salvation destroy everything. Whatever the risk of being misunderstood the Church would be failing in its duty to bring people to God and work with the Lord Jesus restore the whole creation to the Father if it failed to warn of heresy and its dangers.

GLOSSARY

Some of these words and phrases have been described in footnotes. The descriptions below will be slightly fuller than those that occur in footnotes but are by no means exhaustive.

Anakephalaiosis — a Greek noun from the verb, *anakephalaio*, to sum up. It is used to express the belief that the saving work of Christ has the effect of bringing the whole creation to the Father The saving work of Christ can therefore be described as *anakephalaiosis*, that is the act of restoring the whole creation (the "whole" is important) to the Father. That which was separated from God by the Fall is restored by the work of the Son. Two things follow from this. The first is that the Lord had really to be a complete human in every way like us, save for sin. To be a complete human He had to be a man or a woman and He was a man. The completeness of His manhood enables Him to participate fully in the created order and so restore it to the Father. The second thing that follows from this doctrine is that the restored creation is complete. Our souls are not saved. We are saved as whole people. Our minds cannot conceive of what that means but it means that bodies are integral to our salvation now in this life and then in the life of the redeemed and restored. The implications of this for our care of the human body and for the effects of our spiritual condition upon our physical condition are obvious. The reverse is also true, i.e. the effect of our physical condition upon our spiritual condition. This doctrine makes the division between spirit, soul and body a nonsense. Men and women are psychosomatic unities, one reality of spirit, soul and body united. The doctrine of *anakephalaiosis* is to be found in the New Testament letter to the Ephesians (1:10) and in the writings of several of the Fathers and especially of Irenaeus, e.g. *Against the Heretics*, 3.21.10 and 3.22.2.

Apophatic — This is an adjective derived from the Greek verb, *apophemi*, to deny or negate. It is used to describe a way of speaking of God which proceeds by negatives—God does not have a body, does not have parts, is not circumscribable and so on. The human mind cannot grasp the reality of God and so cannot speak positively about God except in Biblical metaphors but even they can be deceptive or misleading; e.g. "Like as a father pitieth his children so is the Lord merciful to those that fear Him" (Psalm 103:13). That description tells us about certain elements in the relationship between God and the one who fears Him. We would be in danger of serious mistakes if we supposed that God is, in any sense other than this, like a human father. Since we cannot adequately frame positive statements about the being of God the best we can do is to deny statements about God that would be misleading. This is the apophatic way of speaking and this apophatic quality is to be seen in all dogmatic statements. We have discussed above the great advantages that this sort of definition has. It has always been a characteristic of Eastern religious thought rather than of the religious thought of the West. It could be argued that the absence of apophatic expression of dogma is the source of many errors in Western religious thought. Positive statements about the being of God and so on lead to the likelihood that we shall fall into the error of reducing God and the things of God to human reason and human analogy and reducing the paradoxes of the truths of God until they seem reasonable to us. It is, perhaps, inadequate to leave it at that but exploring the suggestion would involve another complete study.

Divinisation (theosis) — This can be defined as the final stage in the growth in Christ of a Christian, the point at which the saving work of Christ comes to full effect. St Athanasius and others said that 'God became man that man might become God' (On the Incarnation 54). Without treat-ing that encapsulation of a doctrine as a full statement with all the implications explored we can take it as meaning that the saving work of Christ is designed to bring man to union with God and to participate in the divine nature (2 Peter 1:4). The doctrine is plainly implied in the Epistle to the Romans (8:14–17) and in the doctrine of *anakephalaiosis, which* we have discussed above.

Eschatology — This word comes from the Greek word for the last in a series, *eschatos*, and can be used in two ways. The first way is in a study of what happens either at the end of an individual human life or of what happens at the end of all things, since all created things and beings will come to an end. We can call these two ways of using the word, personal eschatology and cosmic eschatology. These are truly es-chatological studies i.e. they deal with the last things, the last times. The word is also used to apply to the encounter of all time, at each moment of time, with its *telos* — a Greek word meaning "end" in the sense of purpose and fulfilment. It is this sense in which "eschatological" is used mostly in this study. All things find their true nature and meaning in the mind and purpose of God. It is his loving providential care that seeks to bring all things to their fulfilment in union with Him. If we wish to know the truth of anything, its true na-ture, we must examine it in the light of God's purpose for it and as he sees it. This is the eschatological truth of that thing and so the real truth, the truth before God. Whenever a per-son consciously seeks to meet God's purpose for himself in life or when he acts in a way that affects that purpose then he is acting eschatologically, e.g. in prayer, worship and loving self-sacrifice. It is action that reverberates in heaven, so to speak; real action of ultimate significance. The adjective can also apply to those moments in which God discloses Himself, when the truth of reality becomes clear. It is worth noting that the New Testament is eschatological in both senses. The end was expected and the end is seen to be the Lord Jesus and when we read the New Testament, opening ourselves to the revelation of God, we also meet our purpose and end. The belief that the Lord Jesus in his earthly life brought people face to face with their end is sometimes referred to as "realized eschatology", that is that the End has come in the Lord Jesus; the End has been realised in Him.

Hermeneutics — This word means the principles we use to discern the revelation of God in the Scriptures, the principles we use for interpreting the text. Each preacher must have such a principle before he can prepare a sermon. We have discussed these principles in chapter three above. The only observation that needs to be added is that there is no such thing as simple Biblical interpretation. Everyone has a principle of interpretation and to suppose one has not is simply to be blind.

Homoousios — This word was used by the Fathers of the First Council of Nicaea to describe the relationship of the Father to the Son—the Son is *homoousios*, of the same substance—with the Father. It is not a Biblical word but was used as the only one capable of expressing the truth of the relationship of the persons/*hypostases* in the Trinity. The Holy Spirit is also *homoousios* with the Father and the Son. The word flatly denied and contradicted the assertion of Arius that the Son was not divine. The alternative word was *homoiousios* — of like substance — but this was rejected by the Council Fathers. The word is truly apophatic and it would be a grave error to suppose that God has a substance that is shared by the Father and the Son and the Holy Spirit. The Orthodox frequently use the word "essence" instead of "substance" or simply say "one with the Father". The word is simply designed to deny that the Son and the Holy Spirit are inferior to or not equally God with the Father. Spirit.

Myth — A Biblical myth is a type of narrative which describes a present and eternal reality about the nature of man before God – an existential reality - in the form of an historical narrative. For example the creation stories are, in part, more concerned to assert the creatureliness of man and his fall from the goodness of the divine creation i.e. to explain the existence of sin and the consciousness that man has of being part of a good creation, than to describe certain events which occurred in the past at a precise time and in a precise location. The interpretation of a myth concerns, therefore, the discernment of the truth about the standing of man before God now rather than a justification of the view that the narrative is simple, objective, historical writing. The details of the narrative are significant and must be interpreted carefully for they illuminate the basic meaning of the myth. To say a narrative is a myth does not mean that it is untrue but that its truth lies at a level other than the literal truth. It should not be confused with legend that is historical narrative with the descriptive elements heightened to convey the significance of the narrative and the characters in it.

Symbols — Symbols are visible realities that make present an invisible reality. Thus the monarch symbolises in her person the state and so on. The present reality may be an action symbolic of an action that is occurring in the spiritual realm.

Sacraments are like this and effect what they symbolise and signify, e.g. baptism, in part represents washing from sin and at a deeper level entry into the new Israel by passing through the water as Israel passed through the Red Sea. At its most profound level it is dying and rising with Christ and union with Him and the People of God in whose love we know that we have passed from death to life. What is more difficult to discern and explain is the relationship between symbols and reality. This is especially so in the case of the phenomenon in which a spiritual reality and our perception of it change when the symbol that makes it present is changed. We have encountered this in the ordination of women and the Filioque clause. What is clear is that reality and our perception of it do change when symbols are changed. For this reason and because there are frequently plausible reasons for changing a symbol very great caution is necessary. Attempts to change the Church's faith and order so that it is acceptable to modern thought or to reason almost inevitably involves the changing of symbols. We have seen the folly of this enterprise—quite different from bringing the existential truth of a passage of Scripture or a dogma to contemporary man. That concerns the interpretation of symbols not their changing. The very difficulty of tracing the connection between changes in symbols and changes in reality means that we are usually unable to work out in advance what the results of a change of a symbol will be. Even if one can discern it, it is hard to persuade others that one has got it right. Only in the cases of fairly trivial symbols can changes be lightly made in safety. It takes time for changes in symbols to have an effect in the perception of what they symbolize.

Variant Texts — There are, one can say with a fair degree of confidence, no original texts of the Old and New Testament in existence and available to scholars. Some may exist somewhere but they are not known. The oldest are fragments dating from some time after the revelation was recorded in writing. The process of the transmission of the record of revelation was, in the early years, firstly oral and then the result of reducing the oral tradition to writing and then the editing the oral tradition once it had been written down. This process is, in some respects, somewhat hazardous. There may be a considerable number of copies of any particular passage in the Old or New Testament. There are, in very many of these, slight differences so that any particular verse may appear in two or more different forms and some of the forms may differ substantially. These different forms are called variant texts. The best edition of the Greek New Testament, that of the United Bible Societies, lists the many hundreds of textual sources which they employed to arrive at the best text. They also list at the bottom of every page the variants and their origin. The same is true of the best edition of the Hebrew Bible edited by Kittel. Very few variants affect fundamental points of doctrine. Sometimes differences of translation do have an effect however. An obvious one is the translation of the passage at Romans 8:18. Is the glory of God revealed "to" or "in" us? Mary Grosvenor, one of the most distinguished scholars of New Testament grammar says "to." Many translators, equally distinguished, say "in."

SELECT BIBLIOGRAPHY

Bettenson, Henry. *Documents of the Christian Church* (London, 1959).

Bouyer, Louis. *A History of Christian Spirituality* (London, 1968).

Cross, F. L., ed. *Dictionary of the Christian Church* (Oxford, 1958).

Dodd, C. H. *The Authority of the Bible* (London, 1960).

Florovsky, Georges. *The Bible, Church and Tradition: An Eastern Orthodox View* (Belmont, MA, 1987).

Khomiakov, A. S. *The Church is One* (London, 1948).

Lee, P. *Against the Protestant Gnostics* (Oxford, 1986).

Lossky, Vladimir. *The Mystical Theology of the Eastern Church* (London, 1991).

_____. *In the Image and Likeness of God* (London, 1974).

Maximovich, Archbishop John. *The Orthodox Veneration of Mary, The Birthgiver of God* (Platina, CA,1996).

Meyendorff, John. *Living Tradition* (New York, 1978).

Papadakis, Aristeides. *Crisis in Byzantium* (New York, 1997).

Pelikan, Jaroslav. *Jesus Christ through the Ages* (New Haven, 1985).

_____. *The Christian Tradition*, Vols. 1 & 2 (Chicago, 1971).

Piault, B. *What is the Trinity?* (London, 1959).

Rahner, Karl, ed. *Encyclopaedia of Theology* (London, 1981).

Ramsey, Archbishop Michael. *The Gospel and the Catholic Church* (London, 1956).

Runcie, Archbishop Robert. *Authority in Crisis* (London, 1984).

Schmemann, Alexander. *The Historical Road of Eastern Orthodoxy* (London, 1963).

Ware, Bishop Kallistos. *The Orthodox Church* (London, 1963).

THE FAITH SERIES
By Clark Carlton

AN ORTHODOX CATECHISM IN FOUR VOLUMES

Volume One
THE FAITH: *Understanding Orthodox Christianity*

Volume Two
THE WAY: *What Every Protestant Should Know about
the Orthodox Church*

Volume Three
THE TRUTH: *What Every Roman Catholic Should Know
about the Orthodox Church*

Volume Four
THE LIFE: *The Orthodox Doctrine of Salvation*

from

Regina Orthodox Press
1-800-636-2470

THE FAITH
Understanding Orthodox Christianity

An Orthodox Catechism by author Clark Carlton. Quite simply, The Faith is the best single-volume introduction to Orthodoxy in the English language. The Faith is a beautifully written book that truly answers the question, "What is it that you Orthodox believe?" Widely used in all Orthodox jurisdictions, The Faith has become an Orthodox classic.

Perfect for group or individual study. The Faith is written in short chapters with a special section of questions after each chapter for further reflection. Each section also has relevant quotes from the Fathers and suggestions for further reading.

286 pages, paperback   ISBN 0-9649141-1-5

$22.95

Regina Orthodox Press
P.O. Box 5288
Salisbury, MA 01952
1-800-636-2470
FAX: 978-462-5079
www.reginaorthodoxpress.com

THE WAY

What Every Protestant Should Know about the Orthodox Church

The Way is the highly anticipated sequel to Clark Carlton's best selling catechism, *The Faith: Understanding Orthodox Christianity*. In *The Way*, Clark Carlton turns his attention tot he fundamental differences between Orthodoxy and Protestantism. In a clear, well-written style he articulates a broad vision of the Historic Church and gently explains how Protestants may embrace the fullness of the Christian fatih.

"Had Clark Carlton's new book, *The Way*, been available to me when I began to look for the authentic Church it would have saved me years of anguished searching." Frank Schaeffer

222 pages, paperback   ISBN 0-9649141-2-3

$22.95

Regina Orthodox Press
P.O. Box 5288
Salisbury, MA 01952
1-800-636-2470
FAX: 978-462-5079
www.reginaorthodoxpress.com

THE TRUTH
What Every Roman Catholic Should Know about the Orthodox Church

The Truth will enlighten Orthodox Roman Catholics and Protestants about each other's traditions. Building on the foundation he established in The Faith and The Way, Carlton has written the definitive, up to the moment study on Orthodox-Roman Catholic relations, ecumenism and the claims of the Orthodox to be the Historic Church of the ages.

Written in an each to understand style, The Truth explains the theological, cultural, and historical differences between the Roman Catholic and Orthodox communities.

270 pages, paperback   ISBN 0-9649141-2-2

$22.95

Regina Orthodox Press
P.O. Box 5288
Salisbury, MA 01952
1-800-636-2470
FAX: 978-462-5079
www.reginaorthodoxpress.com

THE LIFE
The Orthodox Doctrine of Salvation

The Life is the fourth and last installment in Clark Carlton's catechetical *Faith Series*. *The Life* completes the series with a focus on "the one thing needful:" what must we do to be saved. The author presents the Orthodox doctrine of salvation in an easy-to-understand format, fully supported with scriptural references and quotations from the Fathers. *The Life* addresses many issues related to the doctrine of salvation, including issues that some find confusing. Among these are the immortality of the soul and the resurrection, the relationship of faith and works, and what it means to have a "personal relationship" with Christ. *The Faith Series* has been called the best Orthodox catechism series thus far. *The Life* is the fitting crown of this series.

190 pages, paperback   ISBN 1-928653-02-2

$22.95

Regina Orthodox Press
P.O. Box 5288
Salisbury, MA 01952
1-800-636-2470
FAX: 978-462-5079
www.reginaorthodoxpress.com